Constructing Presidential Legacy

New Perspectives on the American Presidency
Series Editors: Michael Patrick Cullinane and Sylvia Ellis,
University of Roehampton

Published titles
Constructing Presidential Legacy: How We Remember the American President
Edited by Michael Patrick Cullinane and Sylvia Ellis

Forthcoming titles
Presidential Privilege and the Freedom of Information Act
Kevin M. Baron

Obama v. Trump: The Politics of Rollback
Clodagh Harrington and Alex Waddan

Series website: <https://edinburghuniversitypress.com/new-perspectives-on-the-american-presidency.html>

CONSTRUCTING PRESIDENTIAL LEGACY

How We Remember the American President

Edited by Michael Patrick Cullinane and Sylvia Ellis

EDINBURGH
University Press

Edinburgh University Press is one of the leading university presses in the UK. We publish academic books and journals in our selected subject areas across the humanities and social sciences, combining cutting-edge scholarship with high editorial and production values to produce academic works of lasting importance. For more information visit our website: edinburghuniversitypress.com

© editorial matter and organization Michael Patrick Cullinane & Sylvia Ellis, 2018, 2020
© the chapters their several authors, 2018, 2020

Edinburgh University Press Ltd
The Tun – Holyrood Road
12(2f) Jackson's Entry
Edinburgh EH8 8PJ

First published in hardback by Edinburgh University Press 2018

Typeset in 11/13 Adobe Sabon by
IDSUK (DataConnection) Ltd

A CIP record for this book is available from the British Library.

ISBN 978 1 4744 3731 8 (hardback)
ISBN 978 1 4744 3732 5 (paperback)
ISBN 978 1 4744 3733 2 (webready PDF)
ISBN 978 1 4744 3734 9 (epub)

The right of Michael Patrick Cullinane and Sylvia Ellis to be identified as the editors of this work has been asserted in accordance with the Copyright, Designs and Patents Act 1988, and the Copyright and Related Rights Regulations 2003 (SI No. 2498).

Contents

Acknowledgments vii
Notes on Contributors viii

An introduction to presidential legacy 1
Michael Patrick Cullinane and Sylvia Ellis

1. Presidential temples: America's presidential libraries and centers from the 1930s to today 11
Benjamin Hufbauer

2. Presidential legacy: A literary problem 26
Kristin A. Cook

3. Pennsylvania Avenue meets Madison Avenue: The White House and commercial advertising 55
Michael Patrick Cullinane

4. Eisenhower's Farewell Address in history and memory 76
Richard V. Damms

5. Pageantry, performance, and statecraft: Diplomacy and the presidential image 103
Thomas Tunstall Allcock

6. "You've got to decide how you want history to remember you": The legacy of Lyndon B. Johnson in film and television 133
Gregory Frame

7. The farewell tour: Presidential travel and legacy building 158
Emily J. Charnock

CONTENTS

8. Reflecting or reshaping?: Landmark anniversaries and presidential legacy 206
Mark McLay

9. From a "new paradigm" to "memorial sprawl": The Dwight D. Eisenhower Presidential Memorial 227
Patrick Hagopian

10. Top Trumps: Presidential legacies, new technologies, and a new generation 258
Sylvia Ellis

Epilogue: Confessions of a presidential biographer 277
H. W. Brands

Index 284

Acknowledgments

This volume began as a conference at Northumbria University, and the event was enthusiastically supported by the Faculty of Arts, Design and Social Sciences as well as the Department of Humanities. In our years at Northumbria, Sylvia and I owe considerable thanks to those who supported American Studies and modern History. The conference was also funded by the US Embassy and the British Association of American Studies, and supported by the Presidential History Network. We would also like to thank Tom Putnam, John Marszalek, and Bland Whitley for their contributions.

Contributors

H. W. Brands is Professor and Jack S. Blanton Chair in History at the University of Texas at Austin and has written over twenty-five books, including several critically acclaimed presidential biographies such as *Traitor to His Class*, which was a finalist for the Pulitzer Prize.

Emily J. Charnock is Keasbey Research Fellow in American Studies at Selwyn College, University of Cambridge. Her forthcoming book explores the role of interest groups in twentieth-century US election campaigns, and their influence upon the political parties.

Kristin A. Cook is Associate Tutor in US Foreign Policy with SOAS University of London and the Secretary of the Transatlantic Studies Association. She earned her Ph.D. as a Doctoral Fellow with the Institute for Advanced Studies in the Humanities, University of Edinburgh, examining Adam Smith's philosophical ideas in the early United States.

Michael Patrick Cullinane is Professor of US History at the University of Roehampton. He is the author of *Theodore Roosevelt's Ghost: The History and Memory of an American Icon*, *Liberty and American Anti-Imperialism, 1898–1909*, and the co-author of *The Open Door Era: US Foreign Policy in the Twentieth Century*.

CONTRIBUTORS

Richard V. Damms is Associate Professor of History and Head of the Division of Arts and Sciences at Mississippi State University, Meridian. He is the author of *The Eisenhower Presidency, 1953–1961* and *Scientists and Statesmen: Eisenhower's Science Advisers and National Security Policy.*

Sylvia Ellis is Professor of American History at the University of Roehampton. She is the author of *Freedom's Pragmatist: Lyndon Johnson and Civil Rights*, *A Historical Dictionary of Anglo-American Relations*, and *Britain, America, and the Vietnam War.*

Gregory Frame is Lecturer in Film Studies at Bangor University. He is the author of *The American President in Film and Television: Myth, Politics and Representation.*

Patrick Hagopian is Senior Lecturer in History and American Studies at Lancaster University. He is the author of *The Vietnam War in American Memory: Veterans, Memorials, and the Politics of Healing*, and *American Immunity: War Crimes and the Limits of International Law.*

Benjamin Hufbauer is Associate Professor of Art History at the University of Louisville. He is the author of the book *Presidential Temples: How Memorials and Libraries Shape Public Memory.*

Mark McLay is Lecturer in American History at the University of Glasgow. He researches the modern Republican Party and social policy, and is currently writing a monograph, *Poverty Won: The Republican Party and the War on Poverty, 1964–1981.* Mark also co-hosts the *American History Too!* podcast.

Thomas Tunstall Allcock is Lecturer in American History at the University of Manchester. He is the author of *Thomas C. Mann: President Johnson, the Cold War, and the Restructuring of Latin American Foreign Policy.*

An introduction to presidential legacy

Michael Patrick Cullinane and Sylvia Ellis

At the ground breaking of the Robert Frost Library at Amherst College, President John F. Kennedy gave the convocation and reflected on the importance of legacy and memorials. "A nation reveals itself, not only by the men it produces, but by the men it honors," he told the gathering. Kennedy feted Frost as a man of infinite importance to American culture, and congratulated Amherst for commemorating a poet rather than a president. "In America, our heroes have customarily run to men of large and dramatic accomplishment," but the Frost Library, Kennedy noted, memorializes "our spirit."[1] By celebrating a writer rather than a statesman, a critic rather than a general, Kennedy believed that Amherst expanded our memory of the American experience.

That endorsement was especially poignant because little more than a week after he addressed the college, Kennedy was dead. His assassination obscured the thrust of his argument—that in the United States, memorials and tributes skew towards men of dramatic accomplishment like generals and presidents. The public clamor to confer martyrdom on the slain president led to the proliferation of memorials at home and abroad, and the commemorative activities seemed to prove Kennedy's point. If we count the memorials, there are few personalities larger than the president and no single office as emblematic of the American experience. Presidents leave the White House with a weighty legacy derived primarily from their role as head of state, and they often act as emblems of the era in which they serve. It is popular to summarize the national condition with epochal monikers like the "Age of

Jackson" or the "Reagan Revolution," and in doing so bestow an entire era to a president. Times of prosperity or stagnation affect our recollection of their stewardship, as does social progress or lack thereof. Presidential legacies come to embody their achievements, shortcomings, transgressions, and the precedents they set. In addition, the consequences of their decisions—intended or unintended—contribute to our memories of presidential administrations and help construct a legacy.

Successive generations play a considerable role in determining how we consider presidential leadership, and Kennedy's Amherst speech recognized one of the most important factors in legacy production: people. While any president can lay claim to a set of legislative accomplishments or assert their instrumentality in social progress, building a legacy requires buy-in from those who lived through presidential terms of service as well as later generations. Legacy requires mass reflection upon the past and, to a certain extent, a consensus on how we interpret history. Kennedy, for example, left an indelible mark on the national consciousness in myriad ways. We can debate the virtues of his tax cuts, Cold War brinkmanship, or the morality of his romantic dalliances and still recognize what his election represented in an era of striking cultural change, as the first Catholic president, and as a victim of assassination. Indeed, legacies may derive from opposing constituencies, and can produce divergent interpretations of the past. Kennedy's memorial at Runnymede outside London offers a case in point.[2] The stone tablet, placed at the site made famous by King John affixing his seal to the Magna Carta, celebrates Kennedy's commitment to democracy during the Cold War. In 1968, only three years after the dedication of that memorial, anti-Vietnam War protesters attempted to destroy the tablet with a bomb, and a year later vandals spray-painted a swastika on the facade.[3] Legacy is subjective, and changes as our circumstances evolve and perceptions adjust.[4]

Our memories of past presidents create legacy themes that then appear in memorials, and these memorials can be as varied as our memories. Moreover, such diversity in approach to presidential commemoration often produces incongruous impressions. Utilitarian memorials confer meaning by naming spaces, services, and facilities. These differ greatly from artistic memorials such as bronze statues, marble temples, or the landscape and architectural designs so prevalent in Washington, DC. "Living" memorials might be considered a separate category and can take the form of endowments, scholarships, and prizes, or even literally by planting trees. Indeed, the sites and vehicles of memory extend across a range of mnemonic schemes.[5] For presidents, these include regular "rankings" of their leadership, as well as countless depictions in popular culture media.[6]

The goal of this book is to identify and analyze the agents of and means by which presidential legacies are constructed. Because the president occupies a unique place in American consciousness, those who memorialize former presidents have made use of a wide assortment of approaches, and have done so for a variety of reasons that closely relate to a given context and set of objectives. As a result, presidential legacies change frequently and directly correlate with a given historical context and the impulses of memorializers living at that time. Analyzing the people who dedicate themselves to presidential memorialization and the methods they use will shed new light on the presidency, individual presidents, and the ways we remember historical personalities. The virtue of this collection should thus be apparent: if our perception of the past is shaped in any measure by memorialization and memorializers, we owe it to ourselves to consider these sources and their impact.

Academic scholarship has shown a growing interest in the memory and legacy of American presidents, and so does the wider public.[7] Barack Obama's announcement that his presidential center will opt out of traditional management structures that share responsibility between a private foundation and the federal National Archives and Records Administration was received with compliments and controversy. Obama's Chicago-based presidential center will forego tax-payer funding, making the venture cost-neutral for Americans, but in doing so it will free the Obama Foundation from federal scrutiny and regulation. The Foundation can construct an Obama legacy any way it sees fit.[8] And while the thought of a runaway Obama Foundation seeking to bestow sainthood on the 43rd president might not seem a pressing concern to many, consider for a moment the Trump Foundation and its intentions.

The agents and modes of memorialization have a considerable impact on our impression of the past. Presidential legacies can act as historical milestones by which we understand and interpret our contemporary cultural traditions. For example, in 2017, the Theodore Roosevelt statue outside the American Museum of Natural History was splashed with red paint in an apparent effort to bring attention to Roosevelt's "patriarchy, white supremacy, and settler-colonialism."[9] The statue was nearly removed as a result of the protests, and that caused environmentalists to rage. Roosevelt's place at the museum symbolized the president's commitment to conservation and scientific exploration, not imperialism, although many Americans see Roosevelt as the embodiment of an immoral colonial spirit.[10] Who here is right? What public debates did the controversy raise? And how do we reconcile these disagreements? Although somewhat tangential to presidential history, the hundreds of Confederate statues and memorials dismantled by municipal authorities or destroyed by mobs throughout the summer of 2017 show how public art raises fresh questions about American history and culture, long after it is erected.[11]

These grand acts of construction (or destruction) of memorials belong to a range of commemorative activities that stretch far beyond marble statues, presidential centers, and convocations. An assortment of cultural outputs, political acts and invocations, and public activities contribute to presidential legacies, and each chapter of this book examines one of these activities or modes. The first, by Benjamin Hufbauer, examines the presidential library and museum system. These sites of memory emerged from Franklin Roosevelt's desire to tell "his" story to the masses. Hufbauer explains how the rise of a modern "imperial" presidency—defined in no small measure by direct engagement with the public, and appealing to American public opinion—helped create the library and museum system as part of a growing effort to propagandize presidential legacy. We can perhaps find parallels to ancient monuments, Hufbauer contends. Lyndon Johnson's Library and Museum surely compares to an ancient wonder with its ten-storey travertine monolith (140,000 square feet of interior space) set on a groomed fourteen-acre campus. In similar scale and scope, Patrick Hagopian has researched the various plans for a Dwight D. Eisenhower memorial in Washington, DC. The memorial, a grand design for a monument city like Washington, changed considerably over time due to artistic differences and interpretive disagreement. Family, famous architects, city planners, and congressmen debated Ike's legacy and the most appropriate elements to memorialize, and curated a public site to emphasize some aspects of his life over others. Hagopian's analysis demonstrates the contested nature of memorials and the way in which they construct legacy themes.

Bricks-and-mortar memorials like presidential centers and monuments belong to a traditional style of legacy-making, but a host of unorthodox modes of memorialization may have a similar impact on public memory. Michael Patrick Cullinane's chapter on advertising demonstrates how marketing agencies and businesses latch onto presidential legacy in order to sell products. Advertisements need not leave a permanent impression of a former president on the public consciousness; they are instead designed to draw attention to a product by using the president or presidency as a marker of the product's reliability or quality. Marketing agencies and advertising executives may know little or nothing about presidents, in fact, or care little about the consequences of their advertising on presidential legacy, but they construct images that, in effect, depict legacies and influence public opinions. They are ephemeral in nature, but leave a trace that Cullinane argues can reveal the source of public misconceptions and myths about the presidency. Similarly, Gregory Frame examines the contemporary representations of LBJ in motion pictures, showing how producers, directors, writers, and actors shape public memory. Although less fleeting than advertisements, motion picture productions tend to put commercial gain ahead of historical accuracy. The films evaluated by Frame in Chapter 6 span fifteen years, from 2002 to 2017, and give some indication of how visual depictions of the presidency have changed over time and how they remain consistent. Frame concludes that, despite the dynamic nature of film, cinematic portrayals of presidents lean towards singular profiles that contrast with the multitudes inherent in our personalities.

Other non-traditional forms of memorialization come via the literary route, as Kristin Cook writes. If legacy resides in film, art, and advertising, it must also surely reside in the grammar and metaphors of literature. And the types of literary text can include books and poetry as much as lawsuits, editorials, symbols, signs, and new media. Broadly conceived, Cook explores the literary legacy of presidents in sometimes overlooked texts, and argues that such scholarship has the capacity to enlarge our understanding of the past. In literature we find new patterns of legacy, and Cook compels us to consider the esoteric Louisiana Batture case as an instance of literary production that challenges our impression of Thomas Jefferson.

While many of these chapters deal with commemorative activists, each president may be considered an activist for their own legacy. Three chapters of this book reflect on presidential actions that help position their place in history. Emily Charnock and Richard Damms focus on presidential "farewells." Charnock analyzes the data surrounding presidential travel in lame duck terms. Her study shows how presidents aim to communicate achievements and avoid making reference to the failures of their administrations during their last year in office. The farewell tour is an opportunity for the president to set the tone of memorial activities in the post-presidential years, and Damms's chapter considers the power and legacy of Eisenhower's Farewell Address. Penning his farewell gave Ike remarkable personal interest, and the president used polling to gather information on public opinion and took great pains to consider the implications of each word. The term made famous by that speech—"military-industrial complex"—warns of a system that perpetuates war at the expense of domestic prosperity, a system that Eisenhower arguably played a part in sustaining. Damms demonstrates how the speech resonated among anti-war activists, while Ike never lost his appeal among national security stalwarts. In a similar vein, Thomas Tunstall Allcock explains how presidents use diplomacy to shape their image. Diplomatic events such as state visits can play a role in the construction of legacy, be it LBJ's Texas barbecues or Kennedy's gold-plated and celebrity-studded galas. Statecraft not only allows presidents to craft an image of their administrations to the world, it often reacts to domestic public opinion and strengthens a president's image at home. Tunstall Allcock advertently shows how a president uses a team of support staff to shape his image, from the First Lady to foreign dignitaries, and that the staged nature of high-level diplomacy has all the trappings of performance.

A final thread of analysis the book inspects are the prompts that compel us to consider the past. Obvious mnemonic reminders come every so many years with anniversaries of presidential births, deaths, and momentous events. Mark McLay explores the power and significance of anniversaries on public memory. Although the cycles of anniversaries are unstoppable, those that stimulate the largest waves of commemorative activity often arise when multiple decades or a century passes. There is something about the numbers 50 or 100; they trigger popular calls for remembrance, McLay contends. They mobilize our thoughts. In the case of Lyndon Johnson's legacy, which McLay examines most closely, anniversaries can be a boon or a scourge. The fiftieth anniversaries of great achievements like the Civil Rights and Voting Rights acts are followed by the fiftieth anniversary of the war in Vietnam. Which LBJ legacy emerges from our remembrance is as yet unknown. Sylvia Ellis argues that cyberspace is now a crucial site for presidential legacy formation and memorial. Future generations may well form their opinions about past presidents—and sitting presidents—through the lens of new media such as social media and video games.

The book concludes with an epilogue from one of the most prolific presidential biographers: H.W. Brands. Venturing an explanation for all this presidential commemoration, Brands remarks that as presidential power grows, a reverence for the office increases and the public develops a greater interest. Almost like a celebrity, the public thirst for more information about the president creates a market for legacy and memorialization. It also creates a market for biography, a fact that Brands readily admits has led him to write about several former presidents. Had public interest gravitated to the lives of scientists, we might have more biographies of Enrico Fermi and Vera Rubin.

That the presidency captures our attention so completely was exactly the point Kennedy made at the dedication of the Frost

Library. We tend to memorialize presidents because their achievements and failures are so dramatic and grand. Because their lives play out in the pervasive view of the media, their words and deeds seep into our conversations around the dinner table, or interactions with friends and colleagues, and sometimes strangers. As a consequence, we have a stake in the presidency and what we learn from these chapters is that the process of engaging with a president's image makes all of us agents of their legacy.

Notes

1. Annotated Draft of Kennedy's Convocation Speech, prepared by Arthur Schlesinger Jr., John F. Kennedy Presidential Library, President's Office Files, Speech Files, Box 47.
2. Robert Cook and Clive Webb, "Unraveling the Special Relationship: British Responses to the Assassination of President John F. Kennedy," *The Sixties* 8, no. 2 (2015): 179–94.
3. "War Protest Turns Violent: Bomb Mars JFK Memorial," *St. Petersburg Times*, October 28, 1968; "Kennedy Memorial Defaced," *New York Times*, December 2, 1969.
4. As Paul Ricoeur writes, "the recognized past tends to pass itself off as the perceived past." Paul Ricoeur, *Memory, History, Forgetting* (Chicago: University of Chicago Press, 2004), 40. For scholarly views of memory and perception see also Raphael Samuel, *Theatres of Memory: Past and Present in Contemporary Culture* (New York: Verso, 2012), 1–50; Geoffrey Cubitt, *History and Memory* (Manchester: Manchester University Press, 2007), 66–89.
5. Alon Confino, "Collective Memory and Cultural History: Problems of Method," *American Historical Review* 102, no. 5 (December 1997): 1386–1403; Erika Doss, *Memorial Mania: Public Feeling in America* (Chicago: University of Chicago Press, 2010), 17–58.
6. For an excellent summary of the value and biases of presidential rankings, see Iwan Morgan, "Rating America's Presidents: A UK Perspective," in Michael Patrick Cullinane and Clare Frances Elliott (eds.), *Perspectives on Presidential Leadership: An International View of the White House* (London: Routledge, 2014), 1–7. For an excellent take on a presidential image (Lincoln's) in twenty-first-century pop culture, see Jackie Hogan, *Lincoln Inc.: Selling the Sixteenth President in Contemporary America* (New York: Rowman and Littlefield, 2011).

7. From Merrill Peterson's groundbreaking work on Jefferson and Lincoln to failed presidents like Nixon and Harding, a range of scholarship has emerged in the twenty-first century with the aim of understanding the deification and demonizing of individual presidents. See Merrill D. Peterson, *The Jefferson Image in the American Mind* (Charlottesville: University of Virginia Press, 1960); Merrill D. Peterson, *Lincoln in American Memory* (New York: Oxford University Press, 1995); Phillip G. Payne, *Dead Last: The Public Memory of Warren G. Harding's Scandalous Legacy* (Athens: Ohio University Press, 2009); Edward Lengel, *Inventing George Washington: America's Founder, in Myth and Memory* (New York: Harpers, 2011); David Greenberg, *Nixon's Shadow: The History of an Image* (New York: W.W. Norton, 2004); Mark White, *Kennedy: A Cultural History of an American Icon* (London: Bloomsbury, 2013); Jay Sexton and Richard Carwardine (eds.), *The Global Lincoln* (Oxford: Oxford University Press, 2011); Joan Waugh, *U.S. Grant: American Hero, American Myth* (Chapel Hill: University of North Carolina Press, 2009); Michael Patrick Cullinane, *Theodore Roosevelt's Ghost: The History and Memory of an American Icon* (Baton Rouge: Louisiana State University Press, 2017).

8. Blair Kamin, Katherine Skiba, and Angela Caputo, "Obama Presidential Center Breaks from National Archives Model," *Chicago Tribune*, May 11, 2017. Although it might seem strange that the Obama Foundation would pass on a National Archives managed library, the relationship between archive keepers and idolaters has a track record of friction. In 2015, a number of JFK Library staff resigned, including Director Thomas Putnam, when a new team at the Kennedy Foundation took a new direction in fundraising, management, and collaboration with National Archives employees. Jim O'Sullivan, "JFK Library Sees Exodus as New CEO, Strategy Draw Complaints," *Boston Globe*, August 5, 2015; Jim O'Sullivan, "Leaders Critical of Regime in Charge of JFK Library," *Boston Globe*, September 15, 2015.

9. Claire Voon, "Activists Splatter Red Paint on Roosevelt Monument at American Museum of Natural History," *Hyperallergic*, October 26, 2017, <https://hyperallergic.com/407921/activists-splatter-roosevelt-monument-amnh/> (accessed June 13, 2018); Jelani Cobb, "New York City's Controversial Monuments Will Remain, but Their Meaning Will Be More Complicated," *New Yorker*, January 12, 2018.

10. Mayoral Advisory Commission on City Art, Monuments, and Markers, "Report to the City of New York," (January 2018), 25–27.
11. Victor Luckerson, "Dismantling Dixie: The Summer the Confederate Monuments Came Crashing Down," *The Ringer*, August 17, 2017, <https://www.theringer.com/2017/8/17/16160286/charlottesville-richmond-montgomery-confederate-monuments> (accessed June 13, 2018).

1

Presidential temples: America's presidential libraries and centers from the 1930s to today

Benjamin Hufbauer

On April 24, 2013, the $500-million George W. Bush Presidential Center was dedicated on the campus of Southern Methodist University in Dallas, Texas.[1] President Barack Obama and First Lady Michelle Obama were there, as were former President and First Lady Bill and Hillary Clinton, Barbara and George Bush Sr., Jimmy and Rosalynn Carter, as well as a crowd of thousands and—since CNN and other networks transmitted the ceremony live—a television audience of millions. The United States Army Band played "Battle Hymn of the Republic" with its refrain "Glory, Glory, Hallelujah." Later, fireworks exploded forming a giant "W" over the impressive neo-classical complex, which was designed by the award-winning dean of Yale's School of Architecture, Robert A.M. Stern. Since the other, theoretically co-equal branches of the federal government do not get this kind of celebratory commemoration, the dedication of the Bush Presidential Center illuminated a significant problem facing the United States: the excessive and narcissistic aggrandizement of the presidency at the expense of rational thought about the constitutional limits on executive power.

Former President Bush said in his dedication speech—optimistically fantasizing about history's verdict on his presidency—that "when future generations come to this library and study this administration, they're going to find out that we stayed true to our convictions—that we expanded freedom . . . and that when our freedom came under attack, we made the tough decisions required to keep the American people safe."[2] When former President Bill Clinton spoke, however, he deflated Mr. Bush's self-congratulation and earned a knowing laugh from the rich, powerful, and well-connected donors who made up much of the audience by quipping that the Bush Library was just "the latest, grandest example of the eternal struggle of former presidents to rewrite history."[3] Mr. Clinton would know, since he did the same kind of rewriting of history in 2004 when his $250-million Clinton Presidential Library opened in Little Rock, Arkansas. Likewise, former President Obama is working on the Obama Presidential Center in Chicago, which might have a total price tag of as much as one billion dollars when its endowment is included, and which is scheduled to open in 2021.

Presidential libraries and centers (and I will say more about the distinction between these two) are already scattered across the American landscape, from Massachusetts to California, with many more in between and new ones being built every four to eight years for as far as the eye can see. As presidential centers have more or less doubled in cost with each new US president, some questions come to mind: How did we get to this place in history, where former presidents get to create colossal temples of spin dedicated to themselves? What does presidential self-commemoration mean in the larger sweep of history?

Although I've studied presidential libraries and centers for more than twenty years, and written a book about them with a title similar to the one for this chapter, in just the past year I've begun to see presidential centers in a more ominous light than before.[4] Their extraordinary and at times surreal mixture of personal and political narcissism now seem to have built part of the foundation for President Donald J. Trump's rise by helping to normalize his kind of savage political and personal self-promotion. Or, perhaps more accurately, the increasing expense, grandiosity, and self-congratulatory air of presidential libraries and centers is a symptom of an enveloping political disorder that has culminated in Mr. Trump's campaign and presidency. Some of us can now already envision with disturbing vividness the future Trump Presidential Center, largely because it will be a direct outgrowth of what we've already experienced during the eighty-year history of American presidents building monuments to themselves.

These presidential temples are built with privately raised money, but from Herbert Hoover's to George W. Bush's, the federal government runs them in perpetuity. President Bush said in his dedication speech that "This beautiful building has my name above the door, but it belongs to you." Presidents for many decades have claimed that they are bestowing upon us a gift for which we should be grateful, but that may not always be the case.

The upcoming Obama Presidential Center, where the most notable structure on the campus-like setting resembles the base of an Egyptian obelisk, is breaking with tradition by being completely privately funded and operated, and not supported by the federal government. But that is ultimately a small difference. In the analysis of these memorials, the grandeur of the future Obama Presidential Center rests not on whether it is run by the federal government, but on how it has been inspired by examples created by past American presidents. The Obama Center will, like previous presidential centers and libraries, echo the non-democratic past, where autocratic rulers since the dawn of human history have commemorated themselves in elaborate ways.

There are parallels to American presidential self-commemoration in the ancient world. The pyramids, obelisks, temples, and tombs of the pharaohs of ancient Egypt told glorified versions of their reigns, and were tended by paid priests for centuries. And the Imperial Cult of the Roman Empire made most Emperors into gods for political worship. A few Roman Emperors even had a *res gestae* or list of achievements engraved in stone.[5] These self-proclaimed and exaggerated lists of achievements are prequels to the elaborate museum displays in presidential libraries, which are largely curated by the former presidents.[6]

Presidential libraries are an accepted fact of American political life, but what are their deeper meanings? How does the architecture of a presidential library reflect the personality and ideology of a president? And how do presidential libraries use and abuse the raw materials of history? This chapter will try to briefly answer these questions.

Digging deeper, the larger issue for almost all presidential libraries is run-away power, or what historian Arthur Schlesinger Jr. called *The Imperial Presidency*.[7] Presidential libraries don't just commemorate individual presidents, they promote an expansive view of executive power, while usually ignoring excesses, mistakes, and abuses. It's not a coincidence that the federal presidential library was invented by Franklin Roosevelt, identified by Schlesinger as the first modern "imperial president."

Schlesinger was, like many Americans in the late 1960s and early 1970s, disturbed by the abuses of power by Presidents Lyndon Johnson and Richard Nixon. He showed in his book that these abuses went beyond the personality flaws of a few presidents, and were instead systemic. There was a steady gathering of power by presidents during the crises of the Great Depression, World War II, and the Cold War. Even presidents whom Schlesinger admired, like Harry Truman, extended the power of the presidency in ways that violated the Constitution by, for instance, committing the United States to war in Korea without seeking or receiving the constitutionally mandated declaration of war from Congress.

In the decades since Schlesinger's landmark book was published, the questionable use of constitutional powers by presidents of both parties have continued. For instance, after 9/11, the Bush administration authorized the CIA to engage in torture and, starting in 2009, the Obama administration used executive power to conduct extensive domestic surveillance and launch scores of foreign drone strikes. As ineffectual as recent American presidents sometimes seem, abuses of power of the kind that disturbed Schlesinger continue on in new forms. Presidential libraries and centers are, I believe, a symptom of an increasingly dysfunctional American political system, for they serve in large part to excuse the expansion and abuse of presidential power that historians say entered a new era with President Franklin Delano Roosevelt.

FDR helped design the Dutch Colonial style architecture of his presidential library, the first to be federally operated, which opened on his estate at Hyde Park, New York in 1941. In creating his library, Roosevelt looked to the Rutherford B. Hayes Presidential Library in Fremont, Ohio, the first presidential library to be built, but it was Franklin Roosevelt who got the federal government involved. The Hayes Library was founded to honor the nineteenth president and it included a museum as well as an archive of documents. Hayes, who fought in the Civil War, was said by General Ulysses S. Grant to have displayed "conspicuous gallantry on the field of battle," and his presidency (1877–81) marked the end of Reconstruction. The Hayes Library was founded in 1916 by Webb Hayes, the President's son, and has been maintained for a century without federal funding. In a sense, the whole presidential library phenomenon started with Hayes, but it was revolutionized by Roosevelt when he got his wish for his library to be run by the federal government.

The Roosevelt Library was modest in size when compared with succeeding presidential libraries (although since its founding it's been expanded a few times). By creating an institution with an archive for all of the records relating to his life, as well as a popular history museum that has told FDR's story to millions of tourists, Roosevelt changed presidential commemoration in an ambitious way. Previous presidents would only have monuments built in their honor decades after they died. For instance, the Lincoln Memorial was dedicated in 1922, more than fifty years after President Lincoln's death. Washington waited longer: eighty-five years. And many presidents before Roosevelt did not get a national monument at all. This was a better system, for do we need temples dedicated to the memories of Millard Fillmore and Chester Alan Arthur? Or to every single one of our recent presidents? Yet, thanks to Roosevelt, no matter how great, failed, or, most likely, mediocre, every American president gets to create a kind of national monument.

Roosevelt was able to engineer this shift in presidential commemoration for several reasons, including changes in mass media that he used to reimagine and enlarge presidential power in the 1930s. Just as importantly, many presidential records since the time of Washington had been lost in private ownership. The private ownership of presidential papers was a tradition started when George Washington, on his retirement, shipped all of his official and personal documents to Mount Vernon. After Washington's death, his papers were left to his nephew, who confessed that they were "extensively mutilated by rats." The remains of Washington's papers, like the remains of many presidential papers, were eventually purchased by the Library of Congress, but only after some were lost forever. Even the presidential records that found their way to the Library of Congress sometimes had unusual restrictions placed on them by relatives. For instance, many of Abraham Lincoln's papers were unavailable to historians until 1947.[8] If we have to wait until eighty years after a president's death to get at the records, or whatever is left of them, how are we to learn from our own history?

FDR knew this, and also knew that every new government program needs beneficiaries who will lend political support. To create his presidential library, Roosevelt wooed professional historians by saying that his library would be part of the recently created National Archives, and would make available to historians all of his records as soon as possible. But a secret memo that FDR wrote in 1943 makes clear that he wanted all of the most sensitive records sealed away.[9] After Roosevelt's death, a judge ruled that FDR's public statements took precedence, and now any of us can go into the Roosevelt Library's archive and, with the help of professional archivists, look at the personal letters that FDR had sought to restrict, as well as his presidential records. Our understanding of Franklin and Eleanor Roosevelt's public and personal lives has been immeasurably enriched as a result. The recent Roosevelt documentary by Ken Burns was made possible in large part by open access to records at the Roosevelt Library.

The second part of the presidential library was a museum for tourists, and FDR looked forward to the museum serving, as he said, "an appalling number of sightseers." Initially, the museum was filled with relics, from his childhood clothes to mementos of his presidency, including, tellingly, a papier-mâché portrait of Roosevelt himself as an Egyptian sphinx. At the time, some objected to FDR's seemingly narcissistic creation of a monument to himself. One newspaper accused Roosevelt of wanting a "Yankee Pyramid," while a member of Congress said that "only an egocentric maniac would have the nerve to ask" for a presidential library.[10] An editorial comic from the *Chicago Tribune* even pictured FDR as Santa Claus putting a giant present into his own stocking, saying, "Won't he be surprised—Bless His Heart."

The Roosevelt Library cost about $7 million when adjusted for inflation, all privately raised from FDR's supporters. Successive presidents have built their monuments in the same way—with private money—before handing them off to the government to staff and fund (although at times presidential libraries have been expanded with federal money). It costs about $70 million a year to run the thirteen presidential libraries.[11]

Roosevelt was buried next to his library in 1945, and when Eleanor Roosevelt died seventeen years later she was buried next to him. Several other presidents and first ladies have also been buried at their presidential libraries. In 2004, when Ronald Reagan died, there was live TV coverage of his casket being driven up the mountainside in Simi Valley, California, to the Reagan Presidential Library, for a cinematic burial at sunset. These burial ceremonies help make presidential libraries part of what has been called the "civil religion" of the United States.[12] This term, first coined by writer and philosopher Jean-Jacques Rousseau, has been used by historians to describe our political veneration for secular "saints" like George Washington, sacred sites like the Lincoln Memorial, sacred objects like the Declaration of Independence, and rituals like the singing of the national anthem. Presidential libraries are part of this civil religion; they are sites where tourists can make pilgrimages to see the relics and read the hagiographies of presidents who, although recognized as lesser than Lincoln and Washington, are still supposed to be worthy of some degree of patriotic veneration.

After Roosevelt, the construction of a presidential library seemed like a natural and necessary step. Harry S. Truman had built in Independence, Missouri, a library even grander than FDR's, with a facade echoing Queen Hatshepsut's temple in Egypt. As tourists enter the Truman Library, which opened in 1957, they see American artist Thomas Hart Benton's 500-plus-square-foot mural "Independence and the Opening of the West," which frames the entry to the Library's most popular attraction, a 94 percent scale replica of the Oval Office. The mural and replica together create a linked message about the settlement of the West in the nineteenth century, as well as about presidential leadership in the nuclear age. During the era shown in the mural—from the 1840s to the 1860s—Independence was a supply station for American settlers. The painting shows how Truman's future hometown helped the United States to achieve its "manifest destiny." In the mural's center, armed white men prepare to defend the women and children of their camp from two approaching Native Americans.

Western movies and TV programs, which were extremely popular in the 1950s, influenced Benton's "Independence and the Opening of the West." Westerns during the early Cold War recast international tensions into a heroic past. As historian Stanley Corkin writes, "the Western was well-suited to convey ... [the] rationales for post-war US foreign policy, including [those] ... that guided the Truman administration."[13] In other words, just as settlers secured the frontier, the mural seemed to imply, President Truman and NATO helped secure the world against the Soviet Union.

President Truman's contributions to the early Civil Rights movement are also seen in the mural. The two prominent African American blacksmiths refer to a nineteenth-century African American named Hiram Young, a free black man who was the most sought-after wagon-maker in Independence.[14] President Truman, with his Executive Orders to desegregate the Armed Forces and to guarantee fair civil-service employment, had, at that time, made more significant progress on civil rights than any president since Lincoln. Benton's painting presents a microcosm of nineteenth-century American society, and prepares tourists for the Oval Office replica just beyond. As they enter, visitors stand inside the curved walls of the Oval Office where they see Truman's desk next to the American flag and the president's flag, which shows an eagle grasping an olive branch in one talon, and a quiver of arrows in the other. The globe that General Eisenhower gave to Truman at the end of World War II is at the other end of the room, showing the importance of America's global role. And then Truman's voice hails visitors from speakers hidden in the replica: "I am glad you have come to this historical institution. You are very welcome. This is Harry S. Truman speaking. This room is an exact reproduction of the Presidential Office in the West Wing of the White House, as it was in the early 1950s. The furniture, the rug, and the drapes are duplicates of those in use at the White House when I was president of the United States."

One afternoon when I was visiting the replica, a United States Marine and his family entered. As Truman's voice described the reproduction of his Oval Office, a boy about eight years old told his uniformed father, "That's Harry Truman!"[15] But his father replied, "That's not the president, son. That's an actor." In the midst of the largest collection of Truman materials and displays in the world, the sense that Truman's real recorded voice would instead be an actor's impersonation offered an insight. In presidential libraries, where simulations and real history are mixed, historical "truth" is disrupted as much as it is reinforced.

It is noteworthy that the Truman Library's Oval Office replica opened just two years after the first Disneyland in California. As one of my mentors, architectural historian Reyner Banham, wrote, "Disneyland was a set for a film that was never ever going to be made, except in the mind of the visitor."[16] This is essentially the appeal of an Oval Office replica. It is an empty set for tourists to visualize cinematic narratives of presidential power. The replica was so effective at drawing tourists that in the following decades additional Oval Office replicas were built at the Kennedy, Johnson, Ford, Carter, Reagan, Bush, Clinton, and George W. Bush libraries, each highlighting the story of its president with a copy of this famous room.

President Kennedy introduced the next major innovation for presidential libraries by planning to affiliate his with his alma mater, Harvard University. After Kennedy's death, some at Harvard decided they didn't like the idea of tourists on their campus, since only one percent of visitors to presidential libraries are researchers. *New York Times* architecture critic Ada Louise Huxtable humorously lampooned Harvard's fear of "Goths overwhelming the intelligentsia."[17] Harvard did establish the Kennedy School of Government, but the Kennedy Library itself was finally located at the University of Massachusetts, on a spectacular site overlooking Boston Harbor.

The Kennedy Library was also the first to have a "starchitect," when Jacqueline Kennedy chose I.M. Pei to design the building. Pei later designed the East Building of the National Gallery of Art, as well as the expansion of the Louvre. Originally, the Kennedy Library was going to be a large pyramid with the top cut off, representing JFK's tragically truncated achievements, but eventually that plan was scrapped, and Pei reimagined the concept as the glass pyramid at the Louvre. Pei's final design for the Kennedy Library is a futuristic glass, steel, and concrete edifice.

President Lyndon Johnson, with Lady Bird's help, also hired a starchitect for his library. Gordon Bunshaft of Skidmore, Owings & Merrill got LBJ's orders to design "the best presidential library in the world." This stark building, which is brutal and subtle at the same time, represents, as some who knew him say, Johnson's own personality. Lady Bird had told LBJ that the Oval Office replica was the top draw for tourists at the Truman Library, but Bunshaft resisted. And so LBJ called him from the real Oval Office to demand a replica. The conversation, which took place on October 10, 1968, was secretly recorded by Johnson, who said: "That's one of the basic things! [The Oval Office] is gonna be remembered . . . a lot more than some book up there [on] a shelf . . . !" One employee of the National Archives told me that, after retiring from the presidency, LBJ used his replica as his office sometimes: "Johnson could emerge from the door behind his desk into the replica and surprise visitors almost like the Wizard of Oz coming out from behind the curtains."[18]

The grandest space inside the Johnson Library is the so-called "Great Hall of Achievement." There is a spectacular display of some of the thousands of archival boxes that contain the circa 45 million pages of documents from Johnson's career. In 1975, when Pulitzer-prize-winning historian Robert A. Caro first walked into the building to start work on his acclaimed multi-volume biography of Johnson, he felt understandably daunted.[19] The Johnson Library is to a large degree a shrine to Johnson's ego, and to the imperial presidency, but Caro's massive and often disturbing biography has shown that the access to the historical record that this architecture symbolizes is real.

The most remarkable part of the building to me, which is not open to the public, is the private apartment for the Johnsons on the top floor. The Johnson suite is an elegant modernist space, with exquisite pieces of art on display. But it's the chrome and marble bathroom that is the most unusual feature. Inside the large travertine shower are four industrial-strength shower heads, which are like those that Johnson had installed in his real White House bathroom. This shower perplexed his successor President Richard Nixon on his first day in the White House, because "the thing was like a fire hose; it almost knocked him down."[20] As Johnson showered in his library and then dried himself off, mirrors all over the walls and ceilings of the bathroom reflected back his image, multiplied.

Up until 1974, all presidential records were still private property. Although presidents had voluntarily donated their papers to their libraries, they could still edit or destroy parts of their records. They had not done so in any significant way until President Nixon, who resigned from office when his myriad abuses of power collectively known as Watergate came to light. Nixon intended to destroy many of his self-incriminating papers and recordings. Under this threat, Congress seized Nixon's records, and then passed a law that made all future presidential records the property of the nation.[21]

Some might wonder whether presidential libraries make much of a difference to a president's reputation. The short answer is that they do. President Jimmy Carter's reputation, for example, was tarnished when he left office in 1981. But as the *New York Times* put it in a prescient headline in 1986: "Reshaped Carter Image Tied to Library Opening"—and today, Carter is one of the more respected former presidents.[22] It was also Carter who first morphed the presidential library into a presidential center. The Carter Center, which is next to but administratively separate from the Carter Library and Museum in Atlanta, has been so effective at living up to its motto of "Waging Peace. Fighting Disease. Building Hope" that President Carter won the Nobel Peace Prize in 2002. And it also helped when, at the Carter Library's dedication in 1986, then-President Reagan showered Carter with praise; just as President Obama's words for George W. Bush at the Bush Center's dedication, where Obama spoke of Mr. Bush's "incredible strength and resolve" as well as "his compassion and generosity," seemingly gave an immediate boost to Mr. Bush's poll numbers. Presidential libraries help former presidents rise above partisanship, enhancing their reputations.

But most visitors to presidential libraries are not there to do research on a given president and his administration, but instead to make a visit to the museums. Here, the exhibits, not surprisingly, tend to amount to giant campaign commercials in museum form. This is true for presidents from both parties. When the Johnson Library first opened in 1971, for instance, there was little in the museum about the ongoing Vietnam War, and instead there was praise for LBJ and his "Great Society" programs. As *Newsweek* wrote in 1971: "Inside the Library the visage of LBJ is as ubiquitous as Chairman Mao's in Peking."[23] The Nixon Library originally whitewashed Watergate (although the Watergate exhibit has been completely redone in recent years, and now has an accurate account overseen by historian Timothy Naftali). The Reagan Library originally ignored Iran-Contra (also fixed in recent years). Clinton still puts his own spin on his scandals, while the new George W. Bush Library contains bronze statues of the family dogs, but the accounts of our recent wars, Hurricane Katrina, and the Great Recession diverge from those found in history books. As the decades pass, and a president and his supporters pass away, the museums usually become more balanced and accurate. But it often takes forty to fifty years before that happens, and there are no guarantees even then.

Presidential library museums have so much leeway to spin history in part because they open decades before archival records become available, and it is these archival records that can help prove (or disprove) the accuracy of museum exhibits. The number of records generated by the Executive Branch has exploded in the last several decades, but there has been insufficient funding for the archivists who must process these records for release. It will take up to 100 years to fully process and release the records of recent presidents.

Former President Barack Obama, in announcing plans for the future Obama Center, admitted that presidential libraries and centers were ultimately about what he called presidential "ego-tripping."[24] But Mr. Obama offered no assurances that the Obama Presidential Center would refrain from the kind of spin of past presidential centers. The major innovation of the Obama Center—its separation from the National Archives, which, as mentioned, runs the presidential libraries and centers from Herbert Hoover to George W. Bush—was a practical decision based on financial realities. By letting the National Archives house the Obama records in existing facilities, Mr. Obama saved tens of millions of dollars he would have needed to raise to build a new, first-class archive for the records of his administration. And, further, by being privately funded and operated, the Obama Presidential Center escapes from the new legal requirement passed by Congress, and applying for the very first time to President Obama, to raise an endowment equal to 60 percent of the initial construction costs of the complex. That change in law was enacted to help defray the cost to the federal government of maintaining the facility.

The Obama Presidential Center will be the first to completely eliminate the historical records and research spaces that had previously been a key justification for the existence of presidential libraries. Without historians doing research there, what will take their place? According to Mr. Obama, there will be a hill constructed for sledding during the winter, a community center, a studio for people to record music, and a lecture program. To make the land for all this possible and provide parking, Cornell Drive, a six-lane road heavily used by Chicago commuters, will be permanently closed, leading to an unknown increase in commute times and traffic on other roads. But what will ultimately be achieved, according to Mr. Obama, is "not just one building," but a setting "like a campus" devoted to "engaged citizenship."[25] It will almost certainly have a grand interactive museum devoted to the Obama administration; one that will create the impression that Mr. Obama rarely made mistakes in his political life. If so, it will be like other presidential libraries and centers that for eighty years have tended to the legacies and the egos of former presidents. Admitting that a core problem exists with presidential propaganda at presidential centers, as former presidents Clinton and Obama have done, is not the same as solving it.

As presidential libraries have evolved and grown they have become a better deal for presidents, but it's not clear that they are as good a deal for the public. Looking to the future we can say, like the motto under the sculpture in front of the National

Archives, that "what is past is prologue." In other words, presidential libraries are likely to become even more expensive, larger, and glitzier centers of spin in the future, perhaps reminding us of the poem "Ozymandias" by Percy Shelley: "My name is Ozymandias, King of Kings, Look on my works, ye Mighty, and despair!"

Notes

1. Zeke J. Miller, "Bush Raises More than $500 Million For Library," *Time*, April 10, 2013. Mark Langdale, President of the George W. Bush Center, said: "Half of the money was spent to build the Bush Center itself . . . and another portion of the funds will go to Southern Methodist University for an endowment that is intended to strengthen our relationship with their programs."
2. "George W. Bush's Remarks at His Presidential Library Dedication," *New York Times*, April 25, 2013.
3. Peter Baker, "For Bush, a Day to Bask in Texas Sun," *New York Times*, April 25, 2013.
4. Benjamin Hufbauer, *Presidential Temples: How Memorials and Libraries Shape Public Memory* (Lawrence: University Press of Kansas, 2005).
5. Alison E. Cooley, *Res Gestae Divi Augusti* (New York: Cambridge University Press, 2009).
6. Katherine Q. Seelyenov, "Clinton Library Reflects Its Subject's Volatile Era," *New York Times*, November 18, 2004.
7. Arthur M. Schlesinger Jr., *The Imperial Presidency* (Boston: Houghton Mifflin, 1973).
8. "Abraham Lincoln Papers: About This Collection," <https://www.loc.gov/collections/abraham-lincoln-papers/about-this-collection/> (accessed June 13, 2018).
9. Hufbauer, *Presidential Temples*, 33.
10. Ibid. 31–32.
11. National Archives and Records Administration, FY 2014 Congressional Justification, April 10, 2013, <https://www.archives.gov/files/about/plans-reports/performance-budget/2014-performance-budget.pdf> (accessed June 13, 2018).
12. Hufbauer, *Presidential Temples*, 6–8.
13. Stanley Corkin, *Cowboys as Cold Warriors: The Western and US History* (Philadelphia: Temple University Press, 2004), 20.
14. "Young, Hiram (1812–1882)," BlackPast.org, <http://www.blackpast.org/aah/young-hiram-1812-1882> (accessed June 13, 2018).

15. Hufbauer, *Presidential Temples*, 60.
16. Reyner Banham, *Los Angeles: The Architecture of Four Ecologies* (London: Penguin, 1971), 109.
17. Ada Louise Huxtable, "What's a Tourist Attraction like the Kennedy Library Doing in a Nice Neighborhood like This? The Kennedy Library Looms Over Cambridge," *New York Times*, June 16, 1974.
18. Hufbauer, *Presidential Temples*, 100.
19. Robert A. Caro, *The Years of Lyndon Johnson: The Path to Power* (New York: Alfred Knopf, 1982), 777.
20. Richard Reeves, *President Nixon: Alone in the White House* (New York: Simon and Schuster, 2000), 41.
21. Presidential Records Act (PRA) of 1974, <https://www.archives.gov/presidential-libraries/laws/1978-act.html> (accessed June 13, 2018).
22. William E. Schmidt, "Reshaped Carter Image Tied to Library Opening," *New York Times*, September 21, 1986.
23. "Remembering LBJ," *Newsweek*, May 24, 1971.
24. Angela Caputo, Katherine Skiba, and Blair Kamin, "Obamas Unveil Design of Presidential Center in Chicago," *Chicago Tribune*, May 4, 2017.
25. Ibid.

2

Presidential legacy: A literary problem

Kristin A. Cook

What is presidential literary legacy? What does it mean to "read" the life of Washington as Royall Tyler suggests, to interpret a literary sketch authored by Theodore Roosevelt or to discern New Deal realpolitik in the private writings of a Matanuska Valley colonist?[1] What do we discover of presidential legacy in Jefferson's nod to Shakespeare, or Pound's nod to Jefferson? In Reagan's *American Life*, or Carter's *Keeping Faith*?[2] What does it entail, beyond politics of race or reason, for President Barack Obama to invoke Atticus Finch ("a great character in American fiction") in his 2017 Farewell Address: "You never really understand a person until you consider things from his point of view, until you climb into his skin and walk around in it?" And what does it signify that "his" presides as a modifier to the legacy of life in office?[3] These are the concerns of this chapter.

The examination begins with a simple assertion that the broadly political phenomenon of presidential legacy is an inheritance of public memory, and in order to engage it rightly, I suggest, we must admit that memory is a great multiplicity of fictions, as well as a robust cultural voice of heritage. Interpretations of presidential leadership certainly appear in enough texts, either through presidential characters or metaphors for the executive office. One can think of William Wells Brown's entropic novel *Clotel; or The President's Daughter* (1853); L. Frank Baum's *The Wonderful Wizard of Oz* (1900), which recalls the election of 1896; likewise Harper Lee's admonition against "fear itself" in *To Kill a Mockingbird* (1960) repeats FDR's famous adage; Gore Vidal's critical history in

An Evening with Richard Nixon (1972); Philip Roth's provocative counter-imaging in *The Plot Against America* (2004); even *Hamilton*'s enrapt cast on presidential election and administration; or twenty-first-century Mexican American verse, casting slam rhyme to the border.[4] Presidential legacy in statecraft, art, and memorial is, after all, the Technicolor at-home production of a wider transnational story, pictured in its character and office via cross-woven histories, narrative omissions, prevailing scripts, and constituent views of a watching and reading world.

The aims of this chapter are threefold. Firstly, it will demonstrate that there is such a thing as presidential literary legacy and that a "literary-critical" reading of executive history invites more than popular consumption or political unmasking, but constitutes a process of image-making that is essential to legacy-building. Secondly, it identifies twinned notions of literary production and heritable succession as significant ideas central to the historical evolution of the presidency and executive office. Finally, it argues for a more nuanced narrative assessment of presidential scholarship as a multimodal and multivocal production over the long arc of United States history, angling for literature as a critical pattern and conduit of legacy in the national remembrance. It contends that a symphonic host of signifiers, fictive and real, inform presidential image-making and memorialization. Thereby, this study grounds itself in a return to Washington as the founder of this tradition, and derives constructive meaning from an under-examined civil suit from the Early Republic: *Livingston v. Jefferson*. This case, and the precedents set by Washington, set the tone for presidential legacy for centuries to come.

Reading presidential history

Literary legacy offers new inroads into our evaluation of presidential history. The literary view operates at cross-reflective angles, observing and examining executive form and criticism so as to clarify and interconnect written texts and discourses, the substance of narrative and character, and the intricate interlacing of recorded fact with fiction. In the entries compiled in *A New Literary History of America*, editors Greil Marcus and Werner Sollors offer broad scope for capturing its function, expanding traditional literary-critical bounds to contend that "what is at issue [in the new literary history of America] is speech, in many forms."[5] Literature provides rich and essential resources for investigating presidential legacy more intensively, for the executive office is, and has always been, a voiced creation of the will and consent of the people. And in wrestling history backwards to the founding bequest, to the first manner of legacy handed down by the first US president, we find good reason to pursue a literary excavation, not in material substance only, but by manner of rhetorical approach. For at the close of his own inaugural chapter, "we the people" are charged by Washington's contemporaries, within the new national frame, with the high task of close presidential reading.

Delivered in 1800, during the first contested presidential election and in the context of Washington's passing, Royall Tyler published "An Oration, Pronounced . . . In Commemoration of the Death of General George Washington." Tyler, a polymath who fought briefly in the Revolutionary War, served as a jurist in Vermont when the state was entered into the Union, and wrote a number of plays, exhorts "fathers, friends, and fellow citizens" to mourn the loss "of our political father."[6] Whilst turning "the historic page" to read the life of Washington, Tyler's eulogy proclaims that "a thousand [moral] volumes are too few to teach us what is virtuous and honorable. But the life of WASHINGTON is a compendium of instruction. His life is a practical treatise of the cardinal virtues. Would you learn how to live? Read his life."[7] Tracing his tribute through a sequence of memorial conditions, Tyler asks "WOULD you possess that martial courage . . . WOULD you imitate that fortitude which sustains the hero . . . WOULD you learn . . . divine grace of forgiveness . . . WOULD you excel as farmers . . . Are you ambitious of serving your country with reputation in the civil grades of Society?" Each question is accompanied by concrete direction to *"pass with* WASHINGTON," to *"view* WASHINGTON", and to *"follow* WASHINGTON." To see him in action would, Tyler assumed, lead Americans to copy his acts in glory:

> WOULD you possess that dignified virtue of equanimity, in the possession of Dictatorial power, and humility in the resignation of it? *Pursue* WASHINGTON to the tented field, and *read* his Resignation

of his high Commission of Commander in Chief in the armies of the United States.

WOULD you impress modesty, that seal of all the Virtues, upon all your actions? *Peruse* his official Letters.

... remember how like the prophet Elijah he dropt his mantle upon us in his last legacy to the people. Would you learn the true interest of America? Study attentively this precious relic; and as you study, bless, gratefully bless, the sainted lips which pronounced it.[8]

America's republican etymology is established here by virtue and name of its common founder. For insofar as we are permitted by Tyler to read, to peruse, to study the life of Washington, the national community is directly called upon to interpret its representatives rightly as against this original and professed saintly form. The "true interest of America," as Tyler makes plain, would be forever embalmed in close relation to Washington's life, adhering tightly to the character of his office. "If only," as Tyler laments, "mankind were appointed to immortality!" But as mortal sorrow is certain, he projects, such heritage must be preserved in trust by the living—accessible to citizens in each generation so as to protect the "transmitting down entire, those sacred rights which WASHINGTON obtained."[9]

As soon as we introduce the concept of legacy we necessarily admit, as in Tyler's conjuring, any number of heightened and potentially dangerous attributes of myth, where prevailing and disparate politics contend with realms of truth. Approached this way, such eulogistic imagery becomes the stuff of literary affect, emotive appeal aimed at personifying new national urgencies of socio-political construction. Tyler's performative American mythology promotes and distends an ostensibly circumscribed governing narrative, issuing a grammatical framework for republican growth that slides into realms of legend. The presidential myth itself, however, as herein contextualized and passed down in our remembrance of Washington, is neither dissociated from reality nor static in its heritable value, but in its imaging of family resemblance and "property" bequeathed accentuates its own variable shape, and assumes the power to disavow strict limits. Presidential form—the stature and reach of Washington, the first man in office—is rendered contentious and complex in light of changing "civil grades" and civic reception that must be assumed through the outplaying of United States history, the fickle inclusivity of "we" as people, audience, and judge of the past and present. The presidential subject of Tyler's modern mythology is seen to inhere not in logical chains of falsehood or truth, but in a mobile and movable quality found in living personifications that endure as transformative social and political realities, enacted by diverse community networks.

The enduring substance of mythoi, composed over long presidential history, thus highlights the varied and specious powers of fiction, yielding new interpretive problems for scholars of presidential history. Presidential legacy refers after all to a perpetually twinned genealogy, where the legacy of "Mr. President" is ever contoured through the legacy of the office itself. As Tyler demonstrates in his eulogy, fiction in both respects is unavoidable: the character of the man is bound to his office, and his office to the substance of a charactered story. What is more, the fiction of presidential unity may well be the cost of political power. As Tyler suggests, a stable American democracy is a "suspended" reality, a "majestic" idea, a myth of *E Pluribus Unum* personified in the role of chief executive. A president is woven into the office, and Washington into his successors. That process inculcates "a lasting sense" of shared values in the national imagining and generates in perpetuity something akin to F. Scott Fitzgerald's "willingness of the heart."[10] As Fitzgerald conceives it in his modernist short story "The Swimmers" (1929), this willingness to secure the dream of America is harbored in "that quality of the idea" that while holding its own as a fictive unity nevertheless appears set adrift at times from the historied source(s) of its making: "they [his expatriate Americans] go elsewhere and push other water. They spend months in France and they couldn't tell you the name of the President."[11]

As evident in the grammar of Washington's Farewell Address, this projected quality of the American will is no less bound to its presidential heritage and genealogy than it is intertwined with the mobile and variegated makeup of the people, who "with slight shades of difference" and distance, nevertheless command "a persuasive language" of individual liberty and "the continuance of the [national] Union" as one political ideal.[12] How this conceit is transmitted from one generation to the next, who has the power of that transmission, and how it is interpretatively received, as Washington suggests, is the continuing problem of governance; whether at home or abroad, the political strength of the executive office is seen to rely on this imagining.[13] And so in deciphering presidential myth as something manufactured, we mark those moments where man and office fail to integrate and inter-dissolve, and where narrative legacy takes shape in sharp and contrastive measures, despite or in reaction to protest, party, or faction, distance or displacement; or in splits and fissures, as with Washington himself, who while privileging the myth of office nevertheless sought to divest himself of personal fame in its glory.[14] While interpreting presidential pasts in the trajectory of legacy, such disavowals must be consulted; democratic engagement must be taken into account; the performance must be assessed.[15] The written-ness of political history, the agency of literature, the changing methods of cross-generational transmission, and the "warm interest" of character development must be substantively explored, using critical methods of deep literary anthropology.[16]

For this reason, "literary legacy" concedes a blurring of the bounds between the real and the imagined and discovers in their overlapping conceits, as Royall Tyler relates, our present "compendium of instruction."[17] This idea is echoed among Tyler's nineteenth-century contemporaries (those who urged him to publish his "Oration," as well as in common biographical productions and poetics of Washington remembrance) and among earlier transatlantic students of Enlightenment thought.[18] Thomas Jefferson, for instance, conceptualized this in his "literary" common-place book and vivified the overlap in his library catalog prescribed to a fellow Virginian in 1771, where "Hume's History of England," "Blackstone's Commentaries," "Ld. Kaim's Principles of Equity," "Bolingbroke's Philosophical Works", and publications by Montesquieu, Sidney, and Locke sit beside entries by Shakespeare, Congreve, Smollett, Richardson, Chaucer, and Swift.[19] Offering his thoughts on the formation of a private library, Jefferson here underscores the conflation of history writing and the fictive, ascribing the moral value of one's lived inheritance to the natural correspondence between the actual and the conceived. "Considering history as a moral exercise, her lessons would be too unfrequent if confined to real life. Of those recorded by historians few incidents have been attended with such circumstances as to excite in any high degree this sympathetic emotion of virtue. We are therefore wisely framed," he counsels:

> to be as warmly interested for a fictitious as for a real personage. The spacious field of imagination is thus laid open to our use, and lessons may be formed to illustrate and carry home to the mind every moral rule of life. Thus a lively and lasting sense of filial duty is more effectually impressed on the mind of a son or daughter by reading King Lear, than by all the dry volumes of ethics and divinity that ever were written. This is my idea of well-written Romance, of Tragedy, Comedy, and Epic Poetry.[20]

Although the history of American self-making undergoes a dramatic shift with time from early trepidation over moral effects to later modernist concerns with psychological division, such dual interest "for a fictitious as for a real personage" presents itself as an "instructive" and "illustrative" continuance over the long arc of national remembrance, relevant to the study of practical authority in presidential legacy today.[21] Hence Jefferson's notion persists, we might say, in Obama's allusion to the fictional Atticus Finch, calling US citizens to social forbearance via sympathetic conceit; or in his autobiographical *Dreams from My Father* (1995), which finds its near relation, as has been said, in Ralph Ellison's *Invisible Man* (1952).[22] The fact that political "instruction" persists via paternal mandate, as it were, from the origins of presidential history regenerates the myth of the presidential bequest as itself a patrilineal conveyance, instantiating a form of executive governance that prevails at odds with modern democratic nation-building. "He [Washington] was the father of the country," sounds Tyler, "good men . . . like the children of one great family, are come to weep over their father's grave."[23] Such rhetoric arms the "call to sons" that then concludes his *Oration* and privileges the gendered course of the presidential line to date: "if, perchance, your homes salute you with a father's honored name," he exhorts, "go, call your sons, tell them of WASHINGTON; instruct them what a debt they owe their ancestors and vest them executors of his will."[24]

Our twenty-first-century reading of presidential history intertextually maps and intercalates this literary field of performed and recurring values. The most obvious channels of literary legacy thus include all matter of written document and compilation: letters, papers, diaries, notebooks, and correspondence; biographies and memoirs; travel accounts, postcards, and sketches. Literary legacy includes a smattering of campaign slogans such as Harrison's "Tippecanoe and Tyler Too," Obama's "Hope," or Wilson's "He proved the pen mightier than the sword." It might invite transcripts of presidential recordings, such as the Johnson and Nixon tapes; or it might admit the lyrics of 2016 Nobel poet laureate Bob Dylan: "But even the president of the United States / Sometimes must have to stand naked."[25] It might include a bubbled collection of cartoon straplines, or invite Ed Murrow's Allied on-air journalism; it might incorporate William Manchester's *Portrait of a President* or *Death of a President*, or George W. Bush's later presidential citation.[26] Or it might comprise a multitude of fictional, poetic, and dramatic works; the nineteenth-century Anglo-French plays featuring General George Washington; Washington Irving's supposed caricature of Jefferson in the person of William-the-Testy in *A History of New York*, published in 1809; Hawthorne's *The Life of Franklin Pierce*—a "generally correct narrative" published by Ticknor, Reed, and Fields in 1852; or Ezra Pound's intensive modernist *Cantos*, mythologizing the presidency by fragments and memorializing John Adams in poetic dialogue with Adams's original letters.[27] Certainly there is a wealth of discourse to be found in sermon-writing and song, together with that competing array of circulating texts and broadsides read, gifted, written, and arbitrated by family members, campaign hopefuls, lobbyists, judges, and emissaries, orbiting in constellation around the business of office.

Literary legacy is to be increasingly derived as well from an alternate virtual cloud of texts, symbols, and signs, whereby presidential terms are nominated, reconstituted, and reinforced via cross-generational habits, diplomatic forums, and nation branding.

A utopian scripted "Pledge of Allegiance" adopted by Congress in 1945 under FDR fits, or the version amended in 1954 to include "under God" in Eisenhower's term. The inaugural address, the State of the Union, the Oath, mass media coverage, "Twitter diplomacy", and press reports, or the language of Article II whereby the role is foundationally prescribed, all belong to literary-critical assessment. Pursuing such signs into the abstract, we might recur to French theorist Jean Baudrillard's postmodernist tour through what he referred to in the 1980s as an "astral" America, emptying all such signifiers into vast emptiness and simulation, while probing US power or "the Reagan mirage": "As for American reality," he writes, "even the face-lifted variety retains its vast scope, its tremendous scale ... All societies end up wearing masks. Why not the mask of Reagan? But what remains intact is what there was at the beginning: space and the spirit of fiction."[28]

From our present stance, then, which heralds a multimodal and polyvocal American Studies, and an American literary studies more particularly, we can look on this potentially discordant array of texts, performances, and discourses as joint constituents of a new American literary history, in the grand sense of Marcus and Sollors, and we might say with some certainty that "presidential literary legacy" of course incorporates all these things.[29]

Executive proceedings

Turning to a close reading of presidential history, and moving ahead two terms from Washington's administration, it becomes apparent that the diverse texts and discourses which shape our understanding of Thomas Jefferson's actions as the nation's third president, when read in constellation, serve to demonstrate the effects of literary legacy at work, permitting us to recover certain pockets, breaks, and omissions in the narrative account. Two stanzas from William Lambert's "Ode for the Fourth of July, 1810" set the problem and tone:

> Let Jefferson who lately fill'd
> The president's exalted seat,
> For wisdom fam'd, in science skill'd

Our praise and approbation meet,
Hail Columbia, &c.

Detraction's rude and pois'nous tongue
Against his worth has spread its sound;—
The peals of envy may be rung,
But all these arts we shall confound.
Hail Columbia, &c.[30]

A literary-critical approach to Jefferson's early nineteenth-century dispute over the Louisiana Batture (a massive alluvial deposit along the Mississippi River that challenged territorial law and development in the young nation) allows us not only to unearth forgotten histories, but to reclaim notable erasures and rhetorical gaps as sites of new memory—as fertile grounds for reconstituting Jefferson's legacy of individual action, as well as for deepening our treatment of the historiographical evolution of the presidential office.[31]

The matter of *Livingston v. Jefferson* evolved from a civil suit filed against Thomas Jefferson on May 16, 1810, and illustrates in both legal and literary terms the compositional friction that joins Jefferson the private man with the public man in his presidential office.[32] Governed by numerous pleadings over justification, judicial precedent, and jurisdiction, the suit, though filed by the plaintiff in a federal circuit court in Virginia, threatened years of local New Orleans custom and intensified a set of national socio-political disputes over the emerging role and character of the executive.[33]

The case commenced following a presidential action instigated by Jefferson at the request of Louisiana territorial governor William Claiborne in 1807, forcing the removal of private citizen Edward Livingston from beachfront property that had accumulated as deposit along the banks of the Mississippi River—a piece of land referred to in French as the Batture of the Faubourg Ste Marie, or more generally, the batture, or alluvion. Livingston had commenced construction on the riverbank after acquiring an ownership interest in a parcel of the land through a decision by the court in 1805.[34] Local New Orleans residents responded with outrage to Livingston's works and urged Governor Claiborne to intervene, demanding that he arrest building procedures and restore the batture to the public use. Unable to settle the conflict locally, Claiborne petitioned Washington for support, and Jefferson responded to the crisis by asking then Secretary of State James Madison to involve the US Marshal. Livingston was subsequently forced from the site. Following Livingston's eviction, and only after Jefferson had retired from office, Livingston sued Jefferson for $100,000, arguing his right to the alluvial land by asserting title to the adjacent property. This initiated a case against the government and against the public that would persist in variable form for well over a decade. Livingston's 1810 petition, as examined here, would fail on December 5, 1811 for lack of proper jurisdiction.[35]

Notwithstanding the anticlimax, *Livingston v. Jefferson* suffered a literary post-mortem in publications rendered by both parties, principally Jefferson's "Proceedings of the [United States] government," a lengthy analysis of federal action, presidential decision, and law, and Livingston's subsequent "Answer to Mr. Jefferson's Justification," an incensed exposition—each one attending to the case on its merits and devoted to substantive explications of legal theory and fact.[36] Overburdened with pleadings, both real and fictitious, and heavy with legalese of a French, Spanish, and now American case law, the Batture matter proved "frightfully complicated," as one historian writes, and is generally swept into footnotes on the Louisiana Purchase, mentioned in civil procedure case briefs under the "local action" rule, or produced as an aside to *Marbury v. Madison*.[37] Unlike the Sally Hemings scandal, which has been so widely contextualized as to render it almost consistently inconsistent in the Jefferson narrative, *Livingston* has been routinely hung backstage, shielded in some respect from public scrutiny. In the words of nineteenth-century US Supreme Court Justice Joseph Story, "Who ... can remember, without regret, [Jefferson's] conduct in relation to the batture of New Orleans?"[38] Or as twenty-first-century critic Ronan Degnan affirms:

> [I do] not dispute that Thomas Jefferson was a great national hero whose memory is properly revered to this day. Still, if all one knew about Jefferson was his conduct in the matter of the New Orleans batture and his treatment of Edward Livingston, a different conclusion would emerge, a portrait of a petty politician and a contriver

extraordinaire who was not at all above manipulating the federal judiciary to serve his own selfish purposes. I end still admiring Jefferson, but less ardently . . .[39]

Degnan's summary hedges its bets against a simple hero-done-fall scenario by folding the matter into the silhouette of Jefferson immemorial, but reading the case in full permits conflicting narratives to surface. Although dismissed before a trial on the merits, two accounts appear throughout the course of the proceedings that instantiate our current concerns: firstly as to Jefferson's executive action, and secondly as to his presidential character. Venting reason on both fronts, Livingston and Jefferson deploy deep literary-critical and literary-inventive techniques to argue legal principle and to test executive action in form.

Executive action

An analysis of rhetorical strategy reveals a stark contest in the affair over the nature and reach of presidential authority, with Livingston arguing that he was "violently dispossessed [of the alluvion] by the orders of the President of the United States" and Jefferson countering that Livingston acted "in defiance of the general right of the nation."[40] "It became my duty, as charged with the preservation of public property," Jefferson states, "to remove the intrusion, and to maintain the citizens of the United States in their right to a common use of that beach."[41] In his *Proceedings*, Jefferson's seizure of the batture is argued to have been in keeping with the executive's "right to abate" a nuisance or danger to the city of New Orleans, where presidential authority was exercised commensurate with his duty to protect the common good. The "character & office" of the president is rhetorically figured in Jefferson's defence via procedural dialogue with the public safety and right, and is established in legal terms as a conjoined democratic agent of the nation's will and charge. The "Plea in *Livingston v. Jefferson* on Ground of Acting Officially" reads as follows:

> . . . the said Thomas . . . in the year 1807 aforesaid, being then and long before and since President of the said United States, in order to perform his duty as president aforesaid, according to his judgment and

conscience, did acting solely & exclusively in his character & office of President aforesaid, without any malice against the said Edward, direct the Marshal of the said territory, to remove, in the name & for the benefit of the United States, from the said lands messuage [sic] and Close aforesaid, any and every person, who Should have taken possession thereof or of any part thereof . . .[42]

"But how is he," demands Livingston in his "Answer," "in whom the executive power is vested . . . to ascertain that which belongs to the public, what to the individual occupying it? . . . Whenever, then, he [Jefferson] erroneously thinks, or wickedly affects to think, that land in my possession belongs to the public, the president may order a regiment of dragoons to drive me from it at the point of a sabre."[43] Opposing Jefferson's plea, Livingston decries the malicious and perceived unconstitutional exercise of that executive power in force: "Answer: My works did not threaten to drown the city. Mathematical proof of the fact. Mr. J. not high Constable of New Orleans. Local law sufficient to prevent and local authorities to abate nuisances."

Livingston further denounces Jefferson's avowedly presidential conduct by accusing him of secret motives in forcing his removal: "why did he select my *batture* from so many others equally situated?" He also accuses Jefferson of undermining the dignity of his presidential office, of mistranslating records, exercising illegal authority, and "coquetting" political colleagues "over to his opinion." Jefferson's "declamation [was] calculated to excite prejudices against me," Livingston contends, so as to set "his own [unlawful] justification" in false relief against a profoundly "disliked" and "unpopular" individual: "Humane conclusion that I deserved to be *committed to the flames*."[44] Livingston's fiery invective wends its way through Jefferson's nuanced argument for US title in the batture, sequenced through disputed territorial law and code, before folding itself into a so-called "Pathetic" appeal in the following verse by Spenser:

> Ah! little knowest thou, who hast not try'd,
> What hell it is, in suing long to bide,
> To lose good days that might be better spent,

PRESIDENTIAL LEGACY: A LITERARY PROBLEM

> To pass long nights in passive discontent . . .
> To eat thy heart through comfortless despair;
> To fawn, to crouch, to wait, to ride, to run,
> To spend, to give, to want, to be undone;
> Unhappy wight! Such hard fate doom'd to try;
> That curse God send unto mine enemy.[45]

This fictive turn, though couched as an aside, bears weight in our analysis for what it suggests in our reading of Jefferson's actions and for how it braces our comprehension of image-making in presidential legacy more broadly. For in his emotive plea for relief, Livingston attempts to amend his own widely "unpopular" political identity by invoking a moralizing poetics, compelling shared understanding for his plight by urging positive re-evaluation of his suit and detracting from his opposition through imagined cords of (woeful) self-identification. His discursive attempts to realign the public sympathy in his favor are thus significant for their plausible effect in not only challenging Jefferson's narrative claims to constitutionality but in sharpening public expectations of executive political engagement, particularly as to the president's mediation of the contest between individual rights and social democratic protections. Recurring to similar conceits, Jefferson too goads the public sentiment through strategic literary appeal, employing fictive analogy and Shakespearean comedy in his "Proceedings" so as to vilify Livingston's self-interest in the matter, such that his own legacy of individual action, read across both works, is fashioned in the public eye at the interface between competing fictions.[46]

Somewhat unsurprisingly, then, the problem of executive role-play in the affair is centralized, in an arch character, with respect to presidential accountability. Livingston faults Mr. J. for incriminating the members of his Cabinet Council by drawing advisers into the suit to shoulder the weight of his personal responsibility. Not only that, Livingston contends, but Jefferson desired those "servants . . . who committed the trespass" (the government on the ground, as it were) to be "made parties to the suit" for his individual actions in the affair. "The president of the United States wished the innocent ministers of his illegal acts to be made fellow-sufferers with him, for executing his orders!!" Livingston exclaims. From this the plaintiff extrapolates to allege a despotic and royal manner by which Jefferson confused though sheer art of "plurality" the role of President with all other political capacities—"*We* were called," Jefferson avers, and as Livingston objects:

> As LEGISLATOR, he was to make a new law to fit the circumstances of the case; as JUDGE, he was to apply to it those facts which as a JUROR he was to ascertain, and to pronounce that sentence which, as EXECUTIVE OFFICER he was himself to carry into effect; as PRESIDENT, he was to reclaim the lands of the United States; as COMMANDER IN CHIEF of the armies, a sufficient *military force* was to be prepared to over-awe opposition; . . . as MAYOR . . . ; as HIGH CONSTABLE . . . ; as STREET COMMISSIONER . . . [etc.].[47]

That Livingston accommodated Alexander Hamilton's views in these instances (an arrow sharply barbed) concerning powers to be delegated to the executive branch, called into play an intensive dialogue over the manner in which power should be divided within the federal government. And in a rhetorical maneuver designed to shift the weight of blame onto Jefferson alone, Livingston's language exploited Hamilton's suggestion in *Federalist* 70 that the "multiplication of the executive tends to conceal faults and destroy responsibility."[48] Despite Livingston's attempts to deconstruct Jefferson, the late president continued to defend his conduct on the batture as the appropriate outworking of a constitutionally governed Executive, acting in its principal role as chief guardian of the public right. And in a tone reminiscent of Paine ("there is something exceedingly ridiculous"), he challenged the absurdity of Livingston's suit:

> were the Executive, in the vast mass of concerns of first magnitude, which he must direct, to place his whole fortune, on the hazard of every opinion; . . . in short were every man engaged in rendering service to the public bound in his body and goods to indemnification for all his errors, [then] we must commit our public affairs to the paupers of the nation, to the sweepings of hospitals and poor-houses, who, having nothing to lose, would have nothing to risk.[49]

Although Livingston contends that even "a plea of honest error" in this "vast mass of concerns" cannot afford a "general excuse" for executive officers, Jefferson's construction usefully prefigures the problem arising as to sovereign immunity from civil suit: "Great God!" wrote John Adams, "Is a President of the US to be Subject to a private Action of every Individual? This will soon introduce the Axiom that a President can do no wrong; or another equally curious that a President can do no right."[50] Although presidential immunity is not raised as a question of law in the suit, and finds no ruling until later in the century, the issue finds expressive figure here, and churns in literary conceit below the surface of the case.[51]

Presidential character

Implicit in Jefferson's published "Proceedings," then, is a fascinating character defence whereby Jefferson effectively retrieves his fragmented public self-image in order to bind apparent inconsistencies. "Recurring to the tenor of a long life of public service," he writes, "against the charge of malice and corruption I stand conscious and erect."[52] In circulating his argument to key political supporters and members of Congress, Jefferson redresses probable gaps in his exercise of power by inventing new rhetorical linkages—legal, moral, and political—with a host of like minded thinkers, including fellow men of letters. In such manner, he positions (or wrongfully manipulates, as some allege) those who might acquit him on appeal and authors a countervailing history of presidential action in text, character, and form. His "exposition of the Batture question," declares William Wirt, "is by far the best piece of Grecian architecture that I have ever seen, either from modern or ancient times."[53] A return from Elbridge Gerry reads as follows:

> I thank you for the pamphlet this day received, respecting "the intrusion of Edward Livingston"; & for your polite & friendly manner of transmitting it. The publick is much indebted to you on this, & on numerous other occasions, for performances; to which few are equal, & still fewer have a disposition.[54]

And from his predecessor, President John Adams, a vote of confidence by reverse character detraction:

> Yesterday, I received from the Post Office, under an envelope inscribed with your hand . . . a very learned and ingenious Pamphlet, prepared by you for the Use of your Counsel, in the case of Edward Livingston against you. . . . Neddy is a naughty lad as well as a saucy one. I have not forgotten his lying Villany in his fictitious fabricated Case of a Jonathan Robbins who never existed. His Suit against you, I hope has convinced you of his Character.[55]

Whether or not Jefferson planned to arbitrate his multi-varied persona(e) across these transactions, he was clearly concerned to resolve syntactic fractures, and endeavored to offset Livingston's litigious slander through smear tactics of his own, as Livingston contends, as well as through shrewd interpretive discourse on applied executive powers.[56] In setting its ground for posterity, we see Jefferson's language of law in the case struggling to discern its "reasonable [executive] man"—his appropriate mode and manner—even as it presumes "the presidential" construction to hold its original figurative aspect, as a foregone unity in fact: Jefferson did act, his plea contends, "solely & exclusively" in both "his character & office of President," and thus within constitutionally prescribed limits of the executive's role and function.[57] And among a few, at least, Jefferson need not have feared consternation or reprisal. In a letter dated May 19, 1810, William Lambert included two items for Jefferson's perusal: a newspaper containing toasts written and delivered at a meeting of the Tammany Society on May 12, and verse from his next anticipated "Ode for the Fourth of July, 1810" where Jefferson follows Washington in laudatory succession: "Hail Columbia, &c."[58] Even before the Livingston affair reached "high-water" (another legal dispute in the matter), the *National Intelligencer* published the society's proceedings and broadcasted Lambert's fine salute to the nation's late president: "*Thomas Jefferson*—Assailed in his retirement by malicious, unprincipled foes to our republican systems of government. Their persecuting malevolence is and ought to [be] requited by increasing contempt.—*He served his country with applause.*"[59]

PRESIDENTIAL LEGACY: A LITERARY PROBLEM

Grounds of appeal

Stepping back from the intricacies of the case, and with respect to its literary junctures, it serves us well to survey the broader grounds traversed in the course of Jefferson's proceedings. And in this sense I am no longer speaking of the legal grounds of either complaint or appeal, but of the littoral grounds themselves: the batture, the alluvial earth, the Mississippi sod, the deep-rooted relations of the President to the territory, to the soil, to the environment, to the turf that he cultivated and overruled. While Jefferson's disposition of this mantle of earth, relative to his purchase and then executive oversight of the Louisiana territory, was and remained a geo-politically charged investiture, it is possible to demonstrate the cross-connectedness of literary history and the rich possibilities open to us by way of literary legacy by suggesting that his relationship to the earth in this matter signals only one chapter in a much wider heritage concerning presidential connections to the land itself.[60] These "presidential acts of earth," as I will call them, pronounce a literary imperative for interpreting thick presidential history, and supply a vital trans-American and outward-extending global trajectory for our further and future considerations of constructed presidential legacy.

For in heralding its fictions, this case of the batture interweaves its difficult heritage with another narrative arc of presidential succession, where executive history comes down to us in landscape fictions, loss memoirs, and written accounts of executive relief. By way of fictive analogy, new lines of correspondence and conversion appear suddenly visible among seemingly discordant histories. I name only a few in sequence: Andrew Jackson's executive signature of law whereby he catered to cotton possession and set in motion the trail of tears (Indian Removal Act, 1830); Lincoln's ceremonial dedication of the burial ground at Gettysburg, where simple words, spoken over a field, are calibrated with the figural weight of those who gave their "last full measure" (Gettysburg Address, 1863); Theodore Roosevelt's literary sketch called "Hunting the Grisly," which accompanies the American buffalo vanishing into wilderness and the black bear who "Holds his Own Well in the Land" (G.P. Putnam's Sons,

1889).⁶¹ FDR's New Deal realpolitik, captured in the diary of an Alaskan Matanuska Valley colonist: "Cattle have died, farms are ruined . . . all that is left to us is courage to try and carve new homes" (circa 1935); John F. Kennedy's presidential citation at Cape Canaveral, honoring Col. John H. Glenn Jr. by figuring consonance between territorial claims over Mount Suribachi and the hoped-for "American flag on the moon" (February 23, 1962); Jimmy Carter's personal remembrance of the Depression as a child: of "the sand, loam," "red clay", and "soil," he writes, "My most persistent impression as a farm boy was of the earth" (2001).⁶²

We might discern Jefferson's batture legacy in the timeline of environmental development and crisis history, citing a later removal in the annals of literary bequests: "A Noah's Ark of 1927"—that Great Mississippi flood, where executive action again undertook to divert the great course of a river. In a silent film dated 1936, we read small black letters ribboned in celluloid reel across black-and-white frames: "4:10 'The Red Cross moved swiftly. Secretary Hoover on the request of the President took charge April 20'" / "5:00 'Reinforcing the levee at Baton Rouge LA'" / "10:40 'inspecting flood conditions'" / "13.50 'registering the names of refugees'" / "14:25, 'more than half a million people were inoculated with the result that no lives were lost through contagious diseases.'"⁶³ Jefferson's Louisiana trial maps well into the legacy of Coolidge after 1927, Bush after Katrina in 2005, or Trump in the aftermath of Harvey, Irma, and Maria in 2017. It parries with discussions of rising global temperatures, executive orders on leadership and sustainability, or the recent US presidential determination to withdraw from the Paris climate accord. So this muddy affair of *Livingston v. Jefferson* extends beyond any myopic study of Jefferson himself, this gardener farmer who preferred the solace of Monticello to the burdens of the White House, to inform via narrative assessments a more rigorous reading and understanding of presidential action outworked over evolving US executive history.

The problem of and indeed the great fascination with presidential literary legacy across these channels is the extent to which it is powered over time by a great multiplicity of fictions. Literary legacy preserves and supplies an endless font of living relationships that ever inform new democratic proceedings in the present generation; and if the case of the Louisiana Batture offers, in this manner, any form of real or future deposit, then the president's relationship to the earth is most certainly key among them. As with Livingston's legal dispute over the nature of alluvion in consequence and form, it is the very quality of connectedness—the shore with the sea in this instance—that denotes heritable value and right of possession. Is the alluvial earth "so consolidated with the contiguous land," Livingston asks, that it by right belongs to its proprietors? This question metaphorically accentuates the executive office at the same time emerging in formative contest over its grounds of democratic growth and the quest for presidential identity being mapped into the national consciousness by "slow degrees" of dialogical conveyance.[64] To whom does its territory belong? As Livingston stresses, "the same master," if for no other reason than that "the profits and the advantage of the thing" should belong "to him who is exposed to suffer its damages and losses."[65] From Washington's death to Trump's life at work, the peoples' rights, it may be said, inhere via translative acts in the twinned genealogy of presidential accession: for "that augmentation being operated in a slow and [at times] imperceptible manner, remains to the inheritance to which it is found united."[66]

Conclusion

In admitting a state of flux as the fraught balance of the early American Union, we find embedded in the batture case and surrounding politics a host of calibrating measures seeking in diverse ways to check and revitalize the executive as a democratic instrument. The effort to unpack related grammars of presidential constitutionality, the legacy of decision-making, and mythmaking characterizations yield no shortage of literary turns. From chronology to counter-visions, the people transmit a "quality of the idea" in mixed democratic quotient, as the changeable substance of story.[67]

A reading of later US civil rights literature acutely demonstrates the impact of such transmissions, opening new and still challenging avenues into our political comprehension. Take for instance John Lewis's *Memoir of the Movement* (1998), which tracks his personal presidential encounters (in life and imagined memorial) from an early Alabama childhood through varied outworkings of the movement into the 1980s. Lewis's written life here *passes with*, *views*, *reads*, and *follows* the legacies of Lincoln, Kennedy, Johnson, Nixon, Ford, and Carter. In probing these and other White House interactions Lewis admits the strict progress of the executive office over time, thus recomposing its prevailing genealogical myth, while revising the nature and substance of its governing ontology, ascribing its chief powers to new agents and arbiters of democracy. "When Jimmy Carter was elected President that November [of 1976]," Lewis reflects, "I cried . . . But those tears weren't about him. They were about the fact that the hands that picked cotton had now picked a president. The black vote in that election was decisive."[68] Lewis's rhetoric maps into fictional works by James Baldwin who stood with Lewis, or Obama's later election, or US civil rights activism in march and movement today. Certainly this cluster of examples invites us to reassess the generative syntax that facilitates his process of calibration.[69]

The literary impulse is not new, and neither is the quest for authentic power. That fundamental desire to wrestle with presidential character, readership, and plot so as to unveil the "true man" behind the proverbial mask, or that desire to, at the very least, imagine our way into the stories we like best and craft our political reality through them, is a part of history immemorial.[70] But a literary-critical approach to history need not stop there in its interpretive value; it need not tend towards what Dana Nelson has viewed as a "retrospective presidential analysis," or an analysis that is "politically enclaved" in a public array of "democratic engagement[s]."[71] Such a view misses the profound capacity of the literary to cut across the very enclaves it constructs, or to project new forms of meaning. Traditional presidential history studies have spent much time endeavoring to wrestle facts from fiction, rather than setting the fictions at level with fact. If our reading of legacy is vital to understanding the value of the past for the future, or as a mode of political historicization and practical political reconstruction, then the multivocal nature of presidential literary legacy must be centralized as a current operating reality and understood for its narrative capacity to open, enlarge, or disrupt new fields of representative action.

The justification for this takes root not in a conviction that we have altogether ignored literary features in our study of presidential history to date (Sean McCann's *A Pinnacle of Feeling* or Jeff Smith's *The Presidents We Imagine* show that this is not the case), but in a belief that our reading of presidential legacy has yet to provide a comprehensive analytical frame for such investigations, or to seriously incorporate the polyphonic and creative impact of the people's will discharged in the role and character of office.[72] It has yet to unravel the multilayered processes of literary construction that yield or obscure such presidential legacy as *Livingston* relates. Such a study is increasingly necessary as it pertains to political agency, and "appears to me proper," to invoke Washington's own words at resignation, "especially as it may conduce to a more distinct expression of the public voice."[73] The legacy of office reflects after all this contrary, transient production, where America's perplexed democratic unity is transposed fact in hand with its fiction:

> Half of the people can be part right all of the time
> Some of the people can be all right part of the time
> But all of the people can't be all right all of the time
> I think Abraham Lincoln said that.[74]

Notes

1. Royall Tyler, "An Oration, Pronounced at Bennington, Vermont, February 22, 1800, In Commemoration of the Death of General George Washington" (Walpole, NH: Printed for Thomas & Thomas by David Carlisle, 1800), 5. This chapter was first presented at a meeting of the Presidential History Network, May 26–27, 2016, at Northumbria University. I wish to thank Michael Cullinane and members of the PHN for their valuable feedback in that forum, as well as the Institute for Advanced Studies in the Humanities, University of Edinburgh, for supporting earlier research into the Livingston affair.
2. Ronald Reagan, *An American Life: The Autobiography* (New York: Simon & Schuster, 2011); Jimmy Carter, *Keeping Faith: Memoirs of a President* (Little Rock: University of Arkansas Press, 1995).

3. Barack Obama, "Farewell Address," <http://www.presidency.ucsb.edu/ws/index.php?pid=119928> (accessed June 13, 2018). Richard Purcell and Henry Veggian introduce and examine Obama's literary legacy with respect to his political writings in their edited volume. See Richard Purcell and Henry Veggian, *Barack Obama's Literary Legacy: Readings of Dreams From My Father* (New York: Palgrave Macmillan, 2016).
4. Brown, *Clotel* or *The President's Daughter: A Narrative of Slave Life in the United States* (London: Partridge & Oakey, 1853); Harper Lee, *To Kill A Mockingbird* (New York: Harper Collins, 2010), 7; Gore Vidal, *An Evening with Richard Nixon* (New York; Random House, 1972); Philip Roth, *The Plot Against America* (New York: Vintage International, 2005). For example, see Mercedez Holtry, "We're Here to Stay," *Women of the World Poetry Slam* 2016, <https://www.youtube.com/watch?v=TYGxLJK64Cg> (accessed June 13, 2018). The growing significance of performance poetry in the transnational literary arena cannot be understated. Its impact was highlighted to me in profound ways at the American Literature Association Symposium on "Frontiers and Borders in American Literature," San Antonio, TX, February 25–27, 2016. See related borders work by such Texas writers as Jasminne Mendez, *Island of Dreams* (Moorpark, CA: Floricanto Press, 2013) and Natalia Treviño, *Lavando La Dirty Laundry* (Norman, OK: Mongrel Empire Press, 2014).
5. Greil Marcus and Werner Sollors (eds.), *A New Literary History of America* (Cambridge, MA: Harvard University Press, 2009), xxiv.
6. Tyler, "An Oration," 3–4.
7. Ibid. 5. On other eulogistic practices see George E. Kahler, *The Long Farewell: Americans Mourn the Death of George Washington* (Charlottesville: University of Virginia Press, 2008).
8. Tyler, "An Oration," 6–9. Emphasis added by author.
9. Ibid. 8, 3–16.
10. F. Scott Fitzgerald, "The Swimmers," *Saturday Evening Post*, October 19, 1929: I & IV; Tyler, "An Oration," 7.
11. Fitzgerald, "The Swimmers," IV, I.
12. "Washington's Farewell Address," <http://www.presidency.ucsb.edu/ws/index.php?pid=65539> (accessed June 13, 2018).
13. Ibid. Washington speaks of political unity as a matter of national security: "The unity of government which constitutes you one people is . . . a main pillar in the edifice of your real independence, the support of your tranquility at home, your peace abroad . . .

think and speak of it as of the palladium of your political safety and prosperity."
14. Ibid.
15. For one interdisciplinary study of presidential performance, see Jason L. Mast, *The Performative Presidency: Crisis and Resurrection during the Clinton Years* (Cambridge: Cambridge University Press, 2013).
16. Thomas Jefferson, Letter to Robert Skipwith, with a List of Books for a Private Library, August 3, 1771, in Julian P. Boyd (ed.), *The Papers of Thomas Jefferson* (Princeton, NJ: Princeton University Press, 1950), 1, 77.
17. Tyler, "An Oration," 5.
18. Tyler, "An Oration." "*His Excellency Isaac Tichenor, the Hon. Supreme Court, and many other respectable citizens*" are cited among those seeking publication of Tyler's "*Oration*" on "*the Death of our late beloved WASHINGTON.*" See the accompanying letter from Amos Porter, March 3, 1800. See also Parson Mason Locke Weems's *A History of the Life and Death, Virtues and Exploits of General George Washington* (1800). For a discussion of Weems's work in relation to American "self-culture" see Dana D. Nelson, "Commentary," *American Literary History* 24, no. 3 (Fall 2012): 550–60. Other examples include Washington Irving's five-volume *Life of George Washington*, completed in 1859, or James Fenimore Cooper's glowing personification of Washington in the character of Mr. Harper in *The Spy: A Tale of the Neutral Ground* (1821).
19. *Jefferson's Literary Commonplace Book*, Douglas L. Wilson (ed.), *The Papers of Thomas Jefferson* (Princeton, NJ: Princeton University Press, 1989); Jefferson, Letter to Skipwith, *Papers of Thomas Jefferson*, 1, 76–81, see enclosure 78–81.
20. Boyd reflects that Jefferson's "defense of fiction ... represents the views of English critics from Sir Philip Sidney to Addison and Johnson." Jefferson, Letter to Skipwith, *Papers of Thomas Jefferson*, 1, 77, 81.
21. Jefferson, Letter to Skipwith, *Papers of Thomas Jefferson*, 1, 77; Tyler, "An Oration," 5.
22. Obama, "Farewell Address"; Obama, *Dreams from My Father: A Story of Race and Inheritance* (New York: Three Rivers Press, 2004). In 2014, Greg Grandin consulted a range of fictional works read by the president in his youth, including Ralph Ellison's *Invisible Man* (New York: Random House, 1952), which he says provided a model for Obama's memoir. See Grandin, "Obama, Melville and

the Tea Party," *New York Times*, January 18, 2014. For critical literary assessments see Purcell and Veggian.
23. Tyler, "An Oration," 4, 15–16.
24. Tyler, "An Oration," 16. Women are figured in Tyler's pronouncement as complementary bearers of virtue.
25. Bob Dylan, "It's Alright, Ma (I'm Only Bleeding)," *Bringing it All Back Home* (1965). Amidst controversy, Bob Dylan became the first musician to be awarded the Nobel Prize in Literature in 2016: "From an early age, I've been familiar with reading and absorbing the works of those who were deemed worthy of such a distinction: Kipling, Shaw, Thomas Mann, Pearl Buck, Albert Camus, Hemingway. These giants of literature ... housed in libraries around the world and spoken of in reverent tones have always made such a deep impression." Dylan, Nobel Prize acceptance speech, December 10, 2016, <https://www.nobelprize.org> (accessed June 13, 2018).
26. William R. Manchester, *Portrait of a President: John F. Kennedy in Profile* (Boston: MacFadden, 1962); *The Death of a President: November 20–25, 1963* (New York: Harper & Row, 1967); President George W. Bush awarded Manchester the National Humanities Medal, 2001 National Medal of Arts and Humanities Awards Ceremony, C-SPAN, April 22, 2002.
27. Nathaniel Hawthorne, "Preface," *The Life of Franklin Pierce* (Ticknor, Reed and Fields, 1852), 4; Ezra Pound, *The Cantos of Ezra Pound* (Norfolk, CT: New Directions, 1974), LXII-LXXI. For a close study of the Adams Cantos see David Ten Eyck, *Ezra Pound's Adams Cantos*, in the Historicizing Modernism series (London: Bloomsbury, 2012).
28. Jean Baudrillard, "The End of U.S. Power?" and "Astral America" in *America*, trans. Chris Turner (New York; London: Verso, 2010), 117–29 (118, 129); 27–78 (27): "In the image of Reagan, the whole of America has become Californian" (117).
29. See Marcus and Sollors, *A New Literary History*.
30. "William Lambert's, Ode for the Fourth of July, 1810," stanzas six and seven, intended to be "sung at this place [the Tammany Society of Washington] on the fourth of July next to the tune of 'Rule Brittannia.'" Lambert's "Ode" was enclosed in his letter to Thomas Jefferson, City of Washington, May 19, 1810 in J. Jefferson Looney (ed.), *The Papers of Thomas Jefferson*, Retirement Series (Princeton, NJ: Princeton University Press, 2005): 2, 398–401. Stanza three memorialises Washington in Tyler's commemorative style: "But Washington, illustrious sage / Came from the south, by Heav'n inspir'd; / In our defence did more engage, By love of independence fir'd / Hail Columbia, &c."

31. See Peter S. Onuf (ed.), *Jeffersonian Legacies* (Charlottesville: University Press of Virginia, 1993), especially Douglas L. Wilson, "Jefferson and the Republic of Letters," 50–76; Herbert Sloan, "The Earth Belongs in Usufruct to the Living," 281–315; Joyce Appleby, "Introduction: Jefferson and His Complex Legacy," 1–16.
32. *Livingston v. Jefferson*, 15 F. Cas. 660 (C.C.D. Va. 1811). Plaintiff Edward Livingston retained John Wickham as counsel; Defendant Jefferson retained William Wirt, George Hay, and eventually Littleton Waller Tazewell; federal circuit court, Richmond, Chief Justice John Marshall presiding. For a different literary-critical treatment of the case see Kristin A. Cook, *Executing Character: Of Sympathy, Self-Construction and Adam Smith, in Early America, 1716–1826* (Ph.D. dissertation, University of Edinburgh, 2012).
33. Edward Dumbauld, *Thomas Jefferson and the Law* (Norman: University of Oklahoma Press, 1978), 36–74. A famous decision by Lord Mansfield in the 1750s differentiated between a "transitory" and "local" action: when disputing *title* the action needed to be brought where the land was located [thus in Louisiana, not Virginia]; this initial suit did not "present a transitory, rather than a local, cause of action." Dumbauld notes that "a Minnesota case in 1891 took the contrary position."
34. Ronan E. Degnan, "*Livingston v. Jefferson*—A Freestanding Footnote," *California Law Review* 75, no. 1 (January 1987): 115–28.
35. Dumbauld, *Jefferson and the Law*, 36–37.
36. See Edward Livingston, *Address to the People of the United States on the Measures Pursued by the Executive with Respect to the Batture at New Orleans* (New Orleans: Bradford & Anderson, 1808); Thomas Jefferson, "The Batture at New Orleans: The proceedings of the Government of the United States in maintaining the public right to the beach of the Mississippi, adjacent to New Orleans, against the intrusion of Edward Livingston," in Andrew A. Lipscomb and Albert Ellery Bergh (eds.), *The Writings of Thomas Jefferson* (Washington, DC: Thomas Jefferson Memorial Association, 1903–04): 18, 1–132, hereafter cited as "Proceedings"; Livingston, "An Answer to Mr. Jefferson's justification of his conduct in the case of the New Orleans batture" (Philadelphia: William Fry, 1813), hereafter cited as "Answer".
37. Fictitious pleadings were then common, as Degnan reminds us, in such legal proceedings. See related discussions in Dumas Malone, *The Sage of Monticello*, vol. 6, in *Jefferson and His Time* (Charlottesville: University of Virginia Press, 2005), 55–73; George Dargo,

Jefferson's Louisiana: Politics and the Clash of Legal Traditions (Cambridge, MA: Harvard University Press, 1975). See also Dargo, *Law in the New Republic: Private Law and the Public Estate* (New York: Alfred A. Knopf, 1983), 107–36; *Marbury v. Madison*, 5 US 137 (1803).

38. Degnan, citing Story (in W. Story, ed., *Life and Letters of Joseph Story* (Boston: Little and Brown, 1851), 127, footnote 47).
39. Ibid. 127–28.
40. Answer, 2.
41. Proceedings, preface.
42. Plea in *Livingston v. Jefferson* on Ground of Acting Officially, ca. February 28, 1811, in *The Papers of Thomas Jefferson*, Retirement Series: 397–400.
43. Ibid. 146.
44. I was disliked at New Orleans / an unpopular man to be oppressed ("Answer," v, 24).
45. Here artfully compressing verse (and disavowing the final "sentiment") from Edmund Spenser, *Prosopopoia: Or Mother Hubberds Tale* (1591): I quote this passage from memory, writes Livingston, and may not, perhaps, have given every line the exact words of the admirable author ("Answer," 148).
46. In one illustration Jefferson draws on *Henry IV*. See Wilson, in *Jeffersonian Legacies*, 71.
47. "Answer," 112–13, 136. Emphasis added by author. Mr. Jefferson speaks in the plural number, assumes the style of royalty, and why, demands Livingston, 112.
48. Alexander Hamilton, *Federalist* 70, in Isaac Kramnick (ed.), *The Federalist Papers* (New York: Penguin, 1987), 406; Jay Fliegelman, *Declaring Independence: Jefferson, Natural Language, and the Culture of Performance* (Stanford, CA: Stanford University Press), 147–48.
49. Thomas Paine, *Common Sense* (London: Penguin, 1986), 69.
50. "Answer," xi; John Adams to Thomas Jefferson, Quincy, May 1, 1812, in Lester J. Cappon (ed.), *Adams-Jefferson Letters: The Complete Correspondence between Thomas Jefferson and Abigail and John Adams* (Chapel Hill: University of North Carolina Press, 1987), 300–01.
51. The US Supreme Court did not recognize absolute presidential immunity from civil suits until its twentieth-century ruling in *Richard Nixon v. A. Ernest Fitzgerald* (457 US 731, 1982); citing also *Spalding v. Vilas* (161 US 483, 1896).

52. "Proceedings," 132.
53. William Wirt to Thomas Jefferson, April 15, 1812,*The Papers of Thomas Jefferson*, Retirement Series: 4, 615–17; Sowerby, III, 407 in Dumbauld, 56.
54. Elbridge Gerry to Thomas Jefferson, May 1, 1812, *The Papers of Thomas Jefferson*, Retirement Series: 5.
55. John Adams to Thomas Jefferson, May 1, 1812, *Adams-Jefferson Letters*, 300.
56. On Jefferson's reputation in other matters see Francis D. Cogliano, *Thomas Jefferson: Reputation and Legacy* (Edinburgh: Edinburgh University Press, 2006); Merrill D. Peterson, *The Jefferson Image in the American Mind* (Oxford: Oxford University Press, 1960).
57. Although not formalized until 1837, the legal paradigm of the "reasonable man/person" standard appears at issue in this early discussion of Jefferson's individual action. See *Vaughan* v. *Menlove* (132 Eng. Rep. 490, 1837).
58. Lambert, "Ode."
59. William Lambert, "A Toast delivered at the Tammany Society," May 12, 1810 meeting of the Tammany Society of Washington, Washington *National Intelligencer*, May 16, 1810, enclosed in Lambert's letter to Jefferson, *Papers of Thomas Jefferson*: 2, 399.
60. See Robert D. Bush, *The Louisiana Purchase: A Global Context* (New York: Routledge, 2014).
61. Theodore Roosevelt, *Hunting the Grisly and Other Sketches* (New York: The Review of Reviews Company, 1904), 92–144; 3–36; 37–49 (see Contents).
62. Although these examples are listed chronologically, the literary view is most significant for its ability to circumvent temporal bounds and to hold these in different networks of orientation. Arnold R. Alanen, "Midwesterner Colonists in the Matanuska Valley: Colonizing Rural Alaska During the Great Depression," in Sally McMurry and Annmarie Adams (eds.), *People, Power, Places: Perspectives in Vernacular Architecture, VIII* (Knoxville: University of Tennessee Press, 2000), 53; Remarks at the Presentation of NASA's Distinguished Service Medal, <https://www.jfklibrary.org/Asset-Viewer/Archives/JFKPOF-037-019.aspx> (accessed June 13, 2018); Jimmy Carter, *An Hour before Daylight: Memories of a Rural Boyhood* (New York: Simon & Schuster, 2001), 13–47 (15).
63. Signal Corps of the Mississippi Flood, *Mississippi River Flood of 1927*, film, <https://archive.org/details/mississippi_flood_1927> (accessed June 13, 2018).

64. Citing an encyclopedia entry relied on by Jefferson: "Alluvion is an increase of the ground, which takes place by slow degrees, on the shores of the sea, on the borders of *fleuves* and rivers; occasioned by the earth which the water conveys to it, and which becomes so consolidated with the contiguous land, that it forms a *whole with it—an identity*" (38). Livingston uses this passage to refute Jefferson's case respecting US title in the batture.
65. Ibid.
66. Ibid.
67. Fitzgerald, "The Swimmers," IV.
68. John Lewis, with Michael D'Orso, *Walking with the Wind: A Memoir of the Movement* (New York: Simon and Schuster, 1998), 439.
69. Lewis, 239, photo insert no. 38; see James Baldwin, *No Name in the Street* (New York: Vintage, 2007).
70. See Jennifer Szalai, "What Makes a Politician 'Authentic?'" *New York Times Magazine*, July 5, 2016. On authenticity see Lionel Trilling, *Sincerity and Authenticity* (Cambridge, MA: Harvard University Press, 1972); Charles Taylor, *The Ethics of Authenticity* (Cambridge, MA: Harvard University Press, 1992).
71. Nelson, "Commentary," 555.
72. Sean McCann, *A Pinnacle of Feeling: American Literature and Presidential Government* (Princeton, NJ: Princeton University Press, 2008); Jeff Smith, *The Presidents We Imagine: Two Centuries of White House Fictions on the Page, on the Stage, Onscreen, and Online* (Madison: University of Wisconsin Press, 2009). See also Murray Edelman, *From Art to Politics: How Artistic Creations Shape Political Conceptions* (Chicago: University of Chicago Press, 1995).
73. "Washington's Farewell Address." Washington's statement refers to his precedent-setting decision to stand down from re-election to a third term.
74. Bob Dylan, "Talkin' World War III Blues," *The Freewheelin' Bob Dylan* (1963).

3

Pennsylvania Avenue meets Madison Avenue: The White House and commercial advertising

Michael Patrick Cullinane

In 2010, the Chrysler Corporation released a television commercial for the new Dodge Challenger, a much-loved muscle car brand returning to the market after a twenty-five-year hiatus. Expectations for the latest Challenger ran high, and the marketing campaign aimed to capitalize on the anticipation with a commercial that preceded the car's release. Set in Revolutionary-era America, the advertisement opened with the sound of a lone fiddler, and a colonial-era British redcoat running through the woods. When the scout finds his regiment of fellow soldiers, he breathlessly tells the commanding officer what he has seen. The scout's report—muted to the audience, who can only hear the quaint and ominous fiddler—prompts the British officer to order his regiment into columns. The tension builds as a pensive British platoon level and load muskets, gaze into the distance, and take aim, waiting to discover what the scout already knows. The camera pans across a quiet and seemingly vacant American landscape.

The tranquility evaporates with the roar of a V8 engine, and the placid trepidation of British troops turns to abject horror when three marauding Dodge Challengers tear onto the grassy battlefield. One of the cars bears a huge American flag standing upright through the passenger window. Redcoats scramble in utter disorder as General Washington, who sits casually in the driver's seat of a Challenger, slashes through the pitch. When the skirmish ends—we presume, because the advertisement shows no overt violence—the camera returns to General Washington standing victorious alongside his steel and fiberglass stallion with the American flag flapping gloriously. A sonorous narrator concludes, "Here's a couple of things America got right: cars and freedom."[1]

The absurd and anachronistic nature of the commercial prompts viewers to dismiss it, to class it as a clever gag or marketing ploy that purposely strays so far beyond reality that its sole purpose is to grab our attention, and nothing more. But underlying the humor and hyperbole, the ad can tell us more about historical contexts and presidential images. Presidents and the presidency have long featured in commercial advertising, often as a way of connecting contemporary contexts with the past. The Chrysler ad, for example, deliberately overlapped with the 2010 World Cup and the much-hyped clash between England and the United States. The soccer game, billed as a David and Goliath match-up, offered a metaphoric return to the revolutionary battlefield where an underdog United States took on the venerable English. Unlike the War of Independence, however, the football game ended in a draw.

The sporting context had its appeal to the marketing team at Chrysler, but it also had limitations. The popularity of soccer in the US pales in comparison to other sports, and Chrysler opted to re-run the ad on local television stations across the fifty states long after the World Cup ended, as well as during the tournament. The automobile company fixed on an additional context: a mere two months before the USA squared off against the English football team, the Deepwater Horizon oil rig exploded. The industrial disaster killed eleven engineers and spilled more oil than any other environmental catastrophe in American history. Owned and operated by British Petroleum, the platform proved unsafe and the explosion had a negative effect on Anglo-American relations, making the Chrysler ad a timely reminder of the sometimes tumultuous history between the United States and Great Britain. Further still, reporters like Andrew Clark from the *Guardian* credited the popularity of right-wing Tea Party activists who dressed as revolutionary-era minutemen. Certainly, the jingoistic rhetoric of the ad matched the uber-nationalism of Tea Party mobs, and editorialists considered this audience more likely to buy a Challenger than soccer fans or history aficionados. But regardless of Chrysler's motives for the marketing campaign, the commercial tapped into the contemporary context by crafting an image of the past. And, in order to accomplish this, the advertisement invoked the familiar figure of George Washington.[2]

The first president cuts a heroic image for Chrysler, allowing the car manufacturer to associate the Challenger brand with legacies popularly associated with Washington—namely those of reliability, trustworthiness, and patriotism. For much the same reason, the small-time businessman Otto Shipley incorporated the Washington Motor Company in 1921 with the slogan: "A Name That Stands for Character and Strength." It is why Washington Mutual often uses a profile of the first president on their promotional materials; the public memory of George Washington is almost entirely inoffensive, instantly recognizable, and aspirational to many Americans 200 years after his death.[3] Advertising agencies covet historical characters like Washington, with no partisan record, although beyond his reputation for fairness in politics he also represents national unity and strength of character. His legacy is contrived with notions of quality and nostalgia for a bygone era.

Other presidential images similarly spark emotional and mnemonic reactions, a capacity that makes former presidents a valuable symbol for advertisers. After all, the sole purpose of advertising is to make us favorably remember a product, service, or brand, and if advertisers must win our attention, even just momentarily, the presidency is as good a symbol as any to accomplish that.

Advertisers are, therefore, agents of public memory. When they depict historical figures, episodes, or ideas they play a powerful role in shaping our perception of the past. Historian Jackson Lears points out that advertisers do more than "urge people to buy goods," they also "validate a way of being in the world," sometimes by manipulating images of the past to construct "commercial fables."[4] In the late nineteenth century, corporations recognized their ability to create new meaning and value for their products through creative advertising. In addition to marketing, these ads unintentionally directed consumers towards trends in public life, the desires inherent in a given culture, and they reflected popular conceptions of their age. Social theorist Andrew Wernick argues that advertisers, among other marketing professionals, have created a "promotional culture," best defined as the dissemination of prevailing social values to sell commercial goods. Promotional culture has effectively transformed the way we understand our history, traditions, beliefs, and principles by regurgitating them in public relations exercises.[5]

Examples of this abound: Levi-Strauss often used images of the Wild West to market their blue jeans and, during the Cold War, the brand became an iconic consumer good for Germans who saw the jeans as a social marker of Western freedom and democracy. Coca-Cola regularly plasters billboard and print advertisements with Norman Rockwell-esque illustrations that depict fictional episodes of American social history, and the company even described the changing design of the Coke bottle as a cultural marker of American progress. Disney, McDonalds, Microsoft, and many other businesses practice similar brand management. They promote culture to consumers and promise more than a product. Buying a Big Mac, visiting Disney World, or logging into a Windows operating system are all chances to experience the American "way of life."[6]

To the contrary, government offices and officers traditionally steer clear of corporate promotion to ensure their work remains untarnished by conflicts of interest, but images of the presidency and former presidents have appeared regularly in commercial advertising since the end of World War II.[7] Typically, such advertisements reflect popular legacies and public impressions of the past. The Dodge Challenger ad repeated and perpetuated popular perceptions of Washington as a heroic figure. But advertisements also craft exaggerations, myths, and farcical images that can affect public memory. The Challenger ad had no basis in reality, and presented a ridiculous scenario that deliberately distorted the past to promote car sales. False images like the Challenger advertisement should prompt us to pay closer attention to promotional culture. The integration of public relations into our everyday life means that advertisements, as well as the advertisers, play a role in shaping and reflecting our understanding of the past and, in this case, of the presidency and a former president. Indeed, advertisers have as much impact on our memory as the sculptors of bronze statues, the chairs of presidential foundations, of biographers and historians, or of motion picture producers, but while artistic and literary commemorators receive ample treatment from scholars and social critics, advertising agencies and commercial marketing departments attract few studies. Because their production of public images has the same impact on our cultural memory of the past as the work of artists and writers, we must analyze advertisements and advertisers just as scrupulously.

Since the late nineteenth century, when American consumer culture thrived, presidents have appeared in the marketing campaigns of several companies. The automobile industry used presidents prolifically, as did finance and insurance companies.[8] The first mention of a stuffed "teddy bear" appeared in 1902 when Clifford Berryman drew a cartoon of Theodore Roosevelt sparing a bear cub on a hunting trip. The image led Morris Mitcham to start the Ideal Novelty and Toy Company in 1907. Beverages, tobacco, personal hygiene products, and household cleaning goods have all featured presidents in nineteenth-century advertisements, but it was not until the second great boom in consumerism that followed the end of World War II that advertisers began to make wildly exaggerated claims about presidents. New media like television, as well as the growing affluence of American consumers and the evolution of a youth culture, gave rise to a multitude of advertising agencies, all of which attempted to outdo each other in order to capture more clients. The "Mad Men" of Madison Avenue created iconic fictional characters in the 1950s like the Pillsbury Doughboy, Speedy the Alka-Seltzer Kid, and Planters' Mr. Peanut to "help consumers form a personal bond with the represented brand," and the same ad agencies began to adulterate historical characters for the same end.[9] This chapter examines the ways in which advertisers distorted images of the American president after World War II, detailing the lengths to which they went to draw connections to the past, exaggerate history and, in some cases, construct absolute falsehoods. In doing so, the chapter aims to explain how our perceptions of the American presidency and former presidents derive in part from a promotional culture.

Exaggeration and myth-making

In the years following World War II, competition within the food and beverage industry intensified and, consequently, so did industry marketing campaigns. Flour companies were particularly aggressive. During the war they overproduced, and when the war ended, an overabundance of flour prompted the mills to find new ways of selling grains. The growing popularity of cake mix as a convenience product helped accomplish this. General Mills led the way with its Betty Crocker brand mix, while Ballard and Ballard's Pillsbury and Conagra's Duncan Hines brands dominated the remainder of the market in the 1950s. Nabisco (the National Biscuit Company) lagged far behind with their Dromedary cake mix, a slump that persisted until Dromedary began a nationwide advertising campaign showcasing the company's long-standing connections to the Washington family. In the 1930s, Dromedary had called for recipes from the general public and the Daughters of the American Revolution had responded with an obscure, if not delicious gingerbread recipe from Martha Washington. The gingerbread proved to be immensely popular, and Dromedary had their first so-called "historical recipe" cake mix.[10]

When it came time to reconsider the company's marketing strategy in 1941, Dromedary again turned to historic recipes and the presidency. It hired Helen Duprey Bullock, a historian and preservationist who famously said "History isn't just great political events . . . You can feel it in fabrics, taste it in cooking, and see it in architecture."[11] Bullock encouraged Dromedary to re-publicize the gingerbread recipe with a greater emphasis on it being Martha Washington's, and to expand the range of historic recipes. In 1955, Dromedary released a second historic recipe: Martha Washington's "great cake" mix; however, it failed to attract many cooks, primarily because it required beating forty eggs into the mix and could hardly be classed as a convenience. But this setback did not stymie Bullock's advertising strategy. Soon after the great cake release Dromedary began selling Mrs. James Monroe's white cake mix, Martha Jefferson Randolph's pound cake mix, Mary Todd Lincoln's yellow cake mix, and Theodore Roosevelt's devil's food mix. These recipes surpassed Nabisco's expectations and made Dromedary a serious competitor in the lucrative cake mix market.[12]

What distinguishes Nabisco's historical recipe collection is the company's consideration of presidential images as vital to their marketing. The link with reputable historic figures like the presidents and their families generated an air of tradition for a contemporary product; it gave cake a place in American history, and it gave Dromedary's mix an association with the most famous Americans. To ensure the connection had legitimacy, the company donated a portion of the profits to preservation projects or paid a royalty to heritage sites and memorial associations run by foundations or the family of a given president. Kenmore House in Virginia, the home of George Washington's sister, was refurbished on the proceeds of Martha Washington's gingerbread recipe; the Theodore Roosevelt Association sustained its balance sheet in the 1970s in some part with royalties from Dromedary's devil's food cake; and the board of directors at Monticello incorporated advertising for Thomas Jefferson's house in the pound cake advertisements.[13]

Dromedary's historical recipes range is a unique case. Bullock's research allowed Nabisco to conjure up direct links to presidential bakes, but most marketing departments found it difficult to draw out connections to the presidents. Advertisers more frequently exaggerated connections or embellished the facts when promoting products. Again, the food and beverage industry led the way. Since the early twentieth century, Budweiser had advertised as the "King of All Bottle Beers" and deployed the founding fathers as advocates of responsible, yet copious drinking. Anheuser Busch cast Washington as "the purest figure in history," who had a brew house at Mount Vernon; Adams as "a man of stern and unbending rectitude" who "nourished mind and body on health-giving barley beer"; Jefferson's "deeds and written thoughts absolutely and irrefutably prove that good malt beer is not injurious to mind or body"; and Madison and Monroe drank in moderation with a generous supply of beer at their Montpelier and Highland estates. After the end of Prohibition, Anheuser Busch resurrected these ads, and in 1948 they associated Jefferson's appreciation of gourmet cuisine with Budweiser. The brewer implicitly put their lager into the hands of the Founders without mentioning that the King of Beers had only become available to Americans in 1876.[14]

Other alcoholic beverages advertised in similar ways. Philadelphia Whiskey called its potent liquor the taste of the American Revolution, with founding fathers the emblem of that product.

Seagram's produced an elaborate Mount Rushmore sign that had Washington, Jefferson, Theodore Roosevelt, and Lincoln drinking various brands of their whiskey. Even William Henry Harrison, who served a mere thirty days in office, has a whiskey named after him. But one president appears more often than any other in whiskey promotions: Andrew Jackson. The seventh president's appreciation for traditional American whiskey, and the fact that he operated a still at his Hermitage estate, led many advertisers to Jackson's image. In 1959, Old Crow bourbon depicted Jackson advising another Tennessee President, James K. Polk, over a tipple. Another whiskey—Old Hickory—appropriated Jackson's portrait and nickname. It made the claim that its liquor had the character and force of the former president. No evidence exists to suggest that Jackson ever drank Old Crow or Old Hickory, and commercial production of these whiskeys came only after his death.

In marketing terminology, Jackson is a brand ambassador: a figure that embodies the essence of a given product. Modern brand ambassadors also typically use the products they promote, and in almost all cases receive some form of remuneration. Jackson did not, but presidents like John F. Kennedy have taken the role in its full modern meaning, despite doing so from the grave.[15] Kennedy's dapper style, charismatic charm, and handsome appearance make him an irresistible celebrity to advertisers, but his tragic death and status as a national martyr complicate any portrayal. A promotion strategy that uses Kennedy as a brand ambassador runs the risk of disturbing living memory and courting offense from family, memorial foundations, and fan clubs—groups of people who knew Kennedy in life and now work to protect his legacy. Commercial advertisers must tread carefully or insult these groups.

Perhaps the best example of the fine line between paying homage and unfettered promotion comes from Omega watches, a subsidiary of Swatch that, in 2009, ran a series of print and television advertisements for its Speedmaster brand. Employing Kennedy as the brand ambassador, Omega ran a print advertisement that used a photo of Kennedy speaking at a podium, wearing their watch. The integrated campaign also featured a thirty-second television commercial that stitched together footage of Kennedy lecturing an audience on the moon mission while a Saturn V rocket took off—and, of course, both scenes were interspersed with images of the Omega Speedmaster. The marketing promotion coincided with the fortieth anniversary of the Apollo moon landing, and Omega had good reason to claim a connection to the mission. Some of the Apollo astronauts wore, and even tested Omega watches in space, although none wore the limited edition Speedmaster variety. More importantly, Kennedy never wore a Speedmaster. He did, however, proclaim a fondness for the Omega Ultra Thin watch, a timepiece he wore at his inauguration in 1961.[16]

Keen to avoid accusations that they had exploited the connection to Kennedy or the astronauts, Omega sought and gained permission to use the former president's likeness from the Kennedy Presidential Library and Museum. This was the first use of Kennedy's image sanctioned by the Kennedy Foundation.[17] In fact, the JFK Library's brand appeared alongside Omega's, giving the watchmaker more than a patina of cover. That did not stop Jon Stewart of *The Daily Show* from satirizing the murky historical record: the comic called JFK "that guy from the Omega watch ad."[18] Despite his untimely death over forty years earlier, Kennedy became Omega's brand ambassador, embodying the identity of the Speedmaster; and while he did not benefit, his foundation did.

Exaggerating an association with a former president can go beyond celebrity endorsement. In 2008, Citigroup, one of the mega-banks that bore the blame for the 2008 financial crisis brought on by over-leveraged investment in the housing market, attempted to rebrand their image. Citigroup portrayed investment banking and asset management as essential occupations in American history, casting banks as bastions of progress and enterprise (rather than factories of risk and speculation, which is how many Americans viewed them at the time). Advertisers led the rebranding effort, illustrating banks as benevolent lenders catering to the needs of small businesses, fulfilling the ambitions of American inventors, and even smoothing the way for veterans returning from duty or ensuring a comfortable retirement for the elderly.

These scenes broke no boundaries. They remain the hallmark of retail banking marketing, but Citigroup took rebranding to another level in 2010. The conglomerate ran a series of advertisements that claimed its bank played an instrumental role in the "American Century." According to the ads, Citigroup financed American growth from the Civil War to the Cold War and, somewhere in the middle of this timeline, the advertisers pictured President Theodore Roosevelt as the force behind the acquisition and construction of the Panama Canal. Citigroup's promotion proudly declared that the bank financed construction of the canal, a curious boast given the controversial legacy of the Panamanian revolution as a land-grab condemned almost universally by Latin American nations, and indeed by the United States in 1921 (along with an expression of regret and a $25 million indemnity). That oversight aside, the claim also exaggerated Citigroup's role in the financing of the canal's construction. A corporate fusion of retail and investment banks did not exist during Theodore Roosevelt's time. The National City Bank—the institution that gradually became Citigroup over more than eighty years of corporate history—played a tertiary role in financing the canal. Instead, the banking empire of J.P. Morgan organized financing for the canal by enlisting seven subsidiary lenders, among which was included the National City Bank. A junior partner at best, the connection allowed Citigroup to weave a narrative that put it in proximity to Theodore Roosevelt's legacy. Doing so helped in some part to clean up its tarnished image almost a century later.

The exaggeration and myth-making of presidential history in commercial advertising illustrates the lengths to which companies will go to sell their products. Commercialism drives them to invent a historical legacy or attach exaggerated links to a popular figure, and although these advertisements are by nature ephemeral, companies measure the impact of advertisements by sales. For Nabisco, Anheuser-Busch, Swatch, or Citigroup, the appeal of the presidency helped to sell cake mix, beer, watches, and financial products.

Farce and abstraction

While some companies have exaggerated historical truths to erect corporate traditions and product myths, many other commercial advertisers have dispensed with the truth entirely and presented a president in purposely farcical or abstract situations.

Such advertising has great appeal to those businesses that cannot draw on the past to build connections to the present.

One company that provides an example of advertising in historical abstractions is the Container Corporation of America (CCA), a business that began as a small family-run enterprise making wooden crates and other timber shipping products. The company grew considerably when Walter Paepcke, who took over from his father in the 1920s, developed an innovative means of producing cheap, durable, and lightweight cardboard boxes. Paepcke transformed his father's wood-based business into a paper mill at a time when shipping and consumerism were on the rise. The cardboard box made Paepcke one of the most successful businessmen of his generation, but what really distinguished him as a businessperson was his unusual approach to advertising. Convinced by his wife, Elizabeth Nitze Paepcke, a graduate of the Art Institute of Chicago and sister of the influential civil servant Paul Nitze, the CCA promoted its brand through fine art. The Paepckes commissioned artists to design posters that embodied social "leadership" and individual "creativity." They hired advertising firm N.W. Ayer & Son to assist artists in transforming avant-garde designs into popular print media. Initially, the advertising targeted shipping buyers rather than the general public. These buyers included people like scientists who needed packaging for delicate glassware or specimens, and lawyers who stored documents in paper crates.[19] White-collar Americans, Paepcke believed, would buy his packaging because it was a superior product, but they would be drawn to the brand by the cultural connotations found in the advertising.

Paepcke's calculation proved correct. The ads made a big splash and, during World War II, the company began a second campaign with artists. At a time when war consumed public life, the CCA commissioned artists like William de Kooning and Henry Moore to depict defining characteristics of their native European cultures, a task that often highlighted the heroic struggle against fascism. The series reflected the swelling patriotism and sense of international solidarity with America's allies.

After the war, the CCA expanded exponentially when sales in consumer goods surged. The company became the world's largest manufacturer of cardboard and, by the end of the 1940s, the Paepckes had built a reputation for art patronage and avant-garde advertising—no small feat for a product as dull as cardboard boxes. When the Paepckes launched their third major advertising campaign in 1950, the CCA dominated the container market, and yet its public reputation remained stubbornly obscure. Packaging buyers knew the company well, as did the art world, but the average Joe on Main Street, USA paid little attention to the company. To stay atop the cardboard industry and expand the CCA's public image, the Paepckes released a series of advertisements themed around "The Great Ideas of Western Man." The ads came at a time when Cold War tensions ran hot and featured quotes from numerous European and American writers, politicians, and philosophers alongside modern art.

American presidents featured frequently, either in the artwork or as the quoted personality. George Washington appeared twice, as did Thomas Jefferson. Abraham Lincoln and Theodore Roosevelt appeared three times. These ads spoke directly to the legacies of the presidents, not the product for sale. Lincoln's emancipation of the slaves, Jefferson's rebuke of government tyranny, Washington's promise of public morality, and Roosevelt's patriotic call to dare greatly all shone through the modern artwork. In that sense, none of the advertisements exaggerated truths or created myths. Yet the quotes, the art, and the CCA brand shared no discernible association. Contrarian social critic Tom Wolfe judged a number of artworks for the series, and wrote a review of the ads in both contemptuous and complimentary tones:

> Here's our old friend, the Great Ideas of Western Man series. I hadn't come across it since it used to run in the magazines. At the top of the page you'd see a quotation—such as:
> "Hitch your wagon to a star."—Ralph Waldo Emerson.
> And under it would be a painting of a cubistic horse strangling on a banana. I often wondered if the artists were given explicit instructions never to let the artwork have anything to do with the quotation, because they never did. If this was actually a policy, it was a brilliant stroke; because the ads were supposed to have nothing whatsoever to do with what the company actually did. I used to think the company was called the Transcendental Can Corporation, but I see by this entry that I was mistaken about that. Like all

institutional ads, the ads in this series convey the message: "We really don't do what we really do (e.g., make tin cans). What we manufacture is dignity."[20]

To purposefully shroud the identity of the product was revolutionary, and historian Greg Ruth calls the CCA "Great Ideas" series the first guerrilla marketing campaign. It used an unconventional style that promoted the CCA by brandishing aesthetically pleasing and memorable images that grab the attention of observers without making reference to cardboard boxes.[21] In the case of the presidents featured, there is no connection to the packaging products, but the suggestive nature of the ads implies that the values of these presidents are shared by the company.

Sixty years later, advertisers continue to deploy guerrilla advertising that features former presidents. Cadillac's 2015 integrated print, television, and internet campaign asked car buyers to "Dare Greatly" and compares nicely to the Paepckes' style. In magazines, Cadillac printed an excerpt from Theodore Roosevelt's inspirational 1910 "Man in the Arena" speech while featuring a small Cadillac crest at the bottom of the page. In the television and internet videos, a female voiceover reads Roosevelt's speech while a Cadillac drives slowly through a city street, but rather than emphasize the car, the ad focuses on the street life. Similarly, Gaia, a fitness and health video subscription service, uses another quote from Theodore Roosevelt to promote self-reflection—an important concept for Gaia's products, which facilitate personal well-being. In a print ad, with a minuscule Gaia TV icon, an empty chair fills the space below Roosevelt's quote: "If you could kick the person in the pants responsible for most of your trouble, you wouldn't sit for a month."[22]

Cadillac and Gaia offer a convenient contrast for Roosevelt's legacy. In one, he promotes risk and spirited living, and in the other he touts cautious reflection and critical self-awareness. These abstractions in advertising remind us that seemingly value-neutral depictions contain interpretations of presidential legacies, and while the example of the advertisements appear to recite well-known tropes, they can illustrate the contradictory legacies that exist in simple and vague quotations that most observers pass over without consideration.

The ephemeral nature of advertising means that abstractions of presidential images and legacies often go unnoticed or unchallenged, although that is not always the case. Some guerrilla advertising stands out. In 2011, the retail fashion brand United Colors of Benetton launched a foundation to combat global hate and to promote the social responsibility of multinational corporations. Of course, the ads also promoted the fashion brand. The UNHATE Foundation partnered with New York advertising agency 72andSunny to devise the campaign, and an international poster exhibition followed. The campaign began in the melee of mid-town Manhattan, where a team of foundation members unfurled a massive canvas poster of Barack Obama kissing Chinese president Hu Jintao (or was Hu kissing Barack?). Soon after, billboards around the world showed similar scenes of leaders known to share little in common: Pope Benedict XVI with Egyptian imam Ahmed el-Tayeb; North Korea's Kim Jong-Il and South Korea's Lee Myung-Bak; German chancellor Angela Merkel and French president Nicolas Sarkozy; and the Middle East peace plan seemed assured in the passionate embrace of Israeli prime minister Benjamin Netanyahu and Palestinian National Authority president Mahmoud Abbas.[23]

Public reaction to the ads swung from amusement to outrage. "It's not like traditional advertising," marketing executive Steve Jones said. "It's not making a point about the clothes . . . It doesn't obey the rules. You can like it, you can dislike it, you can't ignore it."[24] Like other guerrilla marketing, the UNHATE ads succeeded because they manufactured interest, but as Jones indicates, the relationship to Barack Obama and presidential legacy is entirely absent. Obama's spokesperson Eric Schultz told reporters that the White House had "a longstanding policy disapproving of the use of the president's name and likeness for commercial purposes," and, unlike the Vatican, which sued UNHATE and forced Benetton to remove the ads of the Pope, the White House took no further action.[25] The Obama administration calculated that suing Benetton would only keep the advertising campaign in the headlines. Indeed, Benetton ran a second ad with Obama kissing Venezuelan president Hugo Chavez when the outrage over the first image climaxed. President of the American Catholic League Bill Donohue said of the images that the "damage Benetton did is done," and correctly guessed that the advertisements would not disappear. Despite the Vatican's lawsuit and Benetton's capitulation over the Pope's image, the portrayal of Benedict and Ahmed el-Tayeb proliferated on the internet and social media. The Vatican's lawsuit fueled the media circus and perpetuated the image, whereas ignoring the ads allowed Obama's White House to reject the image in a manner that disarmed the advertising campaign and truncated the spread of his likeness.[26]

More than any other sitting president, Barack Obama faced a number of challenges to his image, but the 2016 election of President Donald Trump—whose campaign of unrestrained guerrilla marketing abstracted the traditional political campaign of platforms and promises into an anti-Washington sound bite and populist trope of social division—has opened the floodgates for advertisers to delve into the political fracas. Airoutdoor billboards in the UK plastered Trump's image on empty signage across England, positing that "Advertising Works . . . Look where it got me."[27] Dove cosmetic products, in response to President Trump's adviser Kellyanne Conway, who said the president offered "alternative facts," launched a campaign of its own alternative facts. "New Dove antiperspirant increases your IQ by 40 points . . . was first used by Cleopatra . . . can plan your next holiday at a competitive rate . . . makes the lift arrive when you feverishly press the button."[28] Commercial advertisers also took on Trump in the biggest marketing forum of the year: the Super Bowl. Budweiser ran a short film that celebrated the immigrant legacy of brewery founders Eberhard Anheuser and Adolphus Busch; 84Lumber showed the experience of Mexicans upon reaching a Trump-styled wall on the border that proclaimed, "The will to succeed is always welcome here"; and Coca-Cola offered a rendition of God Bless America in several languages. Trump supporters rightly gauged the advertising as a slight against the new president. More, they criticized the ads as unrepresentative of Trump's plans for the United States.[29]

Conclusion

Since the 1980s, Jim Warlick has sold presidential memorabilia across from the White House in his store, The American Presidential

Experience. He, perhaps more than anyone, knows that the institution of the presidency, the architecture of the Executive Mansion, and the image of individual American presidents have a commercial value. In fact, his business is predicated on that very idea.

In 2016, Warlick, like so many other observers, expected Hillary Clinton to clinch the election, and the shop owner stocked up on Clinton apparel, bobble heads, hats, magnets, mementos, mugs, and paperweights. Trump's unexpected victory surprised Warlick as much as it did the president-elect, and the shop owner told a reporter in good humor, "If I ever get a hold of Nate Silver," the statistician that promised a Clinton landslide, "I'm gonna choke him."[30] Left with truckloads of Clinton kitsch, Warlick's business quickly recovered from the surplus inventory. He bought in a range of Trump souvenirs for the 2017 inauguration, from iconic red hats with white embroidered "Make America Great Again" stitching to a talking Trump doll replete with the New York businessman's outlandish quips from the election. Warlick even took advantage of the planned protests and supplied anti-Trump items like T-shirts emblazoned with "I'm Still with Her" and mugs that asked "Which Way to Canada?" If consumers will buy it, Warlick will stock it. The souvenirs and memorabilia associated with a president or the White House, much like the advertisements that deploy presidential images to sell other products, show the presidency's innate commercial value. Warlick, in 2008, said anything with Obama's face on it would sell, and while his trade is primarily in contemporary contexts, the historical context is not entirely absent. Sales of Lincolniana increased in 2008 because Obama invoked Lincoln so often during his inauguration and, in 2016, Andrew Jackson figurines appeared in vogue as Trump had readily identified with America's first populist president.

Contemporary invocations remind us of the value of legacy, however it may be interpreted. The past has meaning for the present, and that meaning can be translated into commercial advantage. Advertisers have recognized this for some time. They have exaggerated images, distorted myths, built abstractions of the presidency; and when all this fails, they generate an entirely fictional narrative that serves a commercial purpose. Despite being the pre-eminent symbol of the United States, often replete with dozens of historical biographies that document their lives with precision and care, the American president persistently succumbs to myth-making in public memory by commercial advertisers. At a time when the political climate is referred to as "post-truth," and a celebrity tycoon who has unquestionably mastered the art of self-promotion sits at the Resolute Desk, it is worth reflecting on the idea of promotional culture. While many post-World War II advertisers aimed for integrity and near-truths, the current trend is to fabricate the past and blur the truth to sell more goods. These marketing decisions no longer look so dissimilar to the real political scene. They both aim to shock the senses, to gain our attention and stimulate through the subconscious. They are by nature ahistorical, reshaping the past to imitate or suit the contemporary.

Notes

1. Wieden & Kennedy for Chrysler, "Freedom," Dodge Challenger television advertisement (2010).
2. Andrew Clark, "Does the Dodge Challenger Ad Appeal to Anti-British Sentiment?," *Guardian*, August 16, 2010; Aaron Foley, "Dodge's 'Freedom' Ad for Challenger: Patriotism or Tea Party-baiting?," *MLive*, July 7, 2010, <http://www.mlive.com/auto/index.ssf/2010/07/dodges_freedom_ad_for_challeng.html> (accessed June 13, 2018).
3. For an outstanding treatment of Washington's depiction in popular culture in the twenty-first century, see Edward Lengel's experience with the Greystone's production company that made the short film *We Fight to Be Free*. Edward Lengel, *Inventing George Washington: America's Founder, in Myth and Memory* (New York: Harper Collins, 2011), 200–10.
4. T.J. Jackson Lears, *Fables of Abundance: A Cultural History Of Advertising In America* (New York: Basic Books, 1994), 1–2.
5. Andrew Warnick, *Promotional Culture: Advertising, Ideology and Symbolic Expression* (SAGE Publications, 1991). Aeron Davis contends that Warnick's promotional culture pervades American life in the twentieth and twenty-first centuries and claims that self-promotion has resulted from incessant commercial advertising. He concludes that the ubiquitous promotional culture makes it difficult for audiences to discern the difference between products and services with a commercial value and those products and services with a value beyond

profit. A good example is higher education, which offers intellectual growth for individuals and society, or healthcare, which has an intrinsic value on individual and social well-being. Aeron Davis, *Promotional Cultures: The Rise and Spread of Advertising, Public Relations, Marketing and Branding* (Malden, MA: Polity, 2013), 3–5. See also Jefferson Pooley, "The Consuming Self: From Flappers to Facebook," in Melissa Aronczyk and Devon Powers (eds.), *Blowing up the Brand: Critical Perspectives on Promotional Culture* (New York: Peter Lang, 2010), 71–92.

6. Rance Crain, the editor of *Advertising Age*, said after the Cold War ended, "We won . . . not because we convinced the world our case was just, but because the Soviet Union ran out of money. The job of convincing people around the world that our way of life is best is made more difficult and complex now because of the pervasiveness of our culture. Our movies, music, fashion, consumer brand names such as McDonald's and Coca-Cola, embody what are widely seen as our crass and overly secular society." Laura Belmonte, *Selling the American Way: US Propaganda and the Cold War* (Philadelphia: University of Pennsylvania Press, 2008). Exporting products as cultural symbols as well as products with a consumer value has attracted attention from scholars of international relations, who often refer to this as "cultural imperialism." See John Tomlinson, *Cultural Imperialism: A Critical Introduction* (London: Bloomsbury, 1991), 2–18; Rob Kroes, "American Empire and Cultural Imperialism: A View from the Receiving End," *Diplomatic History* 23, no. 3 (July 1999): 463–77; Lane Crothers, *Globalization and American Popular Culture* (London: Rowman and Littlefield, 2013), 17–31.

7. An exception to this tradition is President Trump, who refuses to concede that a conflict of interest might arise from a president's personal business and corporate affiliations, and the management of government for the benefit of the nation and its people. Joshua Matz, "Trump Conflicts of Interest 'Fix' is no Such Thing," *Guardian*, January 12, 2017.

8. The Jackson Automobile Company formed in 1903, the Lincoln Motor Company and the Harrison Wagon Company two years later, and the Madison Motor Company in 1915. In 1928, a Roosevelt automobile produced by Marmon Motor Car Company even came with a cameo of Theodore Roosevelt on the radiator cap. Insurance and finance companies like Washington Mutual, founded in 1889, and Lincoln National Life Insurance Company in 1905 purposely made use of presidential names and legacies. Lincoln Life

Insurance even had an endorsement from Robert Todd Lincoln, the president's son.
9. Jeffry C. Jackson, "Cartoon Icons: The Michelin Man, Morton Salt Umbrella Girl, and Mr. Peanut," in Danielle Sarver Coombs and Bob Batchelor (eds.), *We Are What We Sell: How Advertising Shapes American Life . . . and Always Has* (Oxford: Praeger, 2014), 98–99.
10. Tansy Elizabeth Matthews, *Selling Captain Smith: 1950s Colonial Revival and the Marketing of the 1957 Jamestown Festival* (M.A. diss., Corcoran College of Art and Design, 2012), 11–15. The story of Dromedary's gingerbread is repeated in popular cookbooks and blogs. See Anne Byrn, *American Cake: From Colonial Gingerbread to Classic Layer* (New York: Rodale, 2016), 17.
11. Robert McG. Thomas Jr., "Helen Duprey Bullock, Historian, Is Dead at 90," *New York Times*, November 11, 1995.
12. For examples of the advertisements see *LIFE Magazine*, September 26, 1955; *McCalls*, February 1957; and *Ladies Home Journal*, October 1956.
13. Heather Baldus, "Kenmore's Famed Gingerbread," *Lives and Legacies Blog: Stories from George Washington's Ferry Farm and Historic Kenmore*, October 28, 2015 <https://livesandlegaciesblog.org/tag/dromedary-cake-mix-company> (accessed June 13, 2018); Michael Patrick Cullinane, *Theodore Roosevelt's Ghost: The History and Memory of an American Icon* (Baton Rouge: Louisiana State University Press, 2017), 149–50; Megan Stubbendeck, "A Woman's Touch: Gender at Monticello," in Jonathan Daniel Wells and Sheila R. Phipps (eds.), *Entering the Fray: Gender, Politics, and Culture in the New South* (Columbia: University of Missouri Press, 2010), 123.
14. For reproductions of the Budweiser advertisements, see Sally Edelstein, "Budweiser Markets America," *Envisioning the American Dream* [blog], <envisioningtheamericandream.com/2016/05/23/budweiser-markets-america> and Al DeFilippo, "Additional Budweiser Ads," *The Long Road* [blog] <https://www.francisasburytriptych.com/john-wesley-budweiser-beer-ad> (accessed June 13, 2018).
15. Samsung, the South Korean technology company, hired Excell Ogilvy to run its Honduran marketing campaign for smartphones. Excell Ogilvy depicted JFK alongside a sunbathing Marilyn Monroe with the slogan "Secrets well kept." The ad was criticized in the United States, as were a number of other advertisements depicting Kennedy. For the Samsung ad and print advertisements see Excell Ogilvy Honduras for Samsung, "Secrets Well Kept," Victor Saravia

art director (2011); Bates Y&R Copenhagen for TeleDanmark, "JFK," Martin Nord art director (1999); Chubb Thailand, "JFK was Killed by" (2005); Duval Guillaume Modem Antwerp, "JFK," Frederic Dupont illustrator (2004); Duval Guillaume Antwerp for IP Press, Men's Magazines, "If Men are Your Target," Gilles de Boncourt art director (2007).

16. Omega purchased JFK's Ultra Thin watch in a 2005 auction. The company's website traced the history of the watch: "In 1960, Grant Stockdale presented to his friend John F. Kennedy an Omega 'Ultra Thin' wristwatch. At that time, he was not yet President of the United States. In a letter addressed to Grant that same year, Jacqueline Kennedy expressed her deepest thanks for this 'thinnest most elegant wristwatch' mentioning how thrilled JFK was about it and how 'promptly he took off the chunky little one' she had given him." Omega, "News Detail: JFK's Ultra Thin Watch," <https://www.omegawatches.com/news/news-detail/1255> (accessed June 13, 2018).

17. Andrew Adam Newman, "Omega's Reminder: J.F.K. Wore One," *New York Times*, August 2, 2009.

18. *The Daily Show*, <http://www.cc.com/episodes/431cxs/the-daily-show-with-jon-stewart-july-20--2009---brian-williams-season-14-ep-14096> (accessed June 13, 2018).

19. Greg Ruth, "Walter Paul Paepcke," *Immigrant Entrepreneurship*, <https://www.immigrantentrepreneurship.org/entry.php?rec=67> (accessed June 13, 2018).

20. Tom Wolfe, "Advertising's Secret Messages," *New York Magazine* 5, no. 29 (July 17, 1972): 23.

21. Ruth, "Walter Paul Paepcke."

22. Cadillac, "Dare Greatly" campaign, <http://www.daregreatly.com>; GaiaM TV.com, "Theodore Roosevelt" advertisement, <https://s-media-cache-ak0.pinimg.com/736x/d2/a3/54/d2a354c224828750f1d8b9c64797af00.jpg> (accessed June 13, 2018).

23. To see the full advertising campaign, see UNHATE Foundation, "Image Gallery," <http://unhate.benetton.com/gallery/china_usa> (accessed June 13, 2018).

24. "Benetton 'Unhate' Campaign, Featuring World Leaders Kissing, Wins Cannes Ad Festival Award," *Huffington Post*, June 20, 2012.

25. "White House Slams Ad Showing Obama-Chavez Kiss," *Reuters*, November 17, 2011; Maura Judkis, "Vatican Takes Legal Action over Pope-Imam, Obama-Chavez Kissing Benetton Ad," *Washington Post*, November 16, 2011.

26. Mark Johanson, "Benetton 'Unhate' Campaign Ads: White House Issues Statement on Obama Kiss," *International Business Times*, November 17, 2011.
27. Simon Gwynn, "Trump Billboard Urges Businesses to Invest in Outdoor Advertising," *US Campaign*, January 23, 2017.
28. Monika Markovinovic, "Dove Releases 'Alternative Facts' Deodorant Campaign In Response To Trump Administration," *Huffington Post*, February 1, 2017.
29. Martin Belam, "Super Bowl ad prompts Trump supporters to #BoycottBudweiser," *Guardian*, February 6, 2017.
30. Patrick Madden, "D.C. Souvenir Shops Stocking Up On Trump Gear," WAMU-American University Radio, <http://wamu.org/story/17/01/12/d-c-souvenir-shops-stocking-trump-gear> (accessed June 13, 2018).

4
Eisenhower's Farewell Address in history and memory

Richard V. Damms

Speaking before a national radio and television audience on the evening of January 17, 1961, President Dwight D. Eisenhower solemnly intoned:

> In the councils of government, we must guard against the acquisition of unwarranted influence, whether sought or unsought, by the military-industrial complex. The potential for the disastrous rise of misplaced power exists and will persist ... Only an alert and knowledgeable citizenry can compel the proper meshing of the huge industrial and military machinery of defense with our peaceful methods and goals, so that security and liberty may prosper together.[1]

This one passage has resonated over the years, so much so that the phrase "military-industrial complex" has become almost synonymous with the entire Farewell Address, of which it was but one component. While Eisenhower scholars have mulled over the genesis and evolution of the speech and the president's intent for decades, relatively few historical analyses of the speech itself have been undertaken.[2] This chapter will delineate the political and policy context from which Eisenhower developed the speech, primarily his long-running efforts to achieve "security with solvency" by pursuing a capital-intensive strategy of containment, with profound implications for American science, technology, and political institutions. To some extent, Eisenhower's speech contained a powerful note of irony, if not regret, because for much of his professional life he had done more to foster the growth of the military-industrial complex and grapple with its consequences than any other American leader. The chapter will also delve into the drafting process, which began almost two years before Eisenhower left office, and offer suggestions as to the president's intent and the origins of some of the concepts and phraseology that constituted the speech. Eisenhower and his speechwriting team deliberately modeled the address on that of George Washington and, like the Founding Father, couched a political message in rhetoric that conveyed an air of wise, apolitical statesmanship. Finally, the chapter will discuss the subsequent reception of the speech, both by contemporaries and in popular memory. It will argue that the subtlety of the language deployed by Eisenhower's team contributed to such ambiguity about the president's precise meaning that the phrase "military-industrial complex" would be taken up predominantly by activists on the left of the political spectrum who co-opted Eisenhower's rhetorical legacy for their own purposes and for ends that Eisenhower would probably never have approved.

The Farewell Address and rhetorical legacy

In the most recent scholarly compendium on Eisenhower, Chester J. Pach characterizes the Farewell Address as "his most eloquent speech as president," and his warning against the danger of the "military-industrial complex" as his "most famous presidential legacy."[3] Indeed, Eisenhower and his speechwriters fully understood the import of the president's last major address to the American people. By the mid-twentieth century, the presidential Farewell Address had become an essential genre of political communication, serving both an institutional and political function. As the bookend to the presidential inaugural address, which set the tone and agenda for the incoming administration, the Farewell Address allowed the outgoing president to formally take his leave of the American people and prepare them for the transition to a new leader. It also provided a unique moment for reflection upon the nation's achievements on his watch, a chance to delineate larger lessons learned that might guide future conduct; and, in the process, it created an opportunity to begin crafting the president's long-term historical legacy.[4] George

Washington's Farewell Address had established the precedent for such a message, and his example resonated particularly forcefully with Eisenhower, who personally admired the Founding Father and envisioned himself as a latter-day equivalent, a military officer who had selflessly assumed the mantle of presidential leadership out of a sense of duty to the nation and had attempted to govern above the fray of partisan politics for the sake of the larger national interest. Washington's speech had reaffirmed faith in the republican experiment in the face of various internal and external dangers, and famously warned against the twin perils of factionalism at home and permanent alliances abroad.[5] Well over a year and a half before his departure from office, Eisenhower expressed interest in delivering a similar valedictory.[6]

As numerous scholars have amply demonstrated, Eisenhower took great personal interest in the public relations and communications aspects of the presidency. According to Craig Allen, he possessed a "public relations mentality" and surrounded himself with "the best and the brightest from the communications field."[7] He ran for office with the backing of several notable friends in the publishing world, employed public relations firms to advise on political campaigns, pioneered the use of weekly tracking polls to gauge public opinion and hired an actor, Robert Montgomery, to coach him on the most effective delivery of presidential speeches. Eisenhower seems to have been well versed in the notion of what political scientists have called "the rhetorical presidency," wherein modern presidents govern by deploying mass rhetoric to mobilize popular opinion.[8] Fred Greenstein's influential study of Eisenhower's "hidden-hand" leadership style highlighted the president's "instrumental use of language" to achieve his intended purpose.[9] According to Martin J. Medhurst, the foremost scholar of Eisenhower's communications, the president was a highly skilled "strategic communicator" who deployed language and imagery for clear political ends.[10] Indeed, internationally, Eisenhower considered public diplomacy and psychological warfare a vital front in the Cold War battle against the Sino-Soviet menace and upgraded the United States Information Agency in an effort to manage Cold War information, or propaganda, activities more effectively. For Eisenhower, rhetoric was an integral part of his "total cold war" at home and abroad.[11]

With regard to the drafting, timing, and delivery of major presidential addresses, Eisenhower's hand was by no means hidden from his speechwriters. He typically discussed broad themes for potential speeches with his chief speechwriter, who then brainstormed with various members of the president's staff and administration whose expertise related to the topic at hand. Eisenhower relied on his speechwriters to develop a complete first draft which he could then "chew on."[12] Having been a speechwriter himself for the secretary of war in the late 1920s and then for General Douglas MacArthur in the 1930s, Eisenhower understood the importance of language and took great pains to ensure that the words he delivered would convey precisely his intended meaning. To the annoyance of some of his speechwriters, he disliked unnecessary verbosity or flowery language, much preferring his "West Point grammar" to make his points easily understandable to a lay audience.[13] As he told his younger brother and confidant, Milton: "I may be temperamental about these matters, but I can never be happy with a talk that in the long run is not developed according to my ideas and not put in my own words."[14] He often edited a dozen or more versions of a major speech, and was "uncannily rigorous in organization," a fact borne out by Eisenhower's extensive marginal notations on numerous draft speeches.[15] Thus, by the time he delivered a speech, "it was *his* speech, every jot and tittle."[16]

Eisenhower's Farewell Address came together gradually over a period of many months. About "two years before leaving office," Eisenhower began contemplating his farewell remarks, apparently spurred by a discussion with chief speechwriter Malcolm Moos regarding a book on presidential speeches that highlighted Alexander Hamilton's role in crafting Washington's Farewell Address. Moos, a political science professor from Johns Hopkins University, had assumed the chief speechwriter role shortly before the 1958 midterm elections at the recommendation of Milton Eisenhower, who was then president of Johns Hopkins. The president told Moos: "I want to have something to say when I leave here, and I want you to be thinking about it . . . I am not interested in capturing headlines but I want to have a message."[17] Eisenhower contemplated a "ten-minute farewell address to the Congress and the American people."[18] Moos began "dropping ideas into a bin" in preparation for the speech. By May 22, 1959, the Farewell Address had made its way onto a proposed schedule of eight major presidential speeches for the remainder of Eisenhower's term, although the intended subject would be "the need for accommodation of a wide range of beliefs in the political spectrum," given the prospect of a federal government continually divided between the two major parties.[19] Eisenhower initially balked at the number of proposed speeches, and mused to Milton that he had "as yet, no fixed idea that I should deliver a so-called 'farewell' talk to the Congress," although he believed that his six years' experience working with an opposition-controlled body gave him the requisite authority to utter "a few homely truths that apply to the responsibilities and duties of a government that must respond to the will of majorities, even when the decisions of those majorities create apparent paradoxes."[20] Significantly, he also noted that the subject matter of some of the proposed talks overlapped and could be consolidated, such as those on the economy, foreign trade and aid, long-term defence planning, and education. He argued that the economy and foreign affairs "cannot be separated from each other," and wanted to impress upon people how "local affairs have a definite relationship to foreign affairs."[21]

As the speechwriters further pondered various ideas, Frederic Fox, who specialized in drafting short presidential statements for ceremonial occasions, made an important intervention. In April 1960 he explicitly suggested Washington's Farewell Address as a model. Specifically, Fox drew attention to several themes in keeping with Eisenhower's principles:

> the call for Constitutional obedience; the warnings about sectionalism; the dangers of "overgrown military establishments" but the necessity of maintaining a "respectable defensive posture"; . . . the necessity of an enlightened public opinion; the ungenerous habit of one generation to spend beyond its means and throw "upon posterity the burden which we ourselves ought to bear."[22]

These themes particularly resonated with Ralph Williams, a Navy captain who had come aboard around the same time as Moos at the recommendation of his former boss, Secretary of the Treasury Robert Anderson, to assist primarily with drafting speeches related to national security and foreign affairs. As the 1960 presidential election campaign heated up, Williams and many administration insiders were especially irked by allegations from Senator John F. Kennedy and the Democrats that Eisenhower's economizing had allowed a dangerous "missile gap" to open up with the Soviets.[23] Just days before the election, Williams proposed what would become the most noted aspect of the speech, "the problem of militarism." As he put it:

> for the first time in its history, the United States has a permanent war-based industry. Not only that, but flag and general officers retiring at an early age take positions in [the] war based industrial complex shaping its decisions and guiding the direction of its tremendous thrust . . . We must be very careful to insure that the "merchants of death do not come to dictate national policy."[24]

Williams's "merchants of death" phrase drew from the title of the notorious 1934 book by H.C. Engelbrecht and F.C. Hanighen condemning the machinations of munitions manufacturers and international financiers who had supposedly pushed the nation into the Great War in their drive for profits, but his particular target was the United States Air Force and their "network of . . . aerospace suppliers, and the congressional people who benefitted—whose districts benefitted—from these contracts."[25] As Moos and Williams fleshed out these ideas into the first draft of a speech in November, Williams dropped the "merchants of death" reference entirely and substituted "military-industrial complex" for "war based industrial complex," because, he said, it more accurately described "what I was complaining about."[26] Congressional liaison Bryce Harlow, who had spearheaded the administration's relations with the Democratic Congress and had cut his teeth as chief of staff of the House Armed Services Committee, fully understood the lobbying power of the Pentagon and strongly endorsed the caution about resisting "the blandishments of the militarists, industrialists, and technologists."[27] More importantly, when Eisenhower received the first substantive draft of the speech in December, he remarked: "I think you've got something here."[28] The warning remained essentially intact throughout the subsequent twenty-plus drafts.[29]

Eisenhower and the military-industrial complex

Eisenhower immediately embraced the major thrust of the initial draft because the newly christened "military-industrial complex" had, in fact, long been the subject of his professional attention. As an Army major in the late 1920s, Eisenhower went to Washington, DC, to work in the War Department on developing plans for industrial mobilization. In this capacity, he became intimately concerned with all aspects of civilian industrial production that might have a bearing on future wartime mobilization. In a paper for the Army Industrial College, Eisenhower noted that any successful wartime mobilization plan would have to be "a joint Army-Navy-Business Man's plan."[30] Such a scheme could only be effective, however, if the federal government assumed responsibility for controlling both production and prices during the wartime emergency, something which came to pass during World War II.[31] After the war, as Army Chief of Staff, Eisenhower argued that: "The armed forces could not have won the war alone. Scientists and business men contributed techniques and weapons which enabled us to outwit and overwhelm the enemy." He therefore insisted that "this pattern of integration must be translated into a peacetime counterpart which will ... draw into our planning for national security all the civilian resources which can contribute to the defense of our country." As such, the Army had a "duty to support broad research programs in educational institutions, in industry, and in whatever field might be of importance," and to that end he created a short-lived Research and Development Division in the General Staff.[32] In other words, Eisenhower himself was one of the architects of the developing Cold War military-industrial complex.

On the other hand, while Eisenhower preached the necessity of preparedness, by the late 1940s he also repeatedly expressed concern about the Harry S. Truman administration's failure to adopt a rational, long-term security strategy for peacetime that effectively balanced means and ends. The true "purpose of America," he wrote, "is to defend a way of life rather than merely to defend property, homes, or lives."[33] For Eisenhower, national security constituted: "Spiritual force, multiplied by economic force, multiplied by military force ... if one of these factors falls to zero, or near zero, the resulting product does likewise."[34] He became increasingly concerned about the propensity of the service chiefs to equate their contribution to the nation's defence to the size of their annual budget allocation. They failed to grasp that American resources were finite, and spending "unconscionable sums" in peacetime on a "program of indefinite duration" could spell economic disaster. Long-term budget deficits would erode business confidence, foster price inflation, weaken the dollar, and eventually necessitate economic controls that would undermine the free enterprise system and even constitutional liberties at home. The end result, Eisenhower feared, would be a "garrison state."[35]

Eisenhower's paradoxical relationship with the military-industrial complex continued during his presidency.[36] His solution to the "Great Equation" of balancing "security with solvency" was the New Look, a capital-intensive defence strategy based on "military formations which make maximum use of science and technology in order to minimize numbers in men." As such, the administration committed the nation to "conduct and foster scientific research and development so as to insure superiority in quantity and quality of weapons systems."[37] Eisenhower's intention was to develop a strong military posture that would be sustainable over the "long haul" without entailing spiraling budget deficits. However, the "technological revolution" of the 1950s—including advances in jet propulsion, nuclear and thermonuclear weapons, guidance systems, and rocketry—made significant budgetary savings problematic. Concerned about the possibility of a window of vulnerability from Soviet long-range bombers, Eisenhower compounded matters in 1955 by reluctantly authorizing four separate long-range missile programs.

Similarly, until 1960, Eisenhower rarely questioned or rejected the military's demands for additional nuclear warheads. Moreover, he struggled to discipline the various service chiefs and their deputies behind the New Look strategy as each branch sought to enhance its own share of the favored strategic mission. In the annual battles over the defence budget, Eisenhower repeatedly complained about the failure of the Joint Chiefs of Staff to adopt a corporate view of national security rather than a narrow service view. Two rounds of Pentagon reforms in 1953 and 1958 designed to strengthen the authority of the Office of the Secretary of Defense over the service chiefs and secretaries hardly seemed to help matters. Interservice rivalry and competitive publicity continued unabated. By late 1957, former assistant secretary of war John J. McCloy reported to Eisenhower: "interservice rivalry is now spreading to industry, universities, etc. which are tending to be tied to particular services."[38] Although Eisenhower largely held the line on overall defence spending, by the end of his term the United States strategic arsenal had mushroomed to the point of "overkill" and military research and development leaped from $2.5 to $7.2 billion per year.[39] In sum, Eisenhower's capital-intensive defence strategy and presidential decisions fostered the exponential growth of the very military-industrial complex that he now wanted to caution against.

The last two years of Eisenhower's term were also characterized by rising levels of partisanship as the 1960 presidential election loomed, and the president was not immune to such considerations. The Soviet sputniks in 1957 first pushed Eisenhower onto the defensive as political opponents alleged that the administration's economizing had allowed a "missile gap" to develop, a theme expounded upon by Democratic Senator Stuart Symington of Missouri, a former secretary of the Air Force with close ties to the aerospace lobby, who had presidential ambitions. Another aspirant, Senate Majority Leader Lyndon B. Johnson (D-TX), held extensive hearings into supposed deficiencies in the nation's missile and rocket programs. Following the Republicans' disastrous showing in the 1958 midterm elections, a defeat which Eisenhower attributed to the irresponsible promises of "the spenders" on the left of the Democratic Party, he vowed, "for the next two years, the Lord sparing me, I am going to fight this as hard as I know how."[40] Working with Republicans and conservative Democrats, Eisenhower managed to balance the budget for 1960, but his administration's policies came under increasing partisan criticism as the election neared. Although not a candidate himself, he was angered that "his administration was being impugned ... he was being made the goat and that really bothered him."[41] When the Democrats selected John F. Kennedy as their presidential candidate, Eisenhower privately called him "incompetent." In his own late intervention in the campaigning for his vice president, Richard M. Nixon, he claimed that Nixon's "preparation for high office . . . has never been equaled," and he sharply critiqued Kennedy's inexperience, arrogance, and impetuosity.[42] He feared "another run [on gold] of catastrophic proportions . . . if the Democrats unbalance the budget."[43]

This, then, provided the context in which Eisenhower's Farewell Address gestated. Like all of his major speeches, it was a team effort. In addition to Moos, Williams, and Harlow, the president used his younger brother, Milton, as a sounding board and to assist with extensive editing throughout the drafting process.[44] Over the course of several weeks in December and January, the president and his brother made significant contributions to the final product. Following Kennedy's victory on November 8, a result which profoundly upset the president because it seemed to represent a repudiation of his philosophy, they decided not to address what was likely to be an unsympathetic Congress but rather to go over their heads and speak directly to the American people, his "fellow countrymen," via radio and television.[45] Thus, instead of urging the Congress to exercise statesmanship, Milton inserted the need for "an alert, knowledgeable, and dedicated citizenry" to patrol the military-industrial complex. The onus would now be upon the American people to elect worthy leaders who could strike the necessary balance between the demands of security abroad and liberty at home. Privately, Eisenhower worried that his Democratic successors would succumb to their own rhetoric about missile gaps and military vulnerabilities and fall prey to "the hard-sell technologists."[46] He was unsure that Kennedy had the necessary strength of character to stand firm against such pressures, or even that he wanted to do so. As Harlow graphically put it, "the thing was to try to protect . . . the presidency against being raped in the future after America's number one military president had retired."[47] In fact, during the election campaign, even the president's own party had implicitly repudiated the New Look's emphasis on fiscal responsibility by asserting that there "must be no price ceiling on America's security."[48] He and Milton therefore inserted one final plea for security with solvency, cautioning against "the temptation to feel that some spectacular and costly action could become the miraculous solution to all current difficulties."[49] Finally, a week or so before delivering the speech, the Eisenhower brothers contemplated but then decided to omit an explicit denunciation of "the radical" or "the extremist, no matter what his persuasion" whose views militated against the "balance" required of true statesmanship.[50]

The speech

As Fox had recommended, in both tone and substance Eisenhower's Farewell Address consciously drew upon Washington's famous precedent, but it also reaffirmed Eisenhower's core beliefs, painted a positive picture of his presidency and both implicitly and explicitly challenged his opponents' critique of his leadership. Like his hero, Eisenhower adopted the self-effacing tone of an elder statesman above party who had simply responded to his nation's call of duty. He reminded his audience of his unique credentials, "half a century in service to our country," thereby establishing his authority to reflect on past accomplishments and draw lessons for the future. Where Washington had warned against faction and the spirit of partisanship, Eisenhower gracefully painted a not entirely accurate picture of general harmony between himself and the opposition-led Congress, asserting that "on most vital issues" they had "cooperated well, to serve the national good, rather than mere partisanship." Momentarily setting aside his personal disdain for some of its members, the president expressed "gratitude that we have been able to do so much together." That said, with an eye to his historical legacy, Eisenhower boldly went on to provide his summary evaluation of his years in office. He asserted that "America today is the strongest, the most influential and most productive nation in the world," implicitly rejecting his political opponents' election-year charges of weakness, stagnation, and decline. Linking his administration with the nation's larger historical mission, he noted the ongoing American purpose to "keep the peace, to foster progress in human achievement, and to enhance liberty, dignity, and integrity among peoples and among nations. To strive for less would be unworthy of a free and religious people."

Like Washington, Eisenhower warned of the perils of a hostile world, and here he returned to his well-honed rhetoric regarding the Cold War and communist culpability. The Cold War struggle was all-pervasive. In contradistinction to the progressive-minded, liberty-loving "free and religious" United States, "We face a hostile ideology—global in scope, atheistic in character, ruthless in purpose, and insidious in method." Moreover, "the danger it poses promises to be of indefinite duration." Eisenhower implicitly reasserted the case for the wisdom of his "long haul" strategy of containment, again calling on Americans to make the necessary sacrifices "which enable us to carry forward steadily, surely, and without complaint the burdens of a prolonged and complex struggle." Temporary provocations should not divert them from "our charted course toward permanent peace and human betterment." Taking a swipe at his critics who had sought to use the Soviet sputniks as a rationale for various emergency measures, Eisenhower emphasized that "the emotional and transitory sacrifices of crisis" were exactly the wrong response. There were no simple, "miraculous solution[s]" to these long-term problems. Eisenhower had criticized such a "crisis" approach to national security policy under his predecessor, Truman, and he worried about its possible reappearance under his successor, Kennedy. What was required was a steady hand at the tiller, "good judgment", and a sense of "balance" among competing priorities given finite resources.

In what became the most widely cited passages of the speech, Eisenhower took up a modern-day version of George Washington's admonition against "those overgrown military establishments . . . which are to be regarded as particularly hostile to republican liberty." Given the realities of the Cold War and the dangers of nuclear conflict, however, Eisenhower considered a powerful military establishment "a vital element in keeping the peace." He reasserted the logic of nuclear deterrence, popularized as "massive retaliation," noting that "Our arms must be mighty, ready for instant action, so that no potential aggressor may be tempted to risk his own destruction." Similarly, the United States "had been compelled to create a permanent arms industry of vast proportions." The conjunction of these two forces permeated every aspect of American life and, while there was "an imperative need" for this development, Americans had to recognize "its grave implications" for "the very structure of our society." For this reason, he cautioned the American people to remain alert to the "unwarranted influence, whether sought or unsought, of the military-industrial complex." Again alluding to his overarching approach to national security, true security required a careful balancing act between the necessities of defence and the requirements of liberty. In their meticulous editing, the Eisenhower brothers went to great pains to avoid an outright denunciation of the military-industrial complex, which Eisenhower had helped to build and which they ultimately regarded as essential to the nation's defence. For that reason, they deliberately inserted the words "whether sought or unsought" after "influence" to avoid the connotation that military and industrial leaders were consciously conspiring to undermine individual liberties. As with the earlier decision by Williams to drop the reference to the "merchants of death," the Eisenhower brothers intended to caution rather than condemn.

Eisenhower issued a related warning regarding the impact of the "technological revolution," which had dramatically affected the nature of warfare and fueled the growth of the military-industrial complex. Here again, the president delved into themes that had characterized much of his presidency, primarily the need for balance. Remarking upon the changing nature of research, notably the shift towards big science and applied research conducted by teams of researchers in dedicated facilities requiring rising levels of funding, Eisenhower expressed concern over the increasing role of the federal government in directing such projects. Although he had sanctioned modest increases in federal support for basic scientific research and education, he had done so warily and, as a former university president, worried about the "prospect of domination of the nation's scholars" by the state. Similarly, as his difficulties in the aftermath of the Soviet sputniks had driven home, there was "the equal and opposite danger that public policy could itself become the captive of a scientific-technological elite." Earlier drafts of the speech had described the conundrum as the problem of striking the appropriate balance between the generalist and the specialist.[51] The solution was wise "statesmanship to mold, to balance, and to integrate these and other forces, new and old, within the principles of our democratic system—ever aiming toward the supreme goals of our free society."

In the final section of the speech, Eisenhower peered into the future but again drew inspiration from Washington's example and his own recent experience. Like Washington, he urged his audience to consider the connection between public finances, security, and their future posterity. Just as Washington had urged avoiding public debt and "throwing upon posterity the burden which we ought to bear," Eisenhower reiterated his concern for fiscal discipline, telling his listeners:

> we—you and I, and our government—must avoid the impulse to live only for today, plundering, for our own ease and convenience, the precious resources of tomorrow. We cannot mortgage the material assets of our grandchildren without risking the loss also of their political and spiritual heritage. We want democracy to survive for all generations to come, not to become the insolvent phantom of tomorrow.

Repeating a major theme of his Second Inaugural Address, Eisenhower pointed to the necessity of a peaceful world, "a proud confederation of mutual respect," grounded in justice and law, where nations great and small could gather together and peacefully resolve their differences at the conference table.[52] What Eisenhower failed to articulate here, although he had done so frequently elsewhere, was that his definition of "peace" necessitated the absolute defeat of international communism and the liberation of peoples held in its thrall. In concluding, Eisenhower expressed personal disappointment at his failure to achieve the "imperative" of disarmament. Nevertheless, employing the passive voice, he modestly drew attention to what he considered his greatest achievement in the perilous years of the early Cold War: "war has been avoided." With that, the old general bade his farewell. Having laid out his considerable accomplishments, he expressed hope that his countrymen "found some things worthy; as for the rest of it, I know you will always find ways to improve performance in the future."

An unintended legacy

If Eisenhower intended his Farewell Address to be a final act of rhetorical statesmanship in which he persuaded the American people to stay the course which his administration had charted, it soon became clear that the military-industrial complex was the element that attracted the greatest attention. Moreover, his warning, which the *New York Times* characterized as "a surprise to many in the capital," quickly began to assume a negative connotation.[53] Perhaps one reason for this was that in his press conference the day after the speech, the president clouded matters. In response to a question about his intent, he observed that: "almost every one of your magazines, no matter what they are advertising, has a picture of the Titan missile or the Atlas or solid fuel or other things, there is becoming a great influence, almost an insidious penetration of our own minds that the only thing this country is engaged in is weaponry and missiles."[54] Although the speech had not specifically addressed the lobbying and advertising conducted by the armed services and defence contractors, speechwriters Moos and Williams recalled that this had been in the forefront of their thinking as they began the drafting process.[55] They also recounted their concern regarding the revolving door whereby defence contractors hired retired military officers to do business with their former services. Within weeks of the presidential transition, Bryce Harlow mischievously reported to Eisenhower and Nixon that the warning against the influence of "the military industrial complex" had proven to be "curiously yeasty" among the Republican minority in Congress. He admitted that he was working behind the scenes with favored reporters "to add fuel to this small flame" in complicating legislative matters for the Kennedy administration.[56] The reporters were not identified. A week after the speech, however, the *New York Times* ran a full-page article analyzing the military-industrial complex. Jack Raymond reported that a congressional inquiry had identified 726 former officers who were employed by the country's top one hundred defence contractors. The piece described their lobbying practices, and noted that 59 percent of the national budget now went for national security purposes. Raymond also fleshed out the president's reference to the rising federal role in research, particularly for defence purposes, and warned that "there has developed a 'cross-fertilization' of men and ideas among the military, industrial and scientific institutions."[57]

Interestingly, within days of the speech, some of Eisenhower's inner circle of scientists expressed concern at the president's language. Several of them contacted Eisenhower's science adviser, George B. Kistiakowsky, to ask whether the president was "turning against science." At a farewell reception, Eisenhower "seemed quite upset" that his words had been interpreted in such a way. He reassured Kistiakowsky that he was strongly in favor of continued basic academic research "and feared only the rising power of military science," a point he subsequently reiterated to Director of Defense Research and Engineering Herbert York and former science adviser and Massachusetts Institute of Technology president James Killian. At the president's request, Kistiakowsky attempted to clarify the president's stance with fellow scientists in an open letter to the editor of *Science*.[58]

Ironically, given his essentially conservative intent to maintain fiscal integrity, Eisenhower's warning resonated most powerfully on the left of the political spectrum among those who would usually have been considered his chief critics. Although there is no evidence that the president was aware of radical sociologist C. Wright Mills's 1956 book *The Power Elite*, it seems highly likely that both Milton Eisenhower and Malcolm Moos were quite conscious of Mills's critique. Mills argued that a triumvirate of corporate leaders, politicians, and high-ranking military officers (including Eisenhower) constituted a virtual hereditary, technocratic elite who had come to monopolize the nation's affairs, effectively spelling the end of participatory democracy. He claimed: "There is no longer, on the one hand, an economy, and on the other hand, a political order containing a military establishment unimportant to politics and to money-making. There is a political economy linked, in a thousand ways, with military institutions and decisions."[59] In effect, the nation had already erected "a permanent war economy." As President Eisenhower and his collaborators crafted their speech, they had touched upon elements of Mills's analysis but given it a more positive twist. Eisenhower's Farewell Address therefore rejected the notion that the United States was already a "garrison state," although that danger certainly lurked over the horizon. Whereas Mills proclaimed the end of democracy, Eisenhower placed faith in an "alert and knowledgeable citizenry."[60]

Nevertheless, these distinctions soon became blurred as other voices on the left embraced Eisenhower for their own purposes and consciously or unconsciously misinterpreted his intent. Shortly after the speech, the left-leaning periodical *The Nation* praised the outgoing president for his prescience and belated attention to the parlous effects of the Cold War on American institutions. "Nothing became Mr. Eisenhower's career in office like the leaving of it . . . now, in the closing days of his Administration he spoke like the statesman and democratic leader we had so long hungered for him to become," intoned the editor.[61] A few months later, the magazine devoted an entire issue to a lengthy piece by investigative reporter Fred J. Cook analyzing the "warfare state" that Eisenhower had supposedly identified. An expanded version of his essay appeared in book form the following year. Labeled a "worthy successor to the late C. Wright Mills" by the *New York Times*, Cook pointed out that the annual military budget of $52 billion accounted for half of all federal spending, noted that 85 percent of military contracts were awarded without competitive bidding, drew attention to the revolving door whereby over 1,400 retired military officers held positions in the 100 top defence contractors, and stated that the Pentagon directly employed 3.5 million military and civilian personnel while defence industries employed a further 4 million. Among the dangers that Cook highlighted were "the grab for military contracts by local communities, self-interested sponsorship of national strategies by military partisans, the latent concern that disarmament might spell economic ruin . . . and the barrage of military-oriented lobbies directed against Congress."[62]

The same year, Eisenhower's warning and Mills's critique became conflated in one of the founding documents of the New Left, Students for a Democratic Society's (SDS) Port Huron statement. Drafted largely by Tom Hayden, who had read Mills closely, the SDS claimed that Eisenhower's "military-industrial complex" was "the most spectacular and important creation of the authoritarian and oligopolistic structure of economic decision-making in America." Whereas Eisenhower had cautioned to be alert for its unwarranted influence, SDS proclaimed that "the militarization of

American society" had already happened. Like Cook, SDS pointed to the dangers of the revolving door of former military personnel taking positions with defence contractors, "the intermingling of Big Military and Big Industry."[63]

Eisenhower's warning about the development of a "scientific-technological elite" and the potentially deleterious impact of federal funding on university research similarly gained traction with the left. Free Speech student leader Mario Savio took up the clarion call by pointing to the complicity of the nation's leading research universities in the military-industrial complex. Drawing upon Eisenhower's concern about federal research contracts, Savio argued that academic scholarship had succumbed to institutional pressure for military research contracts.[64] Not to be outdone, a voice from the Old Left, long-time socialist presidential candidate Norman Thomas, deployed Eisenhower's words almost verbatim in denouncing the corrupting influence of military money on university research.[65] As student unrest mounted, particularly following the escalation of direct United States involvement in Vietnam and growing evidence of the complicity of universities in the war effort, Eisenhower's words were often employed to justify anti-war protests and direct action against the establishment, including universities.[66] At the end of the decade, Moos looked back and noted that the military-industrial complex had become "part of the national debate."[67]

The conspiratorial connotation of the "military-industrial complex" probably reached its apogee in popular culture with two movies released over a decade apart. In 1991, Oliver Stone's controversial movie *JFK* opened with a television clip from Eisenhower's Farewell Address. The reason became apparent in the dramatic denouement when a shady Mr. X. of military intelligence, played by Donald Sutherland, explained to New Orleans District Attorney Jim Garrison (Kevin Costner) just why Kennedy had been assassinated:

> Why was Kennedy killed? Who benefited?
> Who has the power to cover it up? Who? . . .
> Don't underestimate the budget cuts that Kennedy called for in March of 1963.

> Nearly 52 military installations in 25 states.
> Twenty-one overseas bases.
> Big money . . .
> Find out the defense budget since the [Vietnam] war began. $75 going on $100 billion.
> Nearly $200 billion will be spent before it's over . . .
> No war . . . no money.
> The authority of the state over its people resides in its war powers.
> Kennedy wanted to end the Cold War in his second term . . .
> He set out to withdraw from Vietnam.
> But all that ended on the 22nd of November, 1963.
> Like Caesar, he is surrounded by enemies . . .
> Everybody in the power structure . . . has a plausible deniability . . .
> That is a coup d'état.[68]

Fast forward a decade, and Eugene Jarecki's prize-winning 2005 documentary, *Why We Fight*, employed a similar format, opening with the same television clip of Eisenhower's speech. This time, the message was that the military-industrial complex was largely responsible for a series of conflicts culminating in the 2003 Iraq War. Military contractors touting new weaponry, oil interests seeking new opportunities, and military construction companies like Vice President Dick Cheney's Halliburton were the primary architects. "I would think Eisenhower must be rolling over in his grave," the commentator intoned.[69] Quite so.

During the drafting of his Farewell Address, Eisenhower supposedly confided to his chief speechwriter that: "I'm more interested in how this speech reads a generation from now than in the comment it gets in the headlines."[70] By that measure, it was a resounding rhetorical success that seemingly cemented Eisenhower's presidential legacy. On the fiftieth anniversary of its delivery, a slew of generally positive commentaries appeared in various media outlets attesting to the prescience of Eisenhower's words.[71] Mired in a seemingly unending war on global terror, with defence spending in dollar terms over twice as high as in the Eisenhower years and budget deficits mounting, and with raging political battles to protect or augment key weapons systems originally designed to meet a threat that had greatly diminished with the end of the Cold War, the old general's cautionary words about the influence of the military-industrial complex continued to reverberate across the political spectrum. The speech had become something of a Rorschach test for left and right, with each finding elements to their liking.[72] For those on the left, Eisenhower was a belated spokesman for peace who recognized the dangerous drift towards militarism emanating from the "permanent war economy" and wanted to roll it back. For those of a more libertarian bent, he was a wise advocate for limited government and the protection of individual liberties from intrusion by the state. Neither, of course, was entirely accurate.

Eisenhower's legacy with regard to the military-industrial complex is obviously complicated. As both a soldier and statesman, he thought deeply about questions of military preparedness in war and peace and made significant contributions to the Cold War-era structures that constituted the national security state. His Farewell Address reflected his essentially conservative values and reiterated themes that had characterized his presidency: the necessity of containing a military and ideological adversary over the long haul while carefully balancing means and ends to preserve the American way of life. That his "military-industrial complex" phrase should be taken up most forcefully among activists on the left is ironic. Eisenhower presided over what was the largest peacetime military build-up to that point in the nation's history, waged unrelenting economic and psychological warfare against the Soviet bloc, authorized covert actions to eliminate world leaders deemed hostile to American interests, and initiated plans for thermonuclear Armageddon should deterrence fail. He was no dove on Vietnam. While his words were being marshaled to justify anti-war actions by the left, a war which he had indirectly initiated, Eisenhower was advising his successors to pursue the conflict more vigorously. Looking back from the vantage point of the mid-1980s, speechwriter Williams expressed astonishment at the attention still given to "the 'military-industrial complex' portion" of Eisenhower's Farewell Address and lamented that "its true significance has been distorted beyond recognition."[73] Perhaps part of the problem was semantics. As Harlow had suggested, the "military-industrial complex" phrase was just too "yeasty."

Notes

1. *Public Papers of the Presidents: Dwight D. Eisenhower, 1960–61* (Washington, DC: Government Printing Office, 1961), 1038.
2. The major exceptions, and the most useful discussions of the speech are: Charles J.G. Griffin, "New Light on Eisenhower's Farewell Address," *Presidential Studies Quarterly* 22, no. 3 (Summer 1992): 469–80, which draws upon newly available materials in the Eisenhower Library to shed light on the authorship of the speech and its political intent of rebutting Eisenhower's political opponents; Martin J. Medhurst, "Reconceptualizing Rhetorical History: Eisenhower's Farewell Address," *Quarterly Journal of Speech* 80, no. 2 (1994): 195–218, which undertakes a close textual analysis and argues that Eisenhower deliberately drew from Washington's example to add force to what was essentially a critique and warning against the incoming Kennedy administration; James Ledbetter, *Unwarranted Influence: Dwight D. Eisenhower and the Military-Industrial Complex* (New Haven, CT: Yale University Press, 2011), which provides a sweeping intellectual history of the military-industrial complex concept; and Dolores E. Janiewski, "Eisenhower's Paradoxical Relationship with the 'Military-Industrial Complex,'" *Presidential Studies Quarterly* 41, no. 4 (December 2011): 667–92, which argues that Eisenhower was frustrated by the fact that he had been "unable to free the United States from the icy grip of a Cold War dilemma of which he was a creator, a captive, and a critic" (686).
3. Chester J. Pach, "Introduction: Eisenhower, Yesterday and Today," in Chester J. Pach (ed.), *A Companion to Dwight D. Eisenhower* (Malden, MA: Wiley-Blackwell, 2017), 1.
4. On farewell addresses as a genre of presidential rhetoric, see Karlyn Kohrs Campbell and Kathleen Hall Jamieson, *Deeds Done in Words: Presidential Rhetoric and Genres of Governance* (Chicago: University of Chicago Press, 1990), 191–211.
5. On Washington's Farewell Address, see Felix Gilbert, *To the Farewell Address: Ideas of Early American Foreign Policy* (Princeton, NJ: Princeton University Press, 1961); Stephen E. Lucas, "George Washington and the Rhetoric of Presidential Leadership," in Leroy G. Dorsey (ed.), *The Presidency and Rhetorical Leadership* (College State: Texas A&M University Press, 2002), 49–54.
6. Robert J. Donovan, "Moos Recalls Idea for Eisenhower's Militarism Phrase," *Washington Post*, April 1, 1969.

7. Craig Allen, *Eisenhower and the Mass Media: Peace, Prosperity, and Prime-Time TV* (Chapel Hill: University of North Carolina Press, 1993), 8, 214.
8. The foundational work is Jeffrey K. Tullis, *The Rhetorical Presidency* (Princeton, NJ: Princeton University Press, 1987). See also H.W. Brands, "The Golden Age of the Presidency and Why it Ended," unpublished paper at the Presidential History Network Conference on Presidential Legacy, Northumbria University, Newcastle, 2016.
9. Fred I. Greenstein, *The Hidden-Hand Presidency: Eisenhower as Leader* (New York: Basic Books, 1982), 57. For a somewhat more critical analysis by the same author, faulting Eisenhower for ineffectively combating the "missile gap" mythology, see Meena Bose and Fred I. Greenstein, "The Hidden Hand vs. the Bully Pulpit: The Layered Political Rhetoric of President Eisenhower," in Dorsey (ed.), *Presidency and Rhetorical Leadership*, 184–99.
10. See Martin J. Medhurst, *Dwight D. Eisenhower: Strategic Communicator* (Greenwood Press, 1994); Martin J. Medhurst, *Eisenhower's War of Words: Rhetoric and Leadership* (East Lansing: Michigan State University Press, 1994).
11. See Kenneth Osgood, *Total Cold War: Eisenhower's Secret Propaganda Battle at Home and Abroad* (Lawrence: University Press of Kansas, 2006); Shawn J. Parry-Giles, *The Rhetorical Presidency, Propaganda, and the Cold War, 1945–1955* (Westport, CT: Praeger, 2002).
12. Malcolm Moos Oral History, Columbia University Oral History, 1973, 12; Ralph E. Williams Oral History, 1988, 17–18, Dwight D. Eisenhower Presidential Library, Abilene, Kansas (hereafter, DDEL).
13. Moos Oral History, 13; Robert Schlesinger, *White House Ghosts: Presidents and their Speechwriters from FDR to George W. Bush* (New York: Simon and Schuster, 2008), 82–86.
14. Eisenhower to Milton Eisenhower, May 25, 1959, Arthur Larson and Malcolm Moos Records, Box 17, folder: Presidential Speech Planning, DDEL; Milton Eisenhower Oral History, Columbia University, 1976, 51–52.
15. Moos Oral History, 27; William B. Ewald Oral History, 1977, 12–14, DDEL.
16. Ralph E. Williams to Patrick J. Haney, April 6, 1988, Ralph E. Williams Papers, Box 1, folder: Letters 1985–1988, DDEL.
17. Moos Oral History, 33.

18. Moos memo for record, May 20, 1959, Arthur Larson and Malcolm Moos Records, Box 16, folder: Farewell Address (1), DDEL.
19. Subjects for Presidential Talks, May 22, 1959, Arthur Larson and Malcolm Moos Records, Box 17, folder: Presidential Speech Planning, DDEL.
20. Eisenhower to Milton Eisenhower, May 25, 1959, in Louis Galambos (ed.), *The Papers of Dwight David Eisenhower*, vol. 20: *The Presidency: Keeping the Peace* (Baltimore, MD: Johns Hopkins University Press, 2001), 1492–94.
21. Ibid.
22. Frederic Fox to Moos, April 5, 1960, Arthur Larson and Malcolm Moos Records, Box 16, Farewell Address (1), DDEL.
23. Williams Oral History, 34–35, DDEL.
24. Williams memo for file, October 31, 1961, Ralph E. Williams Papers, Box 1, folder: Chronological (1), DDEL.
25. Williams Oral History, 33, DDEL.
26. Williams Oral History, 27, DDEL.
27. Medhurst, "Reconceptualizing Rhetorical History," 208.
28. Moos Oral History, 35.
29. Sam Roberts, "In Archive, New Light on Evolution of Eisenhower Speech," *New York Times*, December 10, 2010.
30. Dwight D. Eisenhower, "Brief History of Planning for Procurement and Industrial Mobilization," October 3, 1930, in Daniel D. Holt and James W. Leyerzapf (eds.), *Eisenhower: The Prewar Diaries and Selected Papers, 1905–1941* (Baltimore: Johns Hopkins University Press, 1998), 184. For an extended discussion, see Kerry E. Irish, "Apt Pupil: Dwight Eisenhower and the 1930 Industrial Mobilization Plan," *Journal of Military History* 70, no. 1 (January 2006): 31–61.
31. Ledbetter, *Unwarranted Influence*, 50–51.
32. Eisenhower to Directors and Chiefs of War Department, General and Special Staff Divisions and Bureaus, and the Commanding Generals of the Major Commands, April 30, 1946, in Louis P. Galambos, ed., *The Papers of Dwight David Eisenhower*, vol. 7: *The Chief of Staff* (Baltimore: The Johns Hopkins University Press, 1978), 1046–50; Thomas C. Lassman, "Putting the Military Back into the History of the Military-Industrial Complex: The Management of Technological Innovation in the US Army, 1945–1960," *Isis* 106, no. 1 (March 2015): 94–120.
33. Diary Entry, January 25, 1952, in Robert H. Ferrell (ed.), *The Eisenhower Diaries* (New York: Norton, 1981), 210.

34. Eisenhower to Lucius D. Clay, February 9, 1952, *Eisenhower Papers* 8: 963.
35. US Department of State, *Foreign Relations of the United States, 1952–1954*, vol. 2, 469; Michael J. Hogan, *A Cross of Iron: Harry S. Truman and the Origins of the National Security State, 1945–1954* (New York: Cambridge University Press, 1998), Chapter 9.
36. The term is from Janiewski, "Eisenhower's Paradoxical Relationship."
37. Basic National Security Policy, NSC 162/2, October 30, 1953, in US Department of State, *Foreign Relations of the United States, 1952–1954*, vol. 2: *National Security Affairs* (Washington, DC: Government Printing Office, 1984), 577–97; Eisenhower to Secretary of Defense Charles E. Wilson, January 5, 1955, *Public Papers, 1955*, 2–6. For detailed discussion of the New Look, see Saki Dockrill, *Eisenhower's New Look National Security Policy, 1953–61* (New York: St. Martin's Press, 1996); H.W. Brands, "The Age of Vulnerability: Eisenhower and the National Insecurity State," *American Historical Review* 94, no. 4 (October 1989): 963–89.
38. Andrew J. Goodpaster memo of conference with the President, November 4, 1957, in US Department of State, *Foreign Relations of the United States, 1955–1957*, 19: *National Security Policy* (Washington, DC: Government Printing Office, 1990), 620–24, McCloy quotation on 622.
39. David Alan Rosenberg, "The Origins of Overkill: Nuclear Weapons and American Strategy, 1945–1960," *International Security* 7, no. 4 (Spring 1983): 3–71; George B. Kistiakowsky, *A Scientist at the White House: The Private Diary of President Eisenhower's Special Assistant for Science and Technology* (Cambridge, MA: Harvard University Press, 1976), 415–16; Richard V. Damms, *Scientists and Statesmen: Eisenhower's Science Advisers and National Security Policy* (Dordrecht: Republic of Letters Publishing, 2015), 268.
40. Iwan W. Morgan, *Eisenhower versus "the Spenders": The Eisenhower Administration, the Democrats, and the Budget, 1953–1960* (New York: St. Martin's Press, 1990); Dwight D. Eisenhower, "The President's News Conference," November 5, 1958, *The American Presidency Project*, <http://www.presidency.ucsb.edu/ws/index.php?pid=11286> (accessed June 13, 2018).
41. William B. Ewald Oral History, 1977, 46, DDEL.
42. Dwight D. Eisenhower, "Address at a Republican Rally in the New York Coliseum," November 2, 1960, *The American Presidency Project*, <http://www.presidency.ucsb.edu/ws/?pid=12004> (accessed June 13, 2018).

43. Kistiakowsky, *Scientist at the White House*, 402.
44. Williams Oral History, DDEL; Milton Eisenhower Oral History, 40–41.
45. After the election, Eisenhower lamented, "All I've been trying to do for eight years has gone down the drain." See John S.D. Eisenhower, *Strictly Personal* (Garden City, NY: Doubleday, 1974), 285. He told speechwriter William Bragg Ewald that: "it was as if someone had hit him in the solar plexus with a baseball bat." See William B. Ewald Oral History, John F. Kennedy Library Oral History Program, 1983, 13; Milton Eisenhower Oral History, 1976, 30.
46. Herbert F. York, *Race to Oblivion: A Participant's View of the Arms Race* (New York: Simon and Schuster, 1970), 10–13.
47. Medhurst, "Reconceptualizing Rhetorical History," 208.
48. Ledbetter, *Unwarranted Influence*, 127.
49. Dwight D. Eisenhower, "Farewell Radio and Television Address to the American People," January 17, 1961, *The American Presidency Project*, <http://www.presidency.ucsb.edu/ws/index.php?pid=12086> (accessed June 13, 2018).
50. Janiewski, "Eisenhower's Paradoxical Relationship," 683.
51. See the draft dated December 16, 1960, Arthur Larson and Malcolm Moos Records, Box 16, folder: Farewell Address (4), DDEL.
52. See Dwight D. Eisenhower, "Second Inaugural Address," January 21, 1957, *The American Presidency Project*, <http://www.presidency.ucsb.edu/ws/index.php?pid=10856> (accessed June 13, 2018).
53. "Vigilance Urged: Talk Bids 'Godspeed' to Kennedy—Voices Hopes for Peace," *New York Times*, January 18, 1961.
54. The President's News Conference, January 18, 1961, *The American Presidency Project*, <http://www.presidency.ucsb.edu/ws/index.php?pid=12087> (accessed June 13, 2018).
55. Moos Oral History; Williams Oral History, 32–35; Stephen Hess, "Eisenhower's Farewell Addresses: A Speechwriter Remembers," Brookings Report, January 9, 2017, <https://www.brookings.edu/research/eisenhowers-farewell-addresses-a-speechwriter-remembers/> (accessed June 13, 2018).
56. Harlow memo for Eisenhower and Richard M. Nixon, March 17, 1961, Dwight D. Eisenhower, Post-Presidential Papers, Special Names Series, Box 6, folder: Harlow, Bryce 1961 (3), DDEL.
57. Jack Raymond, "The 'Military-Industrial Complex': An Analysis," *New York Times*, January 22, 1961.
58. Kistiakowsky, *Scientist at the White House*, 425; Herbert F. York, *Arms and the Physicist* (New York: American Institute of Physics

Press, 1995), 147; Graham DuShane, "Footnote to History," *Science* 133 (February 10, 1961): 355; James R. Killian Jr., *Sputnik, Scientists, and Eisenhower: A Memoir of the First Special Assistant to the President for Science and Technology* (Cambridge: MIT Press, 1977), 241.

59. C. Wright Mills, *The Power Elite* (New York: Oxford University Press, 2000), 7–8.
60. Janiewski, "Eisenhower's Paradoxical Relationship," 672–73; Ledbetter, *Unwarranted Influence*, 43–44.
61. *The Nation*, January 28, 1961, 69–70.
62. Jack Raymond, "The Business of Defense," *New York Times*, November 4, 1962.
63. Ledbetter, *Unwarranted Influence*, 148–50; Port Huron Statement of the Students for a Democratic Society, 1962, <http://coursesa.matrix.msu.edu> (accessed June 13, 2018).
64. Ledbetter, *Unwarranted Influence*, 153–55; Thomas Buckley, "Berkeley Youth Leader Warns of Protests at Other Campuses," *New York Times*, December 12, 1964.
65. "Norman Thomas Scores 'Garrison State Mentality,'" *New York Times*, June 8, 1963.
66. David Brinkley, "Eisenhower the Dove," *American Heritage* 52 (September 2001): 58–64.
67. William McGaffin and Robert Gruenberg, "Ike's Historic 1961 Warning," *Chicago Daily News*, April 14, 1969.
68. *JFK* film script, <http://www.script-o-rama.com/movie_scripts/j/jfk-script-transcript-oliver-stone.html> (accessed June 13, 2018).
69. Ledbetter, *Unwarranted Influence*, 188–89; *Why We Fight*, film, dir. Eugene Jarecki (USA: Sony Pictures Home Entertainment, [2005] 2006).
70. McGaffin and Gruenberg, "Ike's Historic 1961 Warning."
71. For a brief sampling, see Renee Montagne, "Ike's Warning of Military Expansion, 50 Years Later," *Morning Edition* (NPR), January 17, 2011; Guy Raz, "Eisenhower's Warning Still Challenges a Nation," *Weekend All Things Considered* (NPR), January 16, 2011; Fareed Zakaria, "US Defence Spending Out of Control," *Toronto Star*, August 5, 2011; "Military-Industrial Complex, Fifty Years On," Council on Foreign Relations, January 13, 2011, <https://www.cfr.org/interview/military-industrial-complex-fifty-years> (accessed June 13, 2018); Leslie H. Gelb, "The Ike Speech that Eclipses JFK," *Daily Beast*, January 17, 2011; Ira Chernus, "How One Paragraph in a Single Speech has Skewed the Eisenhower Record," *Truthout*, January 19, 2011.

72. This analogy was suggested by Tim Rives, Interim Director of the Dwight D. Eisenhower Presidential Library, during a personal conversation with the author at the library on September 16, 2016. Subsequently, it has appeared in print in Brett Baier, *Three Days in January: Dwight Eisenhower's Final Mission* (New York: HarperCollins, 2017), 283. It is possible that Rives and Baier discussed the idea during the latter's research at the library.
73. Williams to Martin M. Teasley, December 28, 1985, Ralph E. Williams Papers, Box 1, folder: Letters 1985–1988, DDEL.

5

Pageantry, performance, and statecraft: Diplomacy and the presidential image

Thomas Tunstall Allcock

In November 1943, US President Franklin Roosevelt was photographed in Tehran with the leaders of the Soviet Union and Great Britain, Joseph Stalin and Winston Churchill. The picture of FDR, seated in his dark pinstripe suit flanked by Stalin and Churchill in military uniforms, became one of the iconic images of World War II, helping to cement both the concept of the "Big Three" and Roosevelt's status as a great statesman. More than forty years later another president, Ronald Reagan, welcomed Prince Charles and Princess Diana of Great Britain to a star-studded state dinner at the White House, resulting in globally reproduced images of the princess dancing with both the president and movie star John Travolta. These two very different moments highlight the variety of activities a president can undertake as part of their function as "diplomat-in-chief," and the potential of such events in shaping individual reputations and legacies. FDR's leadership during World War II remains central to his place among the presidential greats, while Ronald Reagan's ability to marry personal, earthy charm with Hollywood glamor is central to his enduring popularity with the American public.[1]

Whether through lasting achievements or by providing opportunities to showcase particularly appealing aspects of their personalities, diplomacy can play an integral and often underappreciated role in the construction of a presidential image and in shaping a historical legacy. In order to explore these connections, this chapter has two fundamental goals. The first is to establish, via several case studies, some of the ways in which presidents have actively sought to utilize diplomatic events to project a particular set of images, to emphasize aspects of their leadership and to influence assessments of their legacy. The second goal is to assess the efficacy of such efforts. Given the complex range of factors that can shape a presidential legacy, this is no easy task, and it is therefore helpful to first establish some clarity regarding the key concepts of presidential diplomacy, image, and legacy around which the chapter is built.[2]

No president is in complete control of their public image; too many factors go into its creation, representation, and reception for that to be the case. Nonetheless, this chapter is operating from the basic assumption that while in office a president is continually seeking to manage their image; that they are actively emphasizing aspects of their character, qualities, and personality in order to influence how they are regarded by others. Diplomacy is one arena that provides many opportunities for doing so. In the context of this chapter "presidential diplomacy" is simply taken to mean the instances in which the president is participating in face-to-face diplomacy, whether hosting foreign leaders, attending summit meetings or visiting foreign countries. In this sense, the president's diplomatic function is distinguished, to a degree, from the broader management of foreign affairs.[3] Finally, a presidential legacy will be taken to consist of two main, interrelated strands. The first comprises the items for which a president is remembered either positively or negatively after they have left office, such as legislative accomplishments, international agreements or economic performance. The other is the personal reputation of the president, how they are remembered as an individual and their enduring image in both public and historical memory. Such a definition is certainly not comprehensive, but provides a viable starting point for considering how a legacy is constructed and maintained.[4]

Presidential image, diplomacy, and legacy are deeply interconnected. High-level diplomacy is conducted at least partially in the public eye and provides multiple opportunities for what Bruce Miroff has termed "presidential spectacle," events that enable "the projection of images whose purpose is to shape public understanding and gain popular support." The nature of diplomatic events, most of which involve extensive consideration of staging, performance, and audience, often allow for a rare degree of control over the nature of that spectacle and the aspects a president wishes to emphasize. Reagan's glamorous state dinners are an obvious example. Of particular importance to this process, according to Miroff, are the president's personal qualities, which if established effectively can infuse interpretations of their administration's policies and achievements.[5] Alongside these opportunities for image management, international diplomacy also offers the chance for a president to secure landmark achievements, such as major state visits or the securing of notable international agreements, which can boost contemporary popularity and impact long-term assessments. Costas Panagopolous, for instance, has argued that landmark achievements are a central factor in determining long-term popularity, and are particularly powerful when allied to contemporary approval ratings and the potential of historical nostalgia to inflate a president's reputation. Similarly, Tim Blessing has argued that while the factors that shape a president's public reputation can be varied and complex, ultimately the presidency lends itself to relatively simple and "emotion-laden" narratives in public memory, driven by a few central elements.[6]

High-level diplomacy therefore offers multiple opportunities for a president to further their personal appeal by the projection of particular aspects of their style and personality, as well as the possibility of securing landmark achievements around which a lasting legacy can be constructed. Consequently, there is a great deal of variation between administrations in terms of their approach to presidential diplomacy in both style and substance, and a chapter of this length cannot hope to provide a comprehensive overview of them all. Instead, the first part of the chapter considers three very different presidencies, those of John Kennedy, Lyndon Johnson, and Richard Nixon, in order to highlight some of the ways in which image, diplomacy, and legacy are intimately connected. These administrations have been selected for the contrasting styles and personalities of the three men as well as for the era in which they were in office, beginning with Kennedy's inauguration in 1961 and ending with Nixon's resignation in 1974. Although the terms of US international engagement and the nature of the Cold War shifted substantially throughout this period, each of these presidents faced multiple global challenges and tumultuous relationships with allies and rivals alike. It was also an era that witnessed an increasing awareness of an emerging media landscape. Television and associated satellite technology were transforming the ways in which a president communicated with domestic and global audiences. The combination of these factors meant that each administration was hyper-aware of diplomatic exchanges, and their statecraft provides plenty of examples through which to consider the multifaceted uses of presidential diplomacy and its importance in shaping legacy.[7]

There is also an additional methodological benefit of drawing examples from this era. By the 1960s, polling of the American public regarding presidential performance was regular and widespread, providing a crucial, if somewhat nebulous, insight into the impact of diplomatic efforts on contemporary popularity. Further polls conducted in subsequent decades along with the vast literatures dedicated to each presidency then provide the basis for the second part of the chapter to consider the role of diplomacy in shaping both the views of the public and assessments by academic experts. Consequently, by considering case studies from a relatively short stretch of history it is possible to draw some conclusions regarding the wider importance of presidential diplomacy. A presidential legacy is contingent on a wide range of often interconnected and unpredictable factors, but nonetheless these case studies demonstrate that international diplomacy is a vital and influential arena for a president's image and has the potential to play a substantial role in shaping a lasting and positive legacy.

The spectacle of presidential diplomacy

Writing in a special issue of *The Atlantic* published fifty years after John F. Kennedy's assassination, historian Alan Brinkley noted that despite academics rating him as a relatively average president, Kennedy continued to enjoy widespread popularity with the American public. Kennedy was a youthful "symbol of purpose and hope" for many, and Brinkley identified the fact that perhaps no other president had been so successful in creating and maintaining a recognizable and powerful image and style. For Loren Glass, his style and mystique "allowed him to embody the ideals of the generation that he came to represent" before his untimely death "fixed that image of youthful idealism in the minds of the generation that followed." The myth of "Camelot," the creation of which began during Kennedy's life and was subsequently maintained and furthered by family, friends, and sympathetic chroniclers, prompted future generations of scholars to try and discover the "real" Kennedy, but its power with the public remains largely undiminished. The enduring success of Kennedy's image reflects the degree to which a president with a passion for foreign affairs can integrate diplomatic activities into a wider and coherent effort at image management, with a lasting impact on his legacy and reputation.[8]

Key to the style of presidency that Kennedy sought to create was the embrace of high culture. He invited noted artists, poets, and musicians to the White House to mingle with an administration dominated by the north-eastern political and intellectual elite.[9] The most prominent example of how international diplomacy would play an integral role in these efforts was the relationship between the White House and André Malraux, the distinguished author and Minister of State for Cultural Affairs for the Republic of France. Relations with French President Charles de Gaulle were strained throughout Kennedy's presidency, yet the first family courted Malraux during a state visit to Paris in May 1961. Malraux was charmed by Jackie's fluent French and enthusiasm for art and literature.[10] A year later he would make a return visit to Washington, and was hosted for a dinner that rivaled any held for a head of state. One account of the evening described an "impressive and international" menu being served to a guest list that included Mark Rothko, Saul Bellow, and Tennessee Williams while they enjoyed an evening of Schubert. The president's after-dinner toast incorporated a tribute to Malraux's varied career, a nod to both the rewards and the "difficulties" of dealing with De Gaulle, and a celebration of the "tremendous energy" that infused the intellectual and cultural life of the United States. In his response, Malraux acknowledged the role of the United States as "the country to which is entrusted . . . the destiny of mankind," and emphasized the success of the visit on a personal level, thanking the president for greeting him with the "masterpieces of the world—and ... by having your masterpieces shown to me by Mrs. Kennedy."[11]

The visit also included private discussions between President Kennedy and Malraux, which although frank and good-natured, ultimately changed little in Franco-US relations.[12] The most notable outcome of the visit would instead be revealed the following January, when after months of careful preparations the *Mona Lisa* arrived in the United States from the Louvre, where it would spend several weeks on display at the National Gallery and the New York Metropolitan Museum of Art. At its unveiling Kennedy was able to joke about recent disagreements with de Gaulle over nuclear policy, but also celebrate decades of shared history with France, and declare that the painting and its creator "embodied the central purpose of our civilization."[13] The unveiling attracted global press coverage and hundreds of thousands of Americans to the galleries over the course of its brief stay. It also did much to cement the Kennedys' reputation as patrons of the arts, and fed the image of "Camelot." For decades, newspapers, magazines, and books have regularly retold the story of how the personal diplomacy between the Kennedys and Malraux brought the *Mona Lisa* to the United States.[14]

While the Malraux visit and the loan of the Mona Lisa was perhaps the clearest example of the blending of culture and diplomacy in the Kennedy administration, the melding of symbolic and political goals was evident in conventional diplomatic exchanges, too. The first official state dinner to be hosted at the White House in 1961 was held for Tunisian President Habib Bourguiba, an event for which no formality was spared. The president and first lady were waiting at the airport on the red carpet to welcome the Bourguibas from the plane, before the whole party was driven to the White House via a parade route bedecked by a large crowd waving small Tunisian flags. The subsequent state dinner was also traditional and formal, with a guest list drawn largely from the Washington political elite and a menu inspired by Jackie Kennedy's research in the White House archives. The entertainment that followed the meal was "a patriotic American military panorama staged on the

South Lawn" featuring bands from the Army, Navy, Air Force, and Marine Corps playing and parading in formation under huge klieg lights outside the White House.[15]

One State Department report noted that the successful visit had "served primarily to demonstrate reciprocal respect between Tunisia and US [and] our recognition of Tunisia's efforts in foreign and domestic fields." Such recognition was designed to further Kennedy's broad Cold War strategy of presenting the new administration as a supporter of nations emerging from colonial rule and as a champion of developing economies. Bourguiba was considered politically moderate, having guided his country through a largely peaceful, negotiated independence process from French rule, and his presence allowed Kennedy to strengthen his image as a friend to the developing world, without seriously undermining his relationships with European countries still clinging to colonial possessions elsewhere.[16] The style of the celebrations, incorporating both elegant dining and demonstrations of martial prowess, also reflects that the cultivation of a sophisticated image was regularly complemented by reminders of Kennedy's energetic masculinity and military experience.[17]

These examples provide just a brief insight into the role that diplomacy played in Kennedy's construction of a coherent image and presidential persona. This successful integration also makes it a challenge to assess the specific impact of diplomacy on Kennedy's contemporary popularity, not least because of the relative stability of his approval ratings, which, according to Gallup, rarely dipped below 60 percent and averaged 70 percent across his three years in office. Neither Bourguiba's nor Malraux's visits resulted in any notable fluctuation in public approval ratings, nor did his sole summit meeting with Soviet leader Nikita Khrushchev in Vienna in 1961. By far the biggest jump in Kennedy's ratings, from 61 percent to 74 percent over the course of a month, followed the successful resolution of the Cuban Missile Crisis in October 1962, an example of crisis management and back-channel diplomacy rather than carefully planned public demonstrations of personal charm or cultural refinement. Further complicating matters, Kennedy occasionally received higher marks for his handling of domestic affairs than foreign policy, with a March 1962 poll reflecting a 67 percent approval rating for foreign and 72 percent for domestic matters. Additionally, his higher-profile diplomatic ventures did not always receive widespread approval, with one of the most common criticisms of the president that he let himself be "pushed around" by Khrushchev in Vienna.[18]

The polls can tell a different story, though, reflecting both Kennedy's ability to connect with the public on a personal level, and the potential benefits and pitfalls of prominent diplomatic efforts. For instance, a January 1961 poll showed a substantial majority in favor of holding a summit with the Soviets, suggesting that it was Kennedy's perceived poor performance in Vienna, rather than the diplomatic effort itself, that resonated negatively with the public. Similarly, in a poll taken in July 1963, 82 percent of respondents favored working closely with other nations in world affairs, while only 10 percent favored a "keep independent" position, again suggesting a climate broadly receptive to ambitious, successful diplomacy. While Kennedy's popularity was not necessarily driven by diplomatic achievements, it does seem that his overall efforts to create a consistent public image enjoyed more success. After less than a year in office, the two most common responses to the question "What would you say are President Kennedy's strong points?" were "strong leader, firm, doesn't back down," and "sincere, dedicated, good character," and his appearances on television always provoked positive responses. Kennedy's popularity was of course based on more than just his successful cultivation of a particular image, as the dramatic spike in approval ratings following the Cuban Missile Crisis demonstrates. Nonetheless, throughout the three years of his presidency diplomatic events functioned as an integral part of an administration that was highly skilled at maintaining a consistent public image, the success of which was not wholly reliant on concrete achievements.[19]

As the son of a former ambassador to Great Britain, it is not entirely surprising that Kennedy was largely at ease with the formalities of diplomatic ceremony, able to exude worldliness, intellectual curiosity, and natural style and charm. His successor, Lyndon Johnson, who grew up poor in the Texas Hill Country, was less comfortable in such formal settings. Yet whereas Kennedy's tragic early death meant that his presidency never reached a point of fixating on issues of legacy, Johnson would explicitly seek to secure diplomatic successes in order to bolster his future historical reputation. This is perhaps surprising for a president more associated with domestic legislative achievements, who was often considered ignorant of foreign cultures and reluctant to meet with world leaders.[20] For the Kennedy loyalists in particular, the diplomatic realm exposed Johnson's fundamental inadequacies as president and his inability to truly serve as Kennedy's successor.[21]

Johnson and many of his closest advisers were aware of the negative attention his diplomatic abilities attracted, something the president felt reflected prejudice against his upbringing, a Northern snobbery directed against a Southerner whose education encompassed a one-room school house and a teacher training college rather than prep school and the Ivy League.[22] In truth, Johnson did not always help himself in countering this image, hosting his first major visit of a foreign leader at his ranch, soon known as the "Texas White House." The visit culminated in a barbecue state dinner at a nearby high school gymnasium. The ranch was regularly used for entertaining foreign dignitaries throughout the five years of Johnson's presidency, often in ways that provided a sharp contrast to the style and emphasis on high culture of the Kennedy era, with entertainment ranging from popular singers such as Eddie Fisher to local high school choirs and elaborate sheepdog shows. While this could simply support the traditional narrative of Johnson's clumsiness and parochialism when it came to foreign affairs, there are at least two strong arguments to suggest a more complex interpretation.[23]

Firstly, Johnson sought to emphasize broad continuity with his predecessor, but also privately told aides, "I've got to put my own stamp on this administration in order to run for office on my own." The use of the ranch and emphasis on his Texan background can be interpreted as an effort to provide a clear break with the Kennedy years and establish an identity for the new president, without requiring any immediate disruption to continuity in policy. Secondly, Johnson's diplomacy consisted of more than his Texan-themed celebrations, and while it is undoubtedly true that he lacked Kennedy's affinity for international affairs, it would be a mistake to overstate the impact this had on diplomatic conduct. Using the ranch was the exception rather than the rule, with the State Department website listing twenty-two visits to the United States by foreign leaders in 1964, and only one of them—Mexican President-elect Gustavo Diaz Ordaz—hosted in Texas. Indeed, most Johnson-era state dinners in Washington looked much like Kennedy's, with similar menus and entertainment. Nonetheless, Johnson often complained that his Texan identity was used to criticize his lack of finesse, and there was regular discussion within the administration of ways to counter criticism from Kennedy loyalists that LBJ was "only a good domestic President." Ironically, this often resulted in diplomacy that was heavily influenced by domestic considerations, with the Glassboro summit a prime example.[24]

In June 1967 the Johnson administration was considering the merits of meeting with Soviet Premier Alexei Kosygin while he was in the United States to visit the United Nations.[25] Logistical discussions over an acceptable venue had grown increasingly complex and Johnson was considering whether or not to press ahead. The arguments that ultimately persuaded him to pursue a meeting are revealing. First, White House aide Tom Johnson pushed LBJ to meet Kosygin "at any location," as "even if it blew up into a propaganda device by the Russians, the American people would know that the President did take this step to seek peace for the world." Shortly after, National Security Advisor Walt Rostow was even more explicit regarding the symbolic importance of the summit. He informed Johnson that while there was only a "20% chance that it will have a net favorable effect in US-Soviet policy," domestically the summit would "cover your flank to the left and among the columnists" at a time when criticism of the president's handling of conflict in Vietnam was increasing. Looking ahead to the 1968 presidential election, Rostow also warned that without a meeting "the Republicans will run on: 'I will go to Moscow.'"[26]

Convinced, Johnson arranged to meet with Kosygin for a series of conversations held in Glassboro, New Jersey, commencing on June 23. Glassboro was roughly equidistant from Washington, DC and the United Nations in New York. More historically resonant settings such as Independence Hall in

Philadelphia had been considered, but eventually the Glassboro State College University President's residence, Hollybush, proved the best location available at short notice. White House aides worked tirelessly to prepare for the event, and while there were one or two Johnsonian touches—including barbecuing the lamb chops for lunch in the yard—the overall impression of the summit was of a traditional meeting between heads of state with few Texan flourishes. Furthermore, despite little progress on a number of the major issues discussed, notably conflict in the Middle East and Vietnam, the administration considered the summit to have been a success for its positive atmosphere and symbolic impact. "Hollybush has been heady stuff," NSC staffer Nathaniel Davis gushed in a memo to Rostow, "not just what went on inside the house, but also the cheering crowds, the 500 newsmen, the response of this country." Most media coverage was slightly less euphoric, but still emphasized the significance of the meeting, and the potential it offered for future agreements on more substantive issues.[27]

The most notable consequence of the "spirit of Glassboro" was an improvement in US-Soviet relations that culminated in the signing of the Nuclear Non-Proliferation treaty a year later, but Johnson hoped for another summit meeting with even more substantial results. The pressure of the ongoing conflict in Vietnam and associated domestic protest movements, as well as challenges from within his own party would see Johnson announce in March 1968 that he would not run for the presidency in November, yet throughout his final year in office he repeatedly sought diplomatic victories to build on the Glassboro summit. The shift in emphasis that began with Glassboro is reflected in the increase in foreign visitors during his final years in office, leaping from just fourteen in 1966 to thirty-seven in 1967 and twenty-six in 1968. Without an election campaign to plan for the first time in his adult life, Johnson's diplomatic efforts throughout 1968 were almost exclusively focused on securing a legacy more favorable than that of a president who dragged his country into a disastrous war in South East Asia.[28]

On August 20, 1968, Johnson was poised to present to the world the narrative of his presidency that he hoped would dominate his remaining months in office. A draft press briefing prepared by Rostow declared that "the year since Glassboro has been, certainly, the most intensive and successful post-war year in US-Soviet relations," and that "when President Johnson withdrew from the presidential nomination, he had very much in mind a desire to devote himself . . . to movement towards peace." The statement was to culminate with an announcement that talks were to begin with the Soviets regarding an arms limitation agreement, talks that would likely result in a presidential trip to Moscow later that year. In conjunction with efforts to find a negotiated end to the conflict in Vietnam, Johnson, historian Mitchell Lerner argues, "was on the brink of establishing a legacy as a figure of peace and statesmanship."[29]

Unfortunately for Johnson, that same night the Soviet Ambassador Anatoly Dobrynin informed Washington that Warsaw Pact troops would shortly be entering Czechoslovakia to forcefully end the period of political liberalization known as the "Prague Spring." Plans for any announcements regarding progress on US-Soviet relations were immediately shelved. The timing of the Soviet actions was, according to Secretary of State Dean Rusk, "like throwing a dead fish in the face of the President of the United States." Muted official US condemnation of the Soviet invasion reflected the degree to which Johnson was desperate to rescue an arms limitation agreement, and as late as December he and Rostow had not given up hope of a presidential summit in Moscow, yet ultimately neither proved possible. Still, the degree to which the president and his advisers hoped that high-profile diplomatic achievements could transform his legacy is striking. Whether an arms limitation agreement and a trip to Moscow would have been sufficient to counteract existing assessments of Johnson's diplomatic abilities, achievements, and legacy is impossible to say, but his administration clearly believed in the potential power of landmark, powerfully symbolic events to color historical perspectives. In Johnson's case poll numbers also provide some substance to this belief, with a clearer correlation between diplomatic success and public approval than under his predecessor.[30]

In the early months of his presidency Johnson appears to have done a relatively effective job of establishing a positive interpretation of his personality and identity with the American public.

In June 1964, in response to the open question "Is there anything you particularly like about Lyndon Johnson?," the most common positive answer was "personality and character." Even the fact that some of those asked to name what they disliked about him gave the response "personal conduct (pulling dogs' ears, driving fast etc.)" reflected a degree of success in establishing his own identity in office, particularly as 68 percent were unable to pinpoint anything they particularly disliked about their new president. The following February showed similar results, this time with "personality, character" tied with "experience, ability, dynamic approach to job," as the factors the public liked most. From late 1965 onwards, however, Johnson's handling of Vietnam would come to dominate polling, coinciding with a steady downward progression in his approval ratings. After August 1966 his approval rating rose above 50 percent only twice. One such spike came in early April 1968, following his announcement that he would not be seeking re-election, news which was accompanied by the institution of a bombing pause and more intensive pursuit of negotiations in Vietnam. The other bump was in late June 1967, immediately following the summit with Kosygin, when Johnson's approval ratings jumped from 44 percent to 51 percent, suggesting that the "spirit of Glassboro" had a noticeable if short-term impact on the American public. This is hardly incontrovertible proof that high-profile diplomacy guarantees public approval, but these numbers do lend some credence to Johnson's belief that further summits and agreements with the Soviets, in conjunction with some form of negotiated settlement in Vietnam, would have provided a boost to both his short- and long-term popularity.[31]

Lyndon Johnson only turned his attention emphatically towards foreign affairs and personal diplomacy once he realized that Vietnam, rather than his domestic successes, threatened to shape his legacy. His successor, by contrast, always envisaged his greatest achievements as coming on the world stage as a result of carefully calibrated strategy and diplomacy. During his first term as president, Richard Nixon would succeed where Johnson had failed, signing the first strategic arms limitation agreement with the Soviet Union, and visiting both Moscow and, most dramatically, the People's Republic of China. Returning from his historic travels, Nixon addressed a joint session of Congress and presented his achievements in era-defining terms, claiming that "the historians of some future age will write of the year 1972, not that this was the year America went up to the summit and then down to the valley again, but that this was the year when America helped to lead the world up out of the lowlands of constant war, and onto the highlands of lasting peace."[32] Nixon's bombast owed something to the election due later that year, but he was also a politician acutely aware of the importance of landmark events in shaping presidential legacy. Mentioning what future historians would write and how they would assess his legacy was a semi-regular tic.[33] Nixon was also a man obsessed with image and his ability to control how his actions and personality were interpreted, yet was far less successful at maintaining a public persona than Kennedy, or even Johnson, often coming across as overly studied and awkward.[34]

Nixon's trip to China would be the most famous example of these factors finding form in a grand diplomatic event. Vast amounts of planning went into making the trip a success; gifts were obsessed over, research dossiers produced on every potential location to be visited, and guidelines were drafted regarding correct body language and etiquette for members of the traveling party who did not possess "experience in oriental ways."[35] From the moment it was announced, the president and his team were also constantly monitoring both the domestic and international impact of the visit. White House aide Pat Buchanan warned the president that the "euphoria" that greeted the announcement "will subside in a week or so" and he would likely come in for accusations of "playing with the national interest to advance his political interest." However, Buchanan also argued that the trip would allow Nixon to position himself as a great world statesman, standing above the upcoming throng of primaries and political debate, noting that "a sitting President making peace in Peking is a more attractive figure to all the American people than some squabbling politicians in the snows of New Hampshire." Buchanan's assessment proved accurate, as following the trip Nixon was informed that the pollster Lou Harris had written that the lasting impression of the preceding week was "my God, here is this man who is our

President, our leader and look how well he handles himself," an outcome that would most likely see Nixon "staying locked in as President." Other administration reports noted that thanks to new satellite technology that allowed for global television broadcasts, the China trip had become a worldwide "media phenomenon" that was "frequently compared to another US venture into the unknown—the first landing on the moon."[36]

Nixon's focus on diplomacy extended beyond just landmark overseas visits, though; the hosting of foreign dignitaries was planned with similarly obsessive detail. Just as Johnson had occasionally hosted at his ranch, so Nixon sporadically invited visitors to his home in San Clemente, California. As Nixon was less comfortable than Johnson at offering an insight into his private existence, these visits lacked a defining identity; Nixon focused more effort on perfecting the formal Washington state visit by exercising control over every conceivable aspect of proceedings. Shortly after entering the White House, for instance, he authorized a reversal of the Johnson policy of hosting foreign leaders for two days in Washington "instead of the internationally acknowledged three-day visit." While suggesting that diplomacy took a higher priority in the new administration, Nixon nonetheless remained wary of increasing his personal involvement in the process. It was made clear to the protocol office that even if the additional day allowed the visitors to host a return dinner at their embassy, the president would "prefer not" to attend, and would rather send the vice president.[37]

It is perhaps surprising, then, that according to a *Plain Dealer* article from March 1970, the Nixons "set a record for White House entertainment in 1969, receiving 44,000 guests and more state visitors than any other president." What is less surprising is that the political uses of such events were carefully considered. For instance, when Willis Conover, a long-time Voice of America broadcaster, was consulted by the White House Social Secretary Lucy Winchester regarding possible entertainment for White House events, they discussed how music could be utilized to challenge the perception of the administration as "square," as well as addressing more weighty domestic concerns. A Duke Ellington or Bill Evans performance would bring grudging admiration from the "liberal-intellectual-artistic establishment," Conover claimed, while racial tensions could be eased by "presenting such 'soul music' performers as Aretha Franklin, the Supremes, Sam and Dave."[38] The fine details of hosting were also continually being refined within the administration, with a constant focus on maintaining a dignified and statesman-like persona for the president. For instance, the positioning of photographers when greeting foreign dignitaries from their cars was adjusted after the initial arrangement resulted in shots of the "president squatting like a frog about to launch from a lily-pad." Similarly, the volume of the trumpeters announcing the president's arrival at a state dinner was lowered after it was decided that they had "escalated" to a fanfare "which would properly signal one's arrival to St. Peter at the Pearly Gates," a situation which was "possibly inconsistent with the dignity of the participants and the occasion."[39]

In every presidential administration the protocol office and White House social secretaries pay close attention to seemingly minor elements of diplomatic protocol, but under Nixon the obsessive attention to detail began at the top. After almost every state dinner the president, and often the first lady, would relay a list of observations, complaints, suggestions, and instructions regarding improvements for future events. Issues of importance to the Nixons ranged from the shape of tables to the positioning of various staff members while making introductions, the year of the wine to be served, and the length of entertainers' sets. Particular attention was reserved for any incident that had the potential to embarrass the president, including the names of guests not being provided to him quickly enough, not enough applause greeting his entrance to the East Room, or the vice president wandering into receiving lines he was not intended to be a part of. This can be explained, at least in part, by Nixon's personality and general obsession with appearances, but also reflects the premium that was placed on the president's diplomatic reputation. Nixon admired and sought to emulate past titans of international relations, such as de Gaulle and Churchill, and in order to gain a similarly potent and lasting reputation he not only pursued great diplomatic achievements, but also the maintenance of a style and bearing befitting such a world figure. Perfecting the finer details of protocol, and potentially compensating for personal awkwardness in the process, was therefore an essential part of constructing the presidency that Nixon envisaged for himself.[40]

Nixon's approval ratings while in office tell a clear story regarding the fate of his political career, taking a Watergate-prompted nosedive in mid-1973 from which they would not recover. Before that point though, they also provide the clearest indication that notable diplomatic successes can have an impact with the wider public. Nixon entered 1972, an election year, with his approval ratings hovering at around the 50 percent mark. Polls taken immediately after the China trip, which more than two-thirds of the public viewed as "effective for improving the prospects of world peace," saw him climb to 56 percent, and following his Moscow summit and subsequent address to Congress in May he sat at 62 percent. Given that Nixon's globe-trotting diplomacy was the dominant feature of his presidency during those months, it is no great stretch to attribute the 12 percent rise in approval ratings to the attractiveness of the image of Nixon as the world statesman that Buchanan had identified the previous year. Given the crushing nature of his victory over George McGovern in November, in which he won forty-nine states, it would be foolish to attribute Nixon's gaining a second term solely to one factor, but it is clear that in this case diplomatic successes provided a welcome boost during a crucial election year.[41]

Diplomacy and presidential legacy

While the above examples demonstrate the relationship between diplomacy and public approval during a president's time in office, their relevance in terms of a longer impact on legacy and historical standing is less clear. Given the myriad factors that can shape both contemporary and retrospective popularity, assigning a consistent value to the impact of presidential diplomacy is impossible, but by considering both public and academic polls alongside broad historiographical trends it is possible to draw some general conclusions with a reasonable degree of certainty.

First, John F. Kennedy enjoys much wider popularity with the American public than either of his immediate successors.

A poll taken by Gallup in 2013 asked respondents to rate how they thought the most recent eleven presidents would "go down in history," from "outstanding" to "poor." Kennedy came out comfortably on top, with 74 percent rating him "outstanding" or "above average." Nixon was last, with only 15 percent positive responses, and Johnson was just two places higher, with 20 percent. Kennedy topped similar approval polls taken in 2006 and 2010, while Nixon again found himself last in both, with Johnson just slightly higher. Kennedy also performs well against the full field of American presidents, beating George Washington and Franklin Roosevelt to take fourth place in a 2011 poll that asked "Who do you regard as the greatest United States president?" Johnson and Nixon were chosen by less than 0.5 percent of respondents, placing them below George W. Bush and Jimmy Carter among others.[42]

Unfortunately, public polling is rather opaque regarding the motivations for respondents' choices, leading to various attempts, often by political scientists, to understand the factors that shape presidential popularity. James King has argued that during their time in office, economic performance and unpopular wars have the most impact on approval ratings, but over time other factors, including style and personal conduct, become increasingly important. Historian John Milton Cooper agrees, arguing that after Franklin Roosevelt's terms in office, "personality" became a key determinant in a president's long-term reputation, while Vidal Romero adds that over time "notorious incidents," positive or negative, tend to overshadow the wider performance of an administration. Broadly speaking, these observations correlate to the presidencies considered here. Kennedy has the aura of "Camelot" and an image and personality that retain their appeal for subsequent generations of young people, along with "notorious incidents" in the form of the Cuban Missile Crisis and his assassination that only bolster his reputation and mystique. Johnson might be slightly ahead of Nixon in terms of personal appeal, particularly to those familiar with his civil rights record, but neither compares to Kennedy regarding image, with both tainted by dishonesty and political disgrace as Vietnam and Watergate loom large as the defining aspects of their presidencies.[43]

Surveys amongst academic experts tend to go into more depth, and can produce quite different results. In a poll of UK-based historians of the United States conducted in 2016, Kennedy and Johnson, defying the disparity between them in public ratings, were ranked overall eleventh and twelfth out of all US presidents, while Nixon was a relatively lowly twenty-sixth. These results were broadly similar to a C-SPAN survey of US-based scholars taken the following year, in which Kennedy was ranked eighth, Johnson tenth, and Nixon twenty-eighth. The first survey scored presidents in a variety of categories, and Kennedy performed fairly consistently, with his highest marks coming in "vision and agenda setting" and "foreign policy." Johnson came second only to FDR and Lincoln (one and two in the overall rankings) in domestic policy leadership, and behind only those two and Thomas Jefferson in vision and agenda setting, but scored disastrously in foreign policy and poorly in moral authority. For Nixon, ranked the lowest of any president on moral authority and moderate on domestic issues, any chance of his diplomatic exploits scoring highly enough to substantially boost his overall performance appear to have been undermined by other factors, notably the continuation and geographic expansion of the Vietnam War, leaving him languishing behind eleven other presidents even in foreign policy.[44]

Perhaps unsurprisingly, these results are broadly illustrative of general trends within the literature assessing each president's reputation and legacy. Early hagiographic accounts of Kennedy emphasized his opening of the White House to representatives of newly independent nations, his style and wit, and his coolness during the most stressful of international crises, but following the revisionist attacks of the 1970s onwards, it is fair to say a more balanced picture has emerged that, unlike public assessments, ranks Kennedy as a good but not great leader. The positive aspects of his leadership are still acknowledged, but they are balanced by criticism of his tendency to fall back on Cold War pragmatism when faced with challenges within developing nations, and an awareness of the degree of luck involved in avoiding nuclear catastrophe during his presidency. Additionally, his reputation as a sophisticated consumer of high culture has been questioned, with Mark White in particular demonstrating the degree to which the debonair and learned Kennedy was a product of intense behind-the-scenes efforts on the part of his staff to mask how little the president knew about the poets and musicians he welcomed to the White House. Given his relatively thin legislative record, Kennedy's greatest legacy has increasingly been identified as his ability to inspire admiration, support, and enthusiasm through a carefully crafted image of youthful dynamism and the embrace of television and modern media, shifting the expectations placed on the presidency in the process.[45]

For Johnson, the poll results reflect that historians have traditionally been willing to afford more credit to his legislative achievements than the wider public, often portraying his presidency in tragic terms: the political titan brought low by his vulnerability on foreign policy. As scholars of US foreign relations have increasingly looked "beyond Vietnam," there has also been some moderation of the view that Johnson's diplomatic abilities were entirely lacking, but the broad assessment remains that while his legislative achievements left a legacy of greater racial equality, in legal terms at least, and increased assistance for the nation's most vulnerable citizens, his handling of the Vietnam war resulted in domestic divisions, increased anti-Americanism around the world, mass destruction in Southeast Asia, and a "Vietnam syndrome" that circumscribed US global engagement for decades to come. In such a context, moderate achievements such as the Non-Proliferation Treaty are usually relegated to the status of a relatively minor footnote.[46]

While neither Kennedy nor Johnson would live long enough to play an active role in debates over their legacies, Nixon spent much of his post-presidential career attempting to position himself in the role of a wise elder statesman, playing on his diplomatic successes and establishment connections to offer commentary on global affairs through articles, books, and television appearances. Yet, as the polls demonstrate, any rehabilitation of his reputation with a public that largely associated his presidency with dishonesty and scandal was marginal at best; likewise, it does not appear that Nixon was able to sway many historians to fundamentally rethink their assessments. While some relatively positive biographies of Nixon have been produced, and most scholars would agree with Jussi Hanhimäki's view that the opening to China was a notable success that provided a "durable legacy," ultimately, as David Greenberg has observed, "Nixon's statesman persona did not triumph" and "the negative images of him held sway."[47]

The question remains, then, as to how important diplomatic efforts such as those covered in this chapter are in shaping the views of both the public and academics regarding presidential legacy. Here it is again useful to think of presidential diplomacy as serving two main functions: first, providing lasting "notorious" incidents, and second, contributing to the creation of a positive public image. The relatively limited literature on the connection between diplomacy and approval ratings suggests that successful, high-profile diplomatic efforts can result in notable gains. The examples considered in this chapter broadly support this, as although Kennedy appeared to gain little from his diplomatic ventures, Johnson and Nixon received boosts in approval ratings following successful personal diplomacy. This also suggests that the events have to be high-profile enough to attract extended national or global attention (for instance, hosting Kosygin rather than Bourguiba), and successful or productive enough to receive largely positive coverage (Nixon in Beijing rather than Kennedy in Vienna). The immediate relevance of this to long-term assessments by the public is that a comparison between contemporary ratings and polls conducted retrospectively demonstrates that all presidents since Kennedy have maintained at least their level of approval at the time they left office, and in many cases dramatically improved upon it. While it remains unclear just how important a role diplomatic successes play in retrospective approval ratings, their potential to boost ratings while in office, as Johnson sought to do with increasing desperation in his final months, would seem to make them a wise investment of time and resources, albeit one rendered difficult by the "lame duck" status of an outgoing president. Had Johnson achieved more successes like Glassboro during his final year in office, or made some measurable progress in negotiating an end to the conflict in Vietnam and left with his approval ratings a little higher, perhaps the albatross of his foreign relations failings would not weigh quite so heavily on public assessments of his legacy.[48]

Academic assessments relate less to a president's contemporary popularity, and can of course be influenced by a wide range of issues. A question in the 2016 poll of UK-based scholars asked, "Did the president's legacy have positive benefits for America's development over time?" Abraham Lincoln came out on top, suggesting the predominance of domestic policy in such considerations, an impression furthered by Johnson's presence in eighth place. Yet Woodrow Wilson and Harry Truman, noted more for their influence on decades of foreign policy than their legislative achievements, both made the top six. Both foreign and domestic achievements can influence historians' views, then, and the role presidential diplomacy plays within those assessments is varied and difficult to quantify, but can be substantial. For instance, while Nixon's attempts at creating a lasting legacy based on diplomatic achievements were largely a failure due to the uniquely damaging impact of the Watergate scandal, this should not obscure their function as a mitigating factor in assessments of his presidency. If a brief indulgence of the counterfactual can be forgiven, it is worth considering how much lower his standing would be, particularly in academic rankings, without those landmark trips to China and the Soviet Union.[49]

Perhaps more importantly, the evidence in this chapter also suggests that presidents and their advisers are well aware of the potential of diplomatic spectacle to aid in the construction of a positive public image. Certainly Kennedy's enduring popularity owes much to his successful cultivation of a coherent and appealing public profile, a process in which a variety of diplomatic activities played an important role. Kennedy's style of cultured personal diplomacy fitted neatly, and seemingly effortlessly, into an overall image that has retained much of its potency, with the public at least, to this day. Both Johnson and Nixon attempted something similar, Johnson with his Texan-tinged diplomacy, and Nixon with his obsessive cultivation of a statesmanlike persona. Both appear to have enjoyed limited success early in their presidencies, but ultimately neither was able to sustain an identity with the public that was both appealing and consistent with other aspects of their leadership. The emerging global media and the increasing sophistication of public relations and image management during their presidencies offered all three opportunities to shape their immediate image, but only Kennedy truly took advantage of that fact to any great effect. The contrast between Kennedy and Nixon in this regard is probably starkest in the academic literature. While Kennedy's lower ratings in expert polls reflects a broad assessment that his achievements fell short of his promises, all but the most critical of the Kennedy revisionists would acknowledge the skill with which he was able to manage his public image, and the significance of this, for better or worse, in the development of the presidency. In contrast, Nixon's attempts at creating various personae over the years tend to receive much harsher assessments, treated as another facet of the dishonesty that manifested itself so dramatically during Watergate.[50]

All of the presidents considered here are typical in that none owe their reputations and legacies solely to their achievements or failures in personal diplomacy. Indeed, a president's performance as diplomat-in-chief does not necessarily correlate directly to their overall standing with either the public or academics, as that standing is contingent on too great a variety of factors. Possibly no president demonstrates this more clearly than Richard Nixon, who was responsible for a number of stunning diplomatic achievements but whose lasting reputation with the majority of Americans is of the "crook" who resigned the presidency in disgrace. Any consideration of the factors that shape a legacy will also result in dealing with intangibles to some extent, and face a challenge in drawing too many hard and fast rules. In his consideration of diplomacy and presidential image, Elmer Plischke commented on this problem, observing that successful personal diplomacy also affects a president's legacy in ways that are particularly difficult to measure, such as positive media coverage that adds "luster to his stature" even if it is "not always reflected in opinion sampling."[51]

These challenges do not undermine the importance of considering the relationship between image, diplomacy, and legacy. It is clear that presidents and their advisers are highly cognizant of the ways in which diplomatic performances can be used to address issues both foreign and domestic, or to help shape a positive public image, as well as the potential for diplomatic achievements to play a fundamental role in creating a lasting legacy for their presidency.

The varying efforts of Kennedy, Johnson, and Nixon demonstrate that while there are no guarantees, diplomatic success can have an immediate impact on public approval and a longer influence on assessments of their presidencies, as well as contributing to the construction of a successful presidential image if employed as part of a coherent wider effort. It is clear that myriad factors can determine the success of presidential diplomacy, including individual personality quirks, regional culture, and geopolitical context, and the very nature of presidential legacy is similarly complex. This only suggests the need for further exploration of a broader range of case studies, and ongoing consideration of the intimate ties between diplomacy, image, and presidential legacy.

Notes

1. FDR regularly ranks in the top three in polls of presidential historians, while Reagan consistently performs well in polls of the American public. See C-Span Presidential Historians Survey 2017, <https://www.c-span.org/presidentsurvey2017/>; United States Presidency Centre UK Survey of US Presidents 2016, <http://www.community-languages.org.uk/US-presidency-survey>; Gallup, "Americans Say Reagan Is the Greatest US President," February 2011, <http://www.gallup.com> (all accessed June 13, 2018).
2. The chapter draws inspiration from recent work that employs a wider variety of perspectives to the study of diplomacy, particularly those that could be termed cultural histories of diplomacy. Some good examples are Jason Dittmer and Fiona McConnell (eds.), *Diplomatic Cultures and International Politics: Translations, Spaces and Alternatives* (London: Routledge, 2016); Jessica Gienow-Hecht (ed.), *Decentering America* (Oxford: Berghahn, 2007); Gienow-Hecht and Mark C. Donfried (eds.), *Searching for a Cultural Diplomacy* (New York: Berghahn, 2013); Markus Mösslang and Torsten Riotte (eds.), *The Diplomats' World: The Cultural History of Diplomacy, 1815–1914* (Oxford: Oxford University Press, 2008).
3. Presidential diplomacy is rarely studied as an aspect distinct from broader foreign policy responsibilities. Some recent exceptions include Robert Hutchings and Jeremi Suri (eds.), *Foreign Policy Breakthroughs: Cases in Successful Diplomacy* (New York: Oxford University Press, 2015) and Kristina Spohr and David Reynolds (eds.), *Transcending the Cold War: Summits, Statecraft, and the*

Dissolution of Bipolarity in Europe, 1970–1990 (Oxford: Oxford University Press, 2016). One of the few scholars to attempt a comprehensive consideration of the president as diplomat is political scientist Elmer Plischke, who published several works on the topic in the 1980s. See Elmer Plischke, "The President's Image as Diplomat in Chief," *The Review of Politics* 47, no. 4 (1985): 544–65. See also Plischke, *Diplomat in Chief: The President at the Summit* (New York: Praeger, 1986).

4. For more detailed discussions regarding definitions of presidential legacy see Vidal Romero, "Of Love and Hate: Understanding the Determinants of Presidential Legacies," *Political Research Quarterly* 67, no. 1 (March 2014): 123–35; Michael Nelson, "Evaluating the Presidency," in Nelson (ed.), *The Presidency and the Political System* (Washington, DC: CQ Press 2006), 1–23.

5. Bruce Miroff, "The Presidential Spectacle," in Michael Nelson (ed.), *The Presidency and the Political System*, 9th ed. (Washington, DC: CQ Press, 2010), 211. For further consideration of the performative aspects of diplomatic events see Naoko Shimazu, "Diplomacy as Theatre: Staging the Bandung Conference of 1955," *Modern Asian Studies* vol. 48, no.1 (January 2014), 225–52.

6. Costas Panagopoulos, "Ex-Presidential Approval: Retrospective Evaluations of Presidential Performance," *Presidential Studies Quarterly* 42, no. 4 (December 2012): 719–29; Tim H. Blessing, "Reflections on the Findings of Uscinski and Simon, and Blessing, Skleder and You on Rater Bias and Presidential Rankings," *White House Studies* 11, no. 2 (2011): 95–106.

7. For explorations of the developing media landscape in this era see Sönke Kunkel, *Empire of Pictures: Global Media and the 1960s Remaking of American Foreign Policy* (Oxford: Berghahn, 2016); James Schwoch, *Global TV: New Media and the Cold War, 1946–1969* (Chicago: University of Illinois Press, 2009).

8. Alan Brinkley, "The Legacy of John F. Kennedy," *The Atlantic*, August 2013; Loren Glass, "The Kennedy Legacy: from Hagiography to Exposé and Back Again," in Andrew Hoberek (ed.), *The Cambridge Companion to John F. Kennedy* (New York: Cambridge University Press, 2015), 248; Mark White, *Kennedy: A Cultural History of an American Icon* (London: Bloomsbury, 2013), 111–41.

9. White, *Kennedy*, 31–49.

10. For details of Franco-US relations in this period see Douglas Brinkley and Richard T. Griffiths (eds.), *John F. Kennedy and Europe* (Baton Rouge: Louisiana State University Press, 1999); Erin R.

Mahan, *Kennedy, de Gaulle, and Western Europe* (Basingstoke: Palgrave Macmillan, 2002); Sebastian Reyn, *Atlantis Lost: The American Experience with De Gaulle, 1958–1969* (Amsterdam: Amsterdam University Press, 2010).

11. Marie Smith, *Entertaining in the White House* (Washington, DC: Acropolis Books, 1967), <https://www.jfklibrary.org/Research/Research-Aids/Ready-Reference/JFK-Fast-Facts/Entertaining-in-the-White-House.aspx> (accessed June 13, 2018); John F. Kennedy, "Toasts of the President and Andre Malraux, French Minister for Cultural Affairs," May 11, 1962, *The American Presidency Project*, <http://www.presidency.ucsb.edu/ws/index.php?pid=8648> (accessed June 13, 2018).

12. Memorandum of Meeting, Washington, May 11, 1962, *Foreign Relations of the United States* (henceforth *FRUS*), 1961–1963, Volume XIII, Western Europe and Canada.

13. John F. Kennedy, "Remarks at the National Gallery of Art Upon Opening the Mona Lisa Exhibition," January 8, 1963, *The American Presidency Project*, <http://www.presidency.ucsb.edu/ws/index.php?pid=9545> (accessed June 13, 2018).

14. See, for example, Margaret Leslie Davis, "The Two First Ladies," *Vanity Fair*, November 2008; and *Mona Lisa in Camelot* (Boston: Da Capo Press, 2008); Lisa Liebmann, "Jackie, JFK and the Art of Diplomacy: The Mona Lisa in Washington," *Tate Etc.*, Issue 6 (Spring 2006); "De Gaulle-Kennedy—Malraux le diplomate," *Paris Match*, June 16, 2016.

15. W.H. Lawrence, "Washington Gives a Warm Welcome to Bourguiba," *New York Times*, May 4, 1961; excerpt from Smith, *Entertaining in the White House*.

16. "Circular Telegram from the Department of State to Certain Diplomatic Posts," May 16, 1961; Briefing Paper Prepared in the Department of State, "Morocco and Tunisia," undated, *FRUS*, 1961–1963, Volume XXI, Africa; "US and Tunisia Stress Self-Rule: Kennedy and Bourguiba for Ending of Colonialism," *New York Times*, May 6, 1961. The emptiness of the gesture would be revealed when conflict erupted between Tunisia and France just a few weeks later over access to a Naval base at Bizerte, and the Kennedy administration backed De Gaulle, not Bourguiba, at the UN. See Robert B. Rakove, *Kennedy, Johnson, and the Nonaligned World* (Cambridge: Cambridge University Press, 2012), 73.

17. Robert D. Dean, "Masculinity as Ideology: John F. Kennedy and the Domestic Politics of Foreign Policy," *Diplomatic History* 22, no.1 (January 1998): 29–62; White, *Kennedy*, 40.

18. Historical job approval data for every president since Harry Truman is available through the Gallup Presidential Job Approval Center, <http://www.gallup.com/interactives/185273/presidential-job-approval-center.aspx> (accessed June 13, 2018); George H. Gallup (ed.), *The Gallup Poll: Public Opinion, 1935–1971* (New York: Random House, 1972), 1745–57.
19. Gallup, *The Gallup Poll*, 1703–1954.
20. Classic examples include Larry Berman, *Planning a Tragedy* (New York, 1983); Irving Bernstein, *Guns or Butter: The Presidency of Lyndon Johnson* (Oxford: Oxford University Press, 1996); Eric Goldman, *The Tragedy of Lyndon Johnson* (New York, 1969).
21. For some classic "loyalist" accounts, see Roger Hilsman, *To Move a Nation: The Politics of Foreign Policy in the Administration of John F. Kennedy* (Garden City, NY: Doubleday, 1967); Arthur M. Schlesinger Jr., *Robert Kennedy and his Times* (London: Deutsch, 1978); Theodore C. Sorensen, *The Kennedy Legacy* (London: Macmillan, 1969).
22. Transcript of Telephone Conversation, Johnson and Reedy, April 8, 1964, Michael R. Beschloss, *Taking Charge: The Johnson White House Tapes, 1963–1964* (New York: Simon & Schuster, 1997), 301.
23. Frances Lewine, "Johnson Barbecue," December 30, 1963, MS Washington, DC Bureau Records, 1938–2009: Series I, Presidential Wires AP16, Box 15, Folder 149, *Associated Press Collections Online*; Memo, Bess Abell to Mrs. Johnson, October 1964, Liz Carpenter Files, Box 13, Lyndon Baines Johnson Library, Austin, Texas (henceforth LBJL). For details regarding the ranch see Hal Rothman, *LBJ's Texas White House: "Our Heart's Home"* (College Station: Texas A&M University Press, 2001).
24. Robert A. Caro, *The Years of Lyndon Johnson, Volume 4: The Passage of Power* (New York: Knopf, 2012), 511; State Department Office of The Historian, "Visits by Foreign Leaders in 1964," <https://history.state.gov/departmenthistory/visits/1964> (accessed June 13, 2018); memo, Carpenter to Johnson, August 24, 1966, Liz Carpenter Files, Box 26, LBJL.
25. For more on US-Soviet relations in this period and Johnson's "Bridge Building" efforts, see Nigel Ashton, "Uncertain Decade: US-Soviet Relations, 1961–68," *Diplomacy & Statecraft* 14, no.1 (March 2003): 195–202; John Dumbrell, *President Lyndon Johnson and Soviet Communism* (Manchester: Manchester University Press, 2004); Mitchell Lerner, "'Trying to Find the Guy Who Invited Them': Lyndon Johnson, Bridge Building, and the End of the Prague Spring," *Diplomatic History* 32, no. 1 (January 2008): 77–103.

26. Memo, Tom Johnson to Lyndon Johnson, June 20, 1967, President's Appointment File—Diary Backup, Box 69, LBJL; Memo, Rostow to Johnson, "The case for seeing Kosygin," June 21, 1967, National Security File, Walt W. Rostow Files, Box 10, LBJL.
27. Memo, Wriggins to Rostow, "A Place for LBJ and K to Meet," June 21, 1967, NSF, Country Files—USSR, Box 230, LBJL; Sherwin J. Markman, "Notes on Summit Conference Preparations," June 22–25, 1967, President's Appointment File—Diary Backup, Box 69, LBJL; Memo, Davis to Rostow, "Two Summits and the Niagara as the President's Guest," June 24, 1967, NSF, Country Files—USSR, Box 230, LBJL; Tom Wicker, "In The Nation: Reflections on Glassboro," *New York Times*, June 27, 1967.
28. State Department's Office of the Historian, "Visits by Foreign Leaders," <https://history.state.gov/departmenthistory/visits> (accessed June 13, 2018).
29. Memo, Rostow to Johnson, August 20, 1968, *FRUS*, 1964–1968, Volume XIV, Soviet Union; Lerner, "'Trying to Find the Guy Who Invited Them,'" 77.
30. "Memorandum of Conversation," September 20, 1968; Memo, Rostow to Johnson, Washington, 11 December 1968, both *FRUS*, 1964–1968, Volume XIV, Soviet Union.
31. Gallup, *The Gallup Poll*, 1887–1925; Gallup Presidential Job Approval Center.
32. Richard Nixon, "Address to a Joint Session of the Congress on Return from Austria, the Soviet Union, Iran, and Poland," June 1, 1972, *The American Presidency Project*, <http://www.presidency.ucsb.edu/ws/?pid=3450> (accessed June 13, 2018).
33. During the presidential debates with Kennedy in 1960 he declared, "in the years to come it will be written that one or the other of us was elected and that he was or was not a great president." Television Debates: Transcript, Fourth Debate, <https://www.jfklibrary.org/Asset-Viewer/Archives/JFKCAMP1960-1052-005.aspx> (accessed June 13, 2018).
34. David Greenberg, *Nixon's Shadow: The History of an Image* (New York: W.W. Norton, 2003); Joe McGinniss, *The Selling of the President 1968* (London: Deutsch, 1970).
35. Report, "Chinese-American Rapport During the President's Visit," <https://www.nixonlibrary.gov/forteachers/Chinese-American%20Rappport.pdf> (accessed June 13, 2018). For details of the trip, see Margaret MacMillan, *Nixon and Mao: The Week that Changed the World* (New York: Random House, 2006).

36. Memo, Buchanan to Nixon, July 16, 1971, NSF\NSC President's Trip Files, Box 499, Richard M. Nixon Library, Yorba Linda, CA (henceforth RNL); memo, Colson to Nixon, "Comments from Louis Harris on Your China Trip," March 2, 1972, White House Special File, President's Office Files, President's Handwriting File, Box 16, RNL; USIA Report "Foreign Media Treatment of President Nixon's Visit to China," February 28, 1972, NSF\NSC President's Trip Files, Box 501, RNL.
37. Kunkel, *Empire of Pictures*, 75; memo, Mosbacher to Ehrlichman, "Visits to the United States by Chiefs of State and Heads of Government," February 19, 1969, White House Central File, Lucy Winchester Files, Box 37, RNL.
38. Copy of Dee Wedemeyer, "Dinner with the President," *The Plain Dealer*, March 1, 1970; letter, Conover to Winchester, February 20, 1969, both WHCF, Lucy Winchester Files, Box 4, RNL.
39. Memo, Stuart to Winchester, February 2, 1970; memo, Mosbacher to Hughes, "Signaling the President's arrival at State Dinners," April 29, 1970, and memo, Hughes to Mosbacher, May 6, 1970, WHCF, Lucy Winchester Files, Box 30, RNL.
40. Memo, Haldeman to Winchester, March 26, 1969; memo, Scouten to Butterfield, "Bordeaux Wines for the President," March 25, 1970; memo, Haldeman to Stuart, January 28, 1970; memo, Haldeman to Stuart, February 11, 1970; memo, Chapin to Butterfield, "Pompidou Visit," February 25, 1970, WHCF, Lucy Winchester Files, Box 30, RNL.
41. Plischke, "The President's Image," 556; Gallup Presidential Job Approval Center.
42. Gallup, "Americans Rate JFK as Top Modern President," "Kennedy Still Highest-Rated Modern President, Nixon Lowest," and "Americans Say Reagan Is the Greatest US President," <http://www.gallup.com> (accessed June 13, 2018).
43. James D. King, "Looking Back at Chief Executives: Retrospective Presidential Approval," *Presidential Studies Quarterly* 29, no 1 (March, 1999): 167–68; John Milton Cooper, "Great Expectations and Shadowlands: American Presidents and Their Reputations in the 20th Century," *Virginia Quarterly Review*, vol. 72, no. 3 (Summer 1996); Romero, "Of Love and Hate," 125.
44. Presidential History Network (PHN), UK Survey of US Presidents 2016, <https://presidentialhistorynetwork.wordpress.com> (accessed June 13, 2018); C-Span Presidential Historians Survey 2017.

45. For some good overviews see Mark J. White, "Introduction: A New Synthesis for the New Frontier," in Mark J. White (ed.), *Kennedy: The New Frontier Revisited* (New York: New York University Press, 1998), 1–17, 43; James N. Giglio, "Writing Kennedy," in Marc J. Selverstone, *A Companion to John F. Kennedy* (Chichester: Wiley-Blackwell, 2014), 5–30.
46. Excellent essays on the Johnson historiography can be found in Mitchell B. Lerner (ed.), *A Companion to Lyndon B. Johnson* (Chichester: Wiley-Blackwell, 2012). Of particular relevance are Nicholas Evan Sarantakes, "Lyndon B. Johnson and the World," 487–503, and Andrew L. Johns, "The Legacy of Lyndon Johnson," 504–20.
47. Jussi M. Hanhimäki, "Foreign Policy Overview," in Melvin Small (ed.), *A Companion to Richard M. Nixon* (Oxford: Wiley-Blackwell, 2011), 354; David Greenberg, "Nixon's Image: A Brief History," in Small, *A Companion to Richard M. Nixon*, 533–36.
48. Kenneth L. Adelman, "Summitry: The Historical Perspective," *Presidential Studies Quarterly* 16, no. 3 (Summer 1986): 437–38; Elmer Plischke, "Rating Presidents and Diplomats in Chief," *Presidential Studies Quarterly* 15, no. 4 (Fall 1985): 735–36; Gallup, "History Usually Kinder to Ex-Presidents," <http://news.gallup.com/poll/162044/history-usually-kinder-presidents.aspx> (accessed June 13, 2018).
49. PHN, UK Survey of US Presidents 2016.
50. For examples see Lee Konstantinou, "The Camelot Presidency: Kennedy and Postwar Style," in Hoberek (ed.) *The Cambridge Companion*, 149–63; Greenberg, "Nixon's Image" in Small, *A Companion to Richard M. Nixon*, 519–45.
51. Plischke, "The President's Image," 548–55. For more on the positive impact of media coverage see James P. Todhunter, "The Domestic Fruits of Diplomacy: Mediation and Presidential Approval," *International Negotiation* 18, no. 2 (2013): 195–217.

6

"You've got to decide how you want history to remember you": The legacy of Lyndon B. Johnson in film and television

Gregory Frame

Towards the end of the 2013 film *The Butler*, Cecil Gaines (Forest Whitaker), the eponymous African American servant who waited on every president of the United States from Dwight D. Eisenhower to Ronald Reagan, prepares in his retirement to meet Barack Obama, the first black person to occupy the office.[1] Perhaps sensing the moment is steeped in historical significance, Cecil decides to adorn his attire with mementos given to him by the former bosses that set the United States on the path towards this momentous event. He irons the tie that once belonged to President John F. Kennedy, given to him by Jacqueline Kennedy on the death of her husband. Cecil gives the tie great care and attention, the camera in medium close-up watches him running the iron slowly across it, treating it less as a tie and more as an important historical artifact. Once completed, he holds the tie in his hands, gazing upon it with the awe and reverence it demands. In this moment, the film appears to suggest Obama's victory occurred as a consequence of Kennedy's legacy on civil rights. In this, *The Butler* conforms to other films about the civil rights movement: while many historians view Kennedy's record on civil rights as a timid, incremental, and largely placatory one driven by political necessity rather than moral imperative, in film and television he is viewed as a martyr to the cause.[2] His successor, Lyndon B. Johnson, who achieved far more tangible progress in this area (dragging Kennedy's Civil Rights bill through the Congressional committee stage to pass it in 1964 and subsequently delivering on his promise of voting rights reform a year later) is barely given credit in popular culture. At the moment when Cecil is ironing the tie, it seems *The Butler* will repeat the pattern of celebrating Kennedy at the expense of Johnson, but then Cecil reaches for the tie-clip given to him by LBJ ("LBJ for the USA"). He carries it with care and respect, gazing solemnly into the mirror before the camera tilts down to show him appending the clip to the tie. While historians may balk at the film's idea that Johnson's place in the history of civil rights be viewed as the shiny adornment (the clip) to Kennedy's substance (the tie), *The Butler*'s conclusion is illustrative of a recent shift in film and television towards acknowledging, exploring, and celebrating Johnson's legacy in the area of civil rights.

Recent films and television dramas have begun the process of re-evaluating Johnson's legacy, pivoting away from his disastrous mismanagement of the war in Vietnam and lending equal weight to his domestic record. *Selma* (2014), *All the Way* (2016), and *LBJ* (2017) are three recent examples that reconsider Johnson's presidency.[3] This chapter examines the ways in which film and television struggle to deal with that legacy, wrestling to criticize Johnson's foreign policy on Vietnam as presented in detail by *Path to War* (2002), while simultaneously celebrating his achievements domestically in *Selma* and *All the Way*.[4] It will consider the roles film and television play in the evaluation of presidential legacy, the manner in which techniques of narrative, visual style, and iconography are employed to this end, and how, in the case of Johnson, film and television are forced to contend with a legacy rendered complex and largely unfavorable through a mix of historiography and popular memory.

LBJ and the problem of cultural presidential legacy

As *Variety* asked on the premiere of Rob Reiner's LBJ biopic at the Toronto International Film Festival in 2016: "Why LBJ, why now?"[5] It is, for many, a reassessment that is long overdue. As his domestic adviser Joseph Califano argues in the introduction to the 2015 edition of his 1991 memoir, "we are living in Lyndon

Johnson's America."⁶ The Great Society programs that Johnson's administration implemented survive to this day. They cover education, healthcare, environmental and consumer protection, civil rights, immigration reform, housing and urban affairs, the arts and humanities, and criminal justice, amongst many other areas. They have an impact on every man, woman, and child who lives in the United States. Indeed, as Julian Zelizer argues, "So embedded are the Great Society policies in the nation's fabric that many citizens can no longer conceive of life without them."⁷ Given the extraordinary and enduring achievements of his presidency, it is perhaps surprising that Johnson's legacy has not been afforded much attention in film and television.

According to Andrew L. Johns, historians have not achieved a full perspective on Johnson's presidency because it is a "story being told piecemeal, like an enormous jigsaw puzzle being worked on from different perspectives."⁸ Because its triumphant domestic achievements were accompanied by catastrophic failure overseas, scholars have struggled to assess his presidency, producing books "on a variety of 'Lyndon Johnson and [fill-in-the-blank] topics.'"⁹ The war in Vietnam is the principal reason for the failure to address Johnson's legacy fully. As Califano argues, "for the past half a century, the tragedy of Vietnam has so clouded the public and scholarly vision of Lyndon Johnson that it has been difficult to see what his domestic achievements actually mean for America."¹⁰ As Johns asserts, "Vietnam would cast the darkest shadow over Johnson's presidency, obscuring both his domestic and international successes and magnifying his failures."¹¹

Johnson's reputation has also suffered because of the backlash against the kinds of government intervention he championed. That backlash began with the election of Ronald Reagan and persists during the regime of Donald Trump. As Robert Dallek suggests, "a backlash against Johnson's Great Society, and Federal social programs favoring minorities, has also taken its toll on his standing."¹² Reagan's election in 1980 owed much to the disastrous fallout from the Vietnam War, as well as the conservative assault on liberalism in the form of federal government initiatives championed under Johnson. As Randall B. Woods argues in his sympathetic study of Johnson's Great Society and its failings, "a suprapartisan, centrist consensus favoring liberal programs for the poor, powerless, neglected segments of the American population did not seem to exist."[13] Johns notes that, arguably as a consequence of this, "over forty years after LBJ left the White House, Johnson-style liberal policies have yet to make a successful and complete return to the national political discourse."[14] Although many of Johnson's reforms have survived and even flourished, as in the case of the expansion of Medicaid as part of the Affordable Care Act in 2010, it cannot be said that the Great Society reforms are particularly trumpeted or celebrated in national discourse. Revisionist approaches such as *LBJ's Neglected Legacy: How Lyndon Johnson Reshaped Domestic Policy and Government*, a collection of essays that looks at the multitude of initiatives, policies, and legislation that Johnson pursued in the domestic arena, mean there is greater appreciation for what Johnson achieved among historians.[15] However, the legacy of his policies, in conjunction with the complexity of his character, means it is difficult to tell a simple, let alone straightforwardly heroic story of his presidency in wider culture.

This is a problem, because it is heroic stories of presidents whose legacies reflect the United States' powerful, noble, and righteous self-image that are ordinarily embraced by film and television. This is perhaps why relatively few are portrayed with any great regularity or detail, either receiving one major film or miniseries about their lives (for example, Henry King's biopic of Woodrow Wilson, titled *Wilson*; the HBO film of Harry Truman's presidency, titled *Truman*; the epic miniseries of the life of John Adams, titled *John Adams*), or being relegated to supporting status in the stories of other people where the president is reduced to a caricatured cameo.[16] Indeed, as Iwan Morgan suggests, "movies effectively wrote out of their depiction of American history and politics those presidents that did not fit the mould of heroic shapers of the nation's destiny."[17] This makes Johnson's fate fairly typical of most presidents. Indeed, "Great Men" biopics about post-war leaders are rare.[18]

Until *Path to War*, Johnson had been portrayed in two made-for-television dramas: *LBJ: The Early Years*, and *Lyndon Johnson* (both 1987). He also appeared as a minor character in the stories of other major figures in this period: Martin Luther King in *King*

(1978), J. Edgar Hoover in *The Private Files of J. Edgar Hoover* (1977) and *J. Edgar Hoover* (1987), and the various films and television dramas exploring the lives of the Kennedys, including *Kennedy* (1983), *Robert Kennedy and His Times* (1985), *Hoover vs. The Kennedys* (1987), *A Woman Named Jackie* (1991), *Thirteen Days* (2000), *Jackie, Ethel, Joan: The Women of Camelot* (2001), *RFK* (2002), and *The Kennedys* (2011).[19] In his brief appearances in films about the Kennedys, he is often portrayed as an unsophisticated cowboy, as he is in *Kennedy* and *Thirteen Days*, or a petty, insecure interloper following Kennedy's assassination in *Jackie* (2016).[20] The story of the United States in the 1960s could be Johnson's, but culturally it has not been. The lives and legacies of John F. Kennedy, Robert Kennedy, and Martin Luther King Jr. have been more common subjects. As Nick Kotz argues, these men exist "in the popular imagination as the trilogy of heroes who produced the civil rights triumphs of the 1960s. In sharp contrast, Johnson is often perceived as a crude, self-seeking wheeler-dealer who recklessly plunged his country into a Vietnam quagmire and promised grandiose domestic social programs that mostly failed."[21] Johnson has, until recently, remained a minor player in the lives of others, a fate ridiculously confirmed by his role in *Forrest Gump* (1994).[22] Upon awarding Gump with the Medal of Honor for bravery in Vietnam, Johnson is forced to see the wound the eponymous hero endured—a bullet in the buttocks. His appearance in *Forrest Gump* rather reinforces the caricature of him as buffoonish and unsophisticated, supporting Califano's suggestion that he was an "unforgettable character, but one ready-made for caricature rather than portraiture—not only by political cartoonists but also by political reporters and television commentators."[23]

Furthermore, civil rights stories, when told, have often focused on ordinary people's struggles against racial prejudice: *Mississippi Burning* (1988), *The Long Walk Home* (1990), *Ghosts of Mississippi* (1996), and *The Help* (2011).[24] These films, however problematic they might be in terms of the perspectives they adopt and the use of white protagonists within black stories, attempt within the strictures of mainstream cinema to offer sympathetic portrayals of those who endured the violence at the end of the Jim Crow era. In the decades immediately following the civil rights movement, when the wounds of the conflict were still raw, the story of Johnson's haranguing of recalcitrant members of Congress to pass the Civil Rights Act and Voting Rights Act perhaps did not feature the dramatic tropes necessary to fulfill the demand for socially conscious Hollywood filmmaking about the period. The same arguably is true of the films made about the United States' involvement in Vietnam. Relatively few dwell upon the political decisions that drove the conflict or Johnson's involvement in them, preferring instead to adopt the perspective of the tortured and wounded American soldiers. The most famous and important films about Vietnam necessarily focus on the soldiers Johnson sent to the battlefields: famous examples include *The Deer Hunter* (1978), *Apocalypse Now* (1979), *First Blood* (1982), *Platoon* (1986), and *Born on the Fourth of July* (1989).[25]

Johnson's reputation has also suffered because of Robert Caro's multivolume biography, which explored LBJ's career until the presidency. Caro argued that Johnson had "a hunger for power ... not to improve the lives of others, but to manipulate and dominate them ... It was a hunger so fierce and consuming that no consideration of morality or ethics, no cost to himself—or to anyone else—could stand before it."[26] Television movie *LBJ: The Early Years*, which earned Randy Quaid a Golden Globe for his portrayal of the president, examines the period of Johnson's life covered by Caro's first volume. As biographer Robert Dallek notes, although the film does occasionally acknowledge LBJ as the liberal, pro-civil rights, Great Society reformer, it is primarily interested in portraying Johnson as "a heavy-handed, uncouth, intensely ambitious Texan who wheels and deals his way to political power and wealth," resulting in a "one-dimensional portrait of a complicated man."[27] While lamentable, such inadequacies are unsurprising given that the 1980s were arguably the height of the antipathy towards Johnson. Political subjects were unfashionable in film and television during the 1980s, the prevailing sentiment and industrial structure favoring escapist entertainment, with little appetite for serious biopics about the nation's leaders. Moreover, presidential legacies are not easily or commonly nurtured in film and television.

So while, as Johns suggests, "scholarship on Lyndon Johnson has been characterized by increasing sophistication, greater nuance, and a willingness to look past the inadequacies of the Great Society and the tragedy of Vietnam in reaching a more measured and generally positive appraisal of his presidency and legacy," it is apparent that such sophistication, nuance, and measured appraisal had not yet found its way into film and television.[28] The presidents whose legacies enjoy the most attention in film and television are those that have been largely mythologized in culture already: Lincoln freed the slaves and won the Civil War, and Kennedy was the glamorous, sophisticated liberal and a martyr to the causes about which he was passionate (a debatable conclusion but one that has traction in popular culture). There are self-contained stories to be told about Lincoln and Kennedy: the passage of the thirteenth amendment, as explored in Steven Spielberg's *Lincoln* (2012), or the Cuban Missile Crisis, as examined in *Thirteen Days*. Of course, neither of these events was as simple as their portrayal in either film, but in their reduction to stories of dismantling slavery or saving the world from nuclear annihilation, they satisfy the yearning in popular culture for Manichean stories of good triumphing uncomplicatedly over evil, of people being freed from tyranny and rescued from death.[29] As I have argued elsewhere, because the outcomes of certain presidential decisions and their legacies are already so well known (Lincoln's and Kennedy's are two prominent examples), film and television representations allow the viewer to indulge in the pleasure of a carefully rehearsed iconography and narrative.[30] That process of rehearsing a legacy can be particularly difficult in the case of a president who remains complex and contested in public consciousness.

Johnson and Vietnam: Path to War

The Vietnam War haunts Johnson's legacy because it still plagues the self-image of the United States. The opposition to the war that Johnson faced led him to abandon thoughts of a second term, announcing to the American people in March 1968 that he would not seek re-election later that year. In the public mind, Johnson has taken ownership for the disastrous handling of the

Vietnam War. The extent of his responsibility is difficult to ignore: the incremental, secretive expansion of the war was designed to avoid the scrutiny of Congress and the American people; Johnson's ignorance of foreign affairs led him to defer excessively to military advisers; and he seemed unable to view opposition to the war as anything other than communist agitation.[31] Many of Johnson's worst qualities—belligerent masculinity, self-pity, and paranoia—were brought to bear in his handling of Vietnam and in that sense, Johnson's political instincts failed him.

Path to War offers a full and frank treatise on the decisions Johnson (played by Michael Gambon) took regarding Vietnam following his landslide election in November 1964. It attempts to contextualize those choices and account for them, however, paving the way for the later films that re-evaluate his legacy in broader terms. Much of what is understood of Johnson's judgments on Vietnam is present here: the desire to finish the war quickly to ensure his ambitions for the Great Society; his ignorance of Vietnam, the Vietnamese and their culture; professing a desire, however noble, to "leave the footprint of America in Vietnam"; and his paranoia, frustration, and anger about the quagmire he had a hand in creating.[32] Throughout, *Path to War* presents Johnson as an anguished, impotent leader, incapable of negotiating the situation he has created. He is isolated, passively consuming television news that confronts him with the consequences of his policies, raging at the screen as Robert Kennedy announces his candidacy for president. This construction culminates in a striking sequence in which Johnson rails against his trusted adviser Clark Clifford (Donald Sutherland), who had initially urged the President to withdraw from Vietnam before encouraging him to finish it quickly. Exasperated and paranoid about the prospect of losing to his primary challenger, Eugene McCarthy, Johnson accuses Clifford of trying to "cut and run" just as the war is apparently about to turn in America's favor, and rants about Kennedy sympathizers that he failed to purge from his administration. Johnson blames anyone but himself for this mess, but Clifford quickly brings him back to earth: "They only advised you, Mr. President. You decided. Against all of your natural instincts, against the whole of your life experience, you decided." The two-shot, featuring Clifford standing in the background with Johnson sitting on his desk, turned away and looking off-screen, shows Johnson's face move from angry agitation to fear. His eyes grow wide, staring anxiously and powerlessly as he hears Clifford's assessment of the situation. The look on Johnson's face is of a man beginning to understand that this calamity will first consume him, and then define his legacy.

The film apportions blame for these failures equally among Johnson and his advisers. As Dallek notes in his biography of the president, "The 'wise men'—ten prominent, former foreign policy officials, including Dean Acheson and Clark Clifford—told Johnson that he had no choice but to expand the war to prevent a Communist victory that would jeopoardize America's national security around the world."[33] Robert McNamara (Alec Baldwin) is portrayed as the most vocal advocate of expanding the war, before acknowledging his misjudgments and working to de-escalate the conflict. McNamara's face is frequently framed in close-up on occasions where he is forced to confront the consequences of his decisions, most notably when he witnesses a protestor set himself on fire outside the Pentagon. This visual choice is later repeated in the sequence where he receives the Medal of Freedom from Johnson. In flashback, McNamara confronts Johnson's faith in him as "one of the most humane men" on Election Night 1964, and his strident assertions regarding the expansion of the bombing of North Vietnam and sending soldiers into battle. McNamara's discomfort, doubt, and fear about his failed policies are evident in the close-up as his eyes fill with tears, a single drop sliding down his right cheek. He declines to make a statement after receiving the award. Rather than continue the popular assessment that Johnson should take full ownership for the disaster of Vietnam, *Path to War* tries to apportion the blame more equally.

Path to War also considers the enormous cost of Vietnam to Johnson's overall legacy. As in *The Butler*, this is handled symbolically. While the protests escalate and Johnson faces the disintegration of his presidency, he is shown isolated in the Oval Office, signing condolence letters to the parents of men killed in Vietnam. Mournful orchestral music emerges on the non-diegetic soundtrack as a sombre Johnson lifts his pen to sign another condolence letter. He notices something on the pen, lifting it from the page to give it a closer look. It is inscribed with "Voting Rights Act Signing August 6, 1965." Johnson hangs his head, shaking it from side to side. The pen recalls the jubilant sequences near the beginning of the film in which he celebrates the passage of the Civil Rights Act and Voting Rights Act, but also symbolically confirms that which Johnson had been forced to acknowledge earlier in the sequence, and that which he had worked so hard to avoid: the resources he wanted to change the United States socially and morally have been pressed into serving a ruinous war because of his decisions. While little consensus exists among historians about Johnson's objectives in Vietnam (whether he intended to escalate the conflict in the manner he did, or whether it was all a tragic accident), it is probably fair to say Johnson mishandled the escalation of hostilities. He was guilty of lazy assumptions about the Vietnamese, and fell prey to the political establishment's myopic, pig-headed anti-communism.[34] Given that the American policies in the region had persisted since the 1940s, some form of conflict was probably inevitable. Johnson's administration represents the culmination of two decades of policies derived from a Cold War mindset.[35] In keeping with these assessments, *Path to War* does not absolve the president from blame for the catastrophe, but nor does it find him solely responsible for it. While it reinforces Doris Kearns Goodwin's assessment that the escalation of the conflict was "probably inevitable, given Johnson's nature and convictions," it also suggests that the march to war was the result of many small, poor decisions made with inadequate information by all-too-human decision makers, rather than a grand scheme to hoodwink Congress and the American public.[36] As the film suggests, such fallibility would result in the definition of Johnson's legacy for a generation of people.

Johnson and Martin Luther King Jr.: Selma

Chronicling the campaign for voting rights and the marches from Selma to Montgomery in March 1965, *Selma* is an important film for a number of reasons. It is the first major cinematic release to feature Martin Luther King Jr. as a central character (emerging thirty-six years after Abby Mann's 1978 television miniseries *King*). As Daniel D'Addario observed, "The most surprising thing about the history of Hollywood and Martin Luther King Jr. is that there isn't one."[37] It also bears the distinction of being one of the first films to take as its focus the civil rights movement while avoiding the tendency in mainstream cinema to simplify racial politics and provide "comforting feel-good dramas in which resolution and racial reconciliation are privileged over political struggle."[38] *The Help* and *The Butler*, released in the few years preceding the production of *Selma*, employ the civil rights movement as a decorative backdrop upon which to hang stories of the protagonists' coming to racial consciousness, or reconciliation between black and white Americans. Selma studiously avoids the tendency to revert to melodramatic tropes of this kind, attempting (largely successfully) to understand King's role in the larger movement, the internal political struggles within it, and the often brutal and uncompromising resistance it faced.

Yet in its obvious determination to sidestep the conventions of the civil rights film in mainstream cinema to render King as a dynamic, forceful, independent agent fighting for a just cause against an intractable, racist establishment, *Selma* courted controversy for supposedly misrepresenting his relationship with Johnson. *Selma* portrays Johnson (Tom Wilkinson) as initially resistant to King's (David Oyelowo) pursuit of voting rights reform, putting his Great Society agenda first. According to Mark K. Updegrove, director of the Lyndon B. Johnson Presidential Library, "this characterization of the 36th president flies in the face of history. In truth, the partnership between LBJ and MLK on civil rights was one of the most productive and consequential in American history."[39] Kotz suggests Johnson and King had a sound, albeit complex, understanding, arguing that "the dynamic interaction between the two men was remarkable, as were their willingness and their ability to overcome differences, accommodate each other's political needs, and work in complementary ways."[40] *Selma* is the clearest and most prominent example of the way in which the president's legacy is undermined and marginalized due to the demands of narrative and character in mainstream cinema.

As Sylvia Ellis argues, without Johnson's "considerable talents as an experienced legislator and political operator ... a comprehensive civil rights bill would not have progressed so quickly through the senate."[41] In *Selma*, however, Johnson is rendered as a component of the antagonistic forces impeding the progress of the civil rights movement in a dramatic exercise in which he is not the focus. As Kotz identifies, Johnson was "the consummate Washington insider" who "deplored" the kinds of tactics employed by King and his supporters.[42] Because mainstream film tends to celebrate rebellious outsiders standing against a corrupt and obstinate establishment, it is unsurprising that Johnson's pragmatic shepherding of the Voting Rights Act 1965 might be obscured somewhat.

The film swiftly establishes Johnson as considering King's impatience as harmful to the progress of his overall program of reform, including the Great Society. His introduction portrays him as patronizing towards King, but also reaffirms his reputation as a political pragmatist, telling King that "this voting thing is gonna have to wait" because of the administration's other priorities. What might be considered problematic in *Selma* is that Johnson's commitment to the civil rights movement appears to be born of his renowned political opportunism, rather than any moral imperative. However historically questionable this is, it is vital to the film's rhetorical strategy: King is the heroic figure, and the possessor of moral authority. While the film is keen to construct Johnson as only a reluctant ally of King's (viewing him as less problematic than Malcolm X, for example), it is equally determined to refute any equivalence between Johnson's political expediency and Governor George Wallace's (Tim Roth) racist obstructionism. This is affirmed in a meeting between the two men in which Johnson implores Wallace to allow black people to vote in Alabama, urging him to consider his position in history, in effect asking him to consider his own legacy. Indeed, it does so by literally putting King's words in Johnson's mouth, Johnson employing the same words King used to criticize the president in order to appeal to Wallace's conscience: "In 1985, what do you want looking back? You want people rememberin' you sayin' 'Wait' or 'I can't' or 'It's too hard?'" When Wallace admits he does not care, Johnson responds, "I'll be damned if I'm gonna let history put me in the same place as the likes of you."[43] Johnson is well aware that his approach to civil rights will be a vital component of his legacy, and the film suggests that the president becomes worthy of a favorable assessment only when he succumbs on voting rights legislation.

For all of *Selma*'s celebration of King over Johnson, it chooses Johnson's address to Congress on March 15, 1965, in which the president demanded the passage of voting rights legislation, as one of its moments of triumph. It is an evidently presidential moment: Johnson's words, spoken in front of the American flag, and crosscut with images of black people watching television or listening to the radio in anticipation of a hard-won victory over white supremacy are concluded by the president's echo of the civil rights movement's anthemic cry of "we shall overcome." This underlines the pivotal role he played in the passage of the legislation without reverting to the problematic tendency within stories such as these to sanctify him (as Spielberg's *Lincoln* does) as "the white saviour." In this respect, *Selma* departs significantly from other films about the civil rights movement in which the narrative's resolution is contingent upon the awakening of a white character's racial consciousness, such as *The Long Walk Home* or *The Help*: Johnson's speech is followed by a sequence of archival material featuring the march from Selma to Montgomery underscored by John Legend's "Glory," which celebrates the extraordinary achievements of the civil rights movement, and the film concludes ultimately with an adaptation of King's address in Montgomery itself. This victory belongs unequivocally to King and the civil rights movement. However, Johnson's place in history and his legacy is secured as the film acknowledges his role in passing the Voting Rights Act. *Selma*'s narrative focus and approach to Johnson speaks to the problem of the president's position within the history of the civil rights movement and the way his legacy is represented. Despite what he achieved, he is never the hero of these stories, but nor should he be—the film does not adopt that perspective, and politically speaking to posit the president as such would be enormously problematic given the film's burden of delivering the first major cinematic portrayal of King. *Selma* makes it clear that Johnson's reluctance to support King was not for the same reason as Wallace's refusal to adapt to the new political reality. The film stops short of suggesting Johnson pursued civil rights reform based on conviction, but it does acknowledge that he understood its importance to the future of the nation.

Johnson's Triumphs: All the Way

The film that does most to explore Johnson's character and psychology, his mastery of the legislative process, and his exceptional achievements as president prior to the escalation of the Vietnam War, is *All the Way*, featuring Bryan Cranston as LBJ. In contrast to *Path to War*, *All the Way* takes as its focus the year preceding Johnson's landslide victory in 1964. On display is his determination to wrestle the reactionary forces in Congress to pass the Civil Rights Act, his struggle to ease racial tensions in the country at large prior to the Democratic National Convention, his attempt to prevent Vietnam from overwhelming his presidency, and the tactics he employed to defeat Barry Goldwater. It also focuses far more upon Johnson's character and personality, which are crucial aspects of his legacy: his crude manner, bad temper, and emotional neediness on the one hand, but also his powers of persuasion, political and rhetorical skill are here in abundance. As Johns notes, Johnson "towered over virtually all of his contemporary political rivals . . . yet he could also be a small, petulant, and vindictive man who allowed otherwise minor irritations to become monumental problems."[44] As Dallek suggests, "He was a character out of a Russian novel, one of those human complications that filled the imagination of Dostoyevsky, a storm of warring human instincts: sinner and saint, buffoon and statesman, cynic and sentimentalist, a man torn between hungers for immortality and self-destruction."[45] In *All the Way*, Cranston's voiceover narration and confidential moments with his wife, Lady Bird Johnson (Melissa Leo), and closest aide, Walter Jenkins (Todd Weeks), lay bare Johnson's insecurities.

The focus of *All the Way* reveals how difficult it is to address Johnson's legacy in film and television. In many respects it can be read as a prequel to *Path to War*, illustrating the bifurcated nature of Johnson's presidency: his ascension to the position following Kennedy's assassination in November 1963 until his signing of the Voting Rights Act in August 1965 comprises one part. Thereafter, the legislative successes of the Great Society pale in comparison to Vietnam until he becomes politically redundant in March 1968. *All the Way*, in its determination to celebrate Johnson, focuses far more on the first part of his presidency, but leaves a trail of breadcrumbs that allows viewers with a deeper historical perspective to identify the problematic aspects of his legacy. Furthermore, it reinforces the ways in which film and television employ iconography and visual style to construct presidential legacy.

A crucial aspect of Johnson's legacy in popular memory is the assessment that he was an interloper who appropriated the Kennedy legacy (as explored in Oliver Stone's *JFK*).[46] Johnson is shown to have significant insecurities about the possibility that he might be viewed as such, walking tentatively into the Oval Office upon returning to Washington, DC following Kennedy's death, to find it as it was left. He picks up a framed photograph of JFK with his family before gazing hesitantly at the HMS Resolute Desk. Kennedy was the first president to use the desk in the Oval Office, and it has become an important part of his legacy in popular memory: Stanley Tretick's photograph of JFK's son John playing underneath the desk while his father worked is one of the defining images of the Kennedy presidency. As Johnson stares at the desk, it is apparent that he perhaps does not belong here. The camera cuts to a wider angle of the room, featuring another icon of the Kennedy era—the president's rocking chair—prominently in the center of the frame.[47] Johnson stands awkwardly against the wall, small and somewhat insignificant, almost blending into the background. When Lady Bird finds him there and greets him as "Mr. President," Johnson can only utter, "Accidental president. That's what they'll say." *All the Way* employs the iconography and symbolism of the Kennedy era to hint at a longer view of presidential legacy: monochrome photographs of Kennedy and his family, the Resolute Desk, and the rocking chair are all such recognizable and potent icons that in some ways Johnson's own presidency is doomed to exist in Kennedy's shadow. In popular memory, this has been the case.

However, what *All the Way* seeks to demonstrate is how skilfully Johnson exploited his status as an "accidental president," positioning himself as the inheritor of the Kennedy legacy and the man who could render the promises made in the three previous years a reality. As Goodwin notes, "In the terrible wake of John Kennedy's assassination, Johnson was able to act as both apprentice and caretaker—faithful agent of Kennedy's intentions and the healing leader of a stunned and baffled nation."[48] His address to Congress on November 27, 1963, just five days after JFK's murder, seized the initiative and began the process of building his own legacy under the guise of honoring Kennedy's. The following scene shows the Oval Office being entirely revamped as Johnson speaks colorfully on the telephone to Hubert Humphrey (Bradley Whitford) about the battle the Civil Rights Bill will endure in Congress. Rhetorically and legislatively, Johnson purports to honor the Kennedy legacy, and yet in this sequence every trace of the former president is being swiftly removed from the Oval Office. Johnson is impatient to make his own mark on the room, stating "I mean no disrespect but take down that stuff over there," as he motions to the White House staff to strip the walls and mantelpieces of Kennedy's decoration and furnishing. *All the Way* reinforces how film and television constructs presidential legacy through the careful use of iconography and symbol: in this sequence, Johnson embarks upon constructing his own.

In *All the Way*, the legacy Johnson seeks to emulate is Lincoln's. Lincoln is mentioned at numerous points during the film, the president enthusiastically exclaiming to Humphrey on the phone that he is going to "out-Lincoln Lincoln" in his pursuit of the Civil Rights Act, and suggesting to Martin Luther King (Anthony Mackie) that he should vote for Barry Goldwater if he thinks he is the "legitimate heir to Abraham Lincoln" when King argues the Democratic Party has taken the black vote for granted. In many respects, *All the Way* seeks to position Johnson as a president whose legacy has had as much of an enduring effect on the United States as Lincoln, and does so by emulating many of the rhetorical and structural strategies of Spielberg's 2012 biopic of the Great Emancipator (indeed, *All the Way* was produced by Spielberg's production company, Amblin Entertainment). Like *All the Way*, *Lincoln* shows the president arguing, persuading, and cajoling his advisers and members of Congress to ensure the passage of legislation (in this case, the thirteenth amendment outlawing slavery). *Lincoln*, however, also deified the president by constructing a character that often resorts to homily and analogy in attempting to explain his political positions: Lincoln cites an old case he worked on as a lawyer to explain the Emancipation Proclamation, invokes the universality of Euclid's mechanical law to explain that all human beings are created equal, and tells an old joke about an English water closet being the perfect place for a portrait of George Washington. Such recourse to parable is clearly part of a strategy to construct Lincoln as messianic, helping his people understand greater truths through storytelling. *All the Way*, quite conscious it seems of its similarities to *Lincoln*, approaches Johnson in this fashion, while remaining true to the character of the president it is representing: in convincing King to help him get the Civil Rights Bill out of committee he relays a story about a friend of his who endured many slaps across the face in his pursuit of women in bars, but was also successful in a great deal of his propositions. In trying to win public support for his war on poverty, Johnson relays an emotional story of the impoverished children he taught at a school in Cotulla, Texas. In explaining to his close aide Walter Jenkins about his desire to be loved, Johnson tells a long story about his father's bankruptcy and fall from grace. Therefore, as *All the Way* quite self-consciously strips Johnson's presidency bare of iconographic legacies of Kennedy, it positions him rhetorically as the inheritor of Lincoln's mantle as a man who explained himself and his ideas through stories (albeit considerably less romantic, high-minded ones, reflecting faithfully the coarseness of his character).

The *LBJ* appears to have adopted a similar strategy: the sequence made available for publicity features Johnson (Woody Harrelson) telling a story about a time as a boy when his father kicked him out of the truck for being insolent and, facing a seven-mile walk home in the sweltering heat, he managed to secure a ride home from a beautiful woman with large breasts. Undeniably crude, but attempting to demonstrate to his aides that you should be grateful for any crumbs of comfort that come your way in times of adversity, the construction of Johnson's personality conforms to the popular conception of him as possessing an unpretentious wisdom that helped him become an effective political operator.

In many respects, *All the Way* looks to avoid Vietnam entirely and prefers instead to focus almost entirely on civil rights. Having said this, it cannot avoid the war that cost Johnson the presidency, reinforcing the narrative that he felt hamstrung by the growing conflict. The only scene devoted to Vietnam involves Robert McNamara (Bo Foxworth) informing Johnson of the unconfirmed attack on the USS *Maddox* in August 1964, which came to be known as "the Gulf of Tonkin Incident." Ultimately the response to this possibly fictitious event, and the resulting congressional resolution that granted Johnson full authority over the war, would lead to disaster. *All the Way*, however, constructs this as somehow inevitable: close to the election, without responding to the incident, Johnson would invite relentless attack from Goldwater and the right wing and therefore undermine his chances of winning in November. Johnson rails against Humphrey's criticism of his decisions: "Maybe you think Goldwater ought to be president, is that it? That maniac wants to lob an A-bomb into the Kremlin's bathroom and start World War III! . . . If Goldwater gets elected you can forget about poverty, you can forget about civil rights, is that what you want?" As Goodwin suggested, Johnson deceived himself into thinking he could conclude the war quickly and the Great Society would remain intact.[49] This delusion is clearly in evidence here, but so is the sense that Johnson's decisions were justified in order to prevent Goldwater winning the election and preserve the possibility that he would effect meaningful change in the domestic arena.

In essence, not only does *All the Way* marginalize Vietnam in Johnson's legacy, it positions his underhanded tactics in foreign policy prior to the 1964 election as necessary to ensure the success of his legislative agenda. The film limits accusations of disingenuousness by including a final meeting between Johnson and McNamara on the evening of the president's election victory, in which McNamara hands Johnson a folder of information: "Congratulations, Mr. President. My apologies. From our ambassador in Saigon."

Johnson, in voiceover narration, senses impending doom. Over slow-motion images of dancing, cheering, and jubilant admirers, he states, "Right now we're gonna party like there's no tomorrow ... But the sun will come up, and the knives will come out, and all these smiling faces will be watching me, waitin' for that one first moment of weakness, and then they will gut me like a deer." As Johnson, behind the podium, arms outstretched, soaks up the admiration of the crowd, and "Happy Days Are Here Again" plays on the non-diegetic soundtrack, a sense of the inevitable tragedy that will follow pervades. Because *All the Way* seeks to develop a new perspective on Johnson's legacy that focuses on his domestic achievements, it cannot state this explicitly, but through the use of slow-motion, the ironic song, and Johnson's own paranoid voiceover narration, it hints obliquely at the disasters that will follow.

Ultimately what *All the Way* is most successful in capturing is Johnson's effectiveness as a politician and legislator. That is perhaps the aspect of his legacy that resonates most in the bitter partisan environment of the present, and the primary reason there is a nascent nostalgia for his presidency. As Dallek argues of Johnson, "above all, he was interested in being effective—in learning how to win elections, use government for practical ends, and carve out a niche for himself in the world of politics."[50] Califano suggests that "love him or loathe him, it is widely recognized that Lyndon Johnson was a President who knew how to make Washington work."[51] *All the Way* shows Johnson managing the Democratic Party's divergent wings, embodied on the left by Hubert Humphrey and the right by Dick Russell (Frank Langella). He gives Republican Senator Everett Dirksen (Ray Wise) "The Johnson Treatment" in a particularly noteworthy scene where he uses his imposing height to intimidate Dirksen, before pulling his chair close to the sofa on which Dirksen is sitting to further pressure him into doing what he wants—break the filibuster of the Civil Rights Bill in the Senate. Dirksen has other items on the agenda for the meeting, which Johnson waves away. The camera moves to a hand-held style, first sitting at table level, and then employing medium close-ups of the two men in a shot-reverse-shot pattern. This creates a sense of intimacy and intensity, building to the moment where Johnson leans forward in his chair to come face-to-face with Dirksen. As in *Selma*, Johnson appeals to his opponent's sense of history and legacy. What is apparent is how the film attempts to recreate "the Johnson Treatment" visually, giving one a sense of what it was like to be in the clutches of the president as he sought to cajole and persuade. As Califano argues, "the reason for virtually every LBJ conversation was to get someone to do something," and "no President more effectively meshed the events of his time with his knowledge of the Congress to achieve his legislative, social, and economic goals."[52] *All the Way* is no hagiography, but it is the most substantive and detailed exploration of Johnson's political skill, showcasing his ability to work with Congress to deliver change.

Conclusion

On October 22, 2016, director Rob Reiner, actor Woody Harrelson, and screenwriter Joey Hartstone gathered at the Lyndon B. Johnson Presidential Library in Austin, Texas, to discuss their film *LBJ* and the legacy of the former president. A consensus emerged among the panel participants that Johnson was a leader whose legacy deserved reconsideration. Both Reiner and Harrelson suggested they had some anxiety approaching the project because of the war in Vietnam, but the fuller, more nuanced perspective that has been developed of Johnson's presidency in recent years meant Hartstone's script did not focus solely on the problematics of the conflict. As Harrelson notes, "As I said to Luci [Johnson's daughter], I think he'd be considered maybe our greatest president were it not for Vietnam." As Reiner suggests, "Look at the list. Medicare, Medicaid . . . I mean it just goes on and on, and these are programs that are still around, and still . . . helping society. This is big legacy stuff."[53] As demonstrated by the explorations of *Path to War*, *Selma*, and *All the Way*, film and television are looking to shift focus from blaming Johnson for everything that went wrong in Vietnam towards a greater appreciation for his skill as a leader able to achieve meaningful change within the United States' political system. Nostalgia for Johnson's presidency emerges as a result of the partisan gridlock of the Obama years and the chaos and dysfunction that has thus far characterized the early stages of Donald Trump's presidency. Trump's victory in November 2016 was supposedly the progeny of a frustration with inauthentic, elitist politicians. One could posit the notion that the fond look back to the Johnson era in film and television speaks to the desire for a leader who was plain-speaking, unvarnished, and skeptical of political elites, but (as is certainly not the case with Trump) married these characteristics with a vision of the nation that sought to fulfill its founding promise to be more equal, and possessed the exceptional political skill necessary to deliver it.

As the trailer for *LBJ* attests in its emphasis on Johnson implementing Kennedy's legacy on civil rights, Johnson still struggles to get a full hearing even in films that are ostensibly about him: the story of Johnson in popular culture will always be intertwined with the stories of the other people, movements, and ideas that rendered the 1960s such a vibrant, chaotic, exciting, and calamitous decade in American politics, society, and culture. Yet among the many films and television programs that are produced about Johnson, one wonders whether they will succeed in diverting attention away from the man who sent all those young boys to die in Vietnam, to acknowledge Johnson's legacy in delivering some of the most progressive changes in American history. *Lincoln* was a reasonably large hit at the box office, and Daniel Day-Lewis won the Academy Award for playing the former president. Imagery of Lincoln lingered in popular culture after its release. Whether the same will be true for *LBJ* remains to be seen, but it is doubtful. Lincoln was already as close to sanctified as it is possible to be in American presidential history when Spielberg's film was produced. The same can certainly not be said of Johnson. Film and television struggle to contend with presidential legacies that are complex and multifaceted, and battle to change the popular perception of presidents so firmly entrenched in public memory. Lyndon Johnson may be destined to remain a marginalized, minor, and somewhat maligned figure in film and television's telling and retelling of one of the most turbulent periods in United States history.

Notes

1. *The Butler*, film, dir. Lee Daniels (USA: The Weinstein Company, 2013).
2. Thomas Brown, *JFK: History of an Image* (London: I.B. Tauris, 1988), 58.

3. *Selma*, film, dir. Ava DuVernay (USA/UK: Pathe/Paramount Pictures, 2014); *All the Way*, film, dir. Jay Roach (USA: HBO Films, 2016); *LBJ*, film, dir. Rob Reiner (USA: Castle Rock Entertainment/Electric Entertainment, 2016).
4. *Path to War*, film, dir. John Frankenheimer (USA: HBO Films, 2002).
5. Owen Gleiberman, "Film Review: LBJ," *Variety*, September 15, 2016.
6. Joseph A. Califano, *The Triumph and Tragedy of Lyndon Johnson: The White House Years* (New York: Touchstone, 2015), xiv.
7. Julian E. Zelizer, *The Fierce Urgency of Now: Lyndon Johnson, Congress, and the Battle for the Great Society* (New York: Penguin Press, 2015), 323.
8. Andrew L. Johns, "The Legacy of Lyndon B. Johnson," in Mitchell B. Lerner (ed.), *A Companion to Lyndon B. Johnson* (Chichester: Wiley-Blackwell, 2012), 506.
9. Ibid.
10. Califano, *The Triumph and Tragedy of Lyndon Johnson*, xvi.
11. Johns, "The Legacy of Lyndon B. Johnson," 511.
12. Robert Dallek, *Lone Star Rising: Lyndon Johnson and His Times 1908–1960* (New York: Oxford University Press, 1991), 4.
13. Randall B. Woods, *Prisoners of Hope: Lyndon B. Johnson, The Great Society and The Limits of Liberalism* (New York: Basic Books, 2016), 398.
14. Johns, "The Legacy of Lyndon B. Johnson," 509.
15. Robert H. Wilson, Norman J. Glickman, and Laurence E. Lynn Jr. (eds.), *LBJ's Neglected Legacy: How Lyndon Johnson Reshaped Domestic Policy and Government* (Austin: University of Texas Press, 2015).
16. *Wilson*, film, dir. Henry King (USA: 20th Century Fox, 1944); *Truman*, film, dir. Frank Pierson (USA: HBO Films, 1995); *John Adams*, television drama, dir. Tom Hooper (USA: HBO Films, 2008).
17. Iwan W. Morgan, "Introduction," in Iwan W. Morgan (ed.), *Presidents in the Movies: American History and Politics on Screen* (New York: Palgrave Macmillan, 2011), 8.
18. Ibid.
19. *LBJ: The Early Years*, television drama, dir. Peter Werner (USA: NBC, 1987); *Lyndon Johnson*, television drama, dir. Charles Jarrott (USA: The Susskind Company, 1987); *King*, television drama, dir. Abby Mann (USA: NBC, 1978); *The Private Files of J. Edgar Hoover*, film, dir. Larry Cohen (USA: American International Pictures, 1977); *J. Edgar Hoover*, television drama, dir. Robert L. Collins (USA: Showtime, 1987); *Kennedy*, television drama, dir. Jim Goddard (UK/

USA: NBC, 1983); *Robert Kennedy and His Times*, television drama, dir. Marvin J. Chomsky (USA: Columbia Pictures Television, 1985); *Hoover vs The Kennedys: The Second Civil War*, television drama, dir. Michael O'Herlihy (USA/Canada: Selznick-Glickman Productions, 1987); *A Woman Named Jackie*, television drama, dir. Larry Peerce (USA: NBC, 1991); *Thirteen Days*, film, dir. Roger Donaldson (USA: New Line Cinema, 2000); *Jackie, Ethel and Joan: The Women of Camelot*, television drama, dir. Larry Shaw (USA: NBC, 2001); *RFK*, television drama, dir. Robert Dornhelm (USA: 20th Century Fox Television, 2002); *The Kennedys*, television drama, dir. Jon Cassar (USA/Canada: Reelz, 2011).
20. *Jackie*, film, dir. Pablo Larraín (USA/Chile/France/Hong Kong: Fox Searchlight Pictures, 2016).
21. Nick Kotz, *Judgment Days: Lyndon Baines Johnson, Martin Luther King Jr., and the Laws that Changed America* (New York: Mariner, 2006), xiv.
22. Ibid. xiv; *Forrest Gump*, film, dir. Robert Zemeckis (USA: Paramount Pictures, 1994).
23. Califano, *The Triumph and Tragedy of Lyndon Johnson*, xvi.
24. *Mississippi Burning*, film, dir. Alan Parker (USA: Orion Pictures, 1988); *The Long Walk Home*, film, dir. Richard Pearce (USA: Miramax Films, 1990); *Ghosts of Mississippi*, film, dir. Rob Reiner (USA: Columbia Pictures, 1996); *The Help*, film, dir. Tate Taylor (USA: Walt Disney Studios, 2011).
25. *The Deer Hunter*, film, dir. Michael Cimino (USA: EMI, 1978); *Apocalypse Now*, film, dir. Francis Ford Coppola (USA: Omni Zoetrope, 1979); *First Blood*, film, dir. Ted Kotcheff (USA: Orion Pictures, 1982); *Platoon*, film, dir. Oliver Stone (USA: Orion Pictures, 1986); *Born on the Fourth of July*, film, dir. Oliver Stone (USA: Universal Pictures, 1989).
26. Robert Caro, *The Years of Lyndon Johnson: The Path to Power* (New York: Alfred A. Knopf, 1982), xix–xx.
27. Robert Dallek, "LBJ: The Early Years," *Journal of American History* 74, no. 3 (December 1987), 1121–22.
28. Johns, "The Legacy of Lyndon B. Johnson," 514.
29. *Lincoln*, film, dir. Steven Spielberg (USA: DreamWorks Pictures/20th Century Fox, 2012).
30. Gregory Frame, "The Myth of John F. Kennedy in Film and Television," *Film & History* 46, no. 2 (Winter 2016): 21–34.
31. Robert Dallek, *Lyndon B. Johnson: Portrait of a President* (London: Penguin Books, 2005), 211, 224; Doris Kearns Goodwin, *Lyndon*

Johnson and the American Dream (New York: St. Martin's Griffin, 1991), 268.
32. Goodwin, *Lyndon Johnson and the American Dream*, 260–82.
33. Dallek, *Portrait of a President*, 218.
34. Frederik Logevall, *Choosing War: The Lost Chance for Peace and the Escalation of War in Vietnam* (Berkeley: University of California Press, 1999); David Kaiser, *American Tragedy: Kennedy, Johnson and the Origins of the Vietnam War* (Cambridge: Harvard University Press, 2000).
35. Mark Atwood Lawrence, *The Vietnam War* (Oxford: Oxford University Press, 2005).
36. Goodwin, *Lyndon Johnson and the American Dream*, 263.
37. Daniel D'Addario, "Making Selma History," *Time*, January 19, 2015.
38. Sharon Monteith, "Civil Rights Movement Film," in Julie Armstrong (ed.), *The Cambridge Companion to American Civil Rights Literature* (New York: Cambridge University Press, 2015), 124.
39. Mark K. Updegrove, "What Selma Gets Wrong," *Politico*, December 22, 2014.
40. Kotz, *Judgment Days*, xii.
41. Sylvia Ellis, *Freedom's Pragmatist: Lyndon Johnson and Civil Rights* (Gainesville: University Press of Florida, 2013), 3.
42. Kotz, *Judgment Days*, xvi.
43. According to Nick Katzenbach, Johnson's Attorney General, the president's appeal to Wallace's sense of his own legacy was considerably more pointed in the meeting. Reportedly Johnson said, "What do you want left after you, when you die? Do you want a great big marble monument that reads, 'George Wallace—He Built.' Or do you want a little pine piece of board lying across that harsh caliche soil that reads, 'George Wallace—He Hated.'" Ellis, *Freedom's Pragmatist*, 203.
44. Johns, "The Legacy of Lyndon B. Johnson," 504.
45. Dallek, *Lone Star Rising*, 7.
46. *JFK*, film, dir. Oliver Stone (USA: Warner Brothers, 1991).
47. Gregory Frame, "Seeing Obama, Projecting Kennedy: The Presence of JFK in Images of Barack Obama," *Comparative American Studies* 10, no. 2–3 (2012): 163–76.
48. Goodwin, *Lyndon Johnson and the American Dream*, 173.
49. Ibid. 263.
50. Dallek, *Portrait of a President*, 23.
51. Califano, *The Triumph and Tragedy of Lyndon Johnson*, xiii.

52. Ibid. xxv.
53. *LBJ* film discussion with Rob Reiner, Woody Harrelson, and Joey Hartstone, Lyndon B. Johnson Presidential Library, October 22, 2016, <https://www.youtube.com/watch?v=V5FsNyk9rDo> (accessed June 13, 2018).

7

The farewell tour: Presidential travel and legacy building

Emily J. Charnock

In March 2016, President Barack Obama made a historic trip to Cuba, the first time in nearly ninety years that an American president had set foot on its soil. The visit reflected Obama's efforts to set a "new course" in US relations with this neighboring island state. But his presence there received as much criticism as it did praise. Writing in the *Washington Post*, conservative columnist Charles Krauthammer denounced Obama's decision to travel to a country known for its repressive communist regime. Moreover, the visit revealed Obama's skewed sense of priorities, Krauthammer said, elevating Cuba's diplomatic status (and Obama's concern with the US prison at Guantanamo Bay) over more pressing international issues.[1] Warming to this theme, Krauthammer observed that the president "could not bestir himself to go to Paris in response to the various jihadi atrocities" of 2015, but he could rouse himself to "make an ostentatious three-day visit there for climate change"—referencing the United Nations agreement Obama helped negotiate.[2] Thus Obama's trips provided a window into the issues he really cared about, Krauthammer said: "climate change, Gitmo and Cuba." And more than that, at this late stage in his presidency, what he hoped to be known for. "With time running out, he wants these to be his legacy."[3]

This chapter examines that claim: the extent to which presidents use travel, both domestic and international, to emphasize their political priorities and the issues or achievements for which they hope to be remembered. It considers, in essence, to what extent a president's itinerary late in their administration offers insight into their desired legacy. To assess this possibility in its likeliest cases, the chapter only looks at presidents who know their administration is coming to an end: those elected to a second term since ratification of the Twenty-second Amendment in 1951, which limits the president to two full terms in office. For comparability, it considers only those presidents who completed two full terms: Dwight D. Eisenhower, Ronald Reagan, Bill Clinton, George W. Bush, and Barack Obama, assessing how their public activities might shape their entries in the history books.

A (brief) tour through presidential travel

Presidential travel has long been of interest to journalists. They report widely on the president's whereabouts, but also consider the broader mechanics, allocation, and implications of these visits across the country and around the world. The costs of Air Force One, the deployment of Secret Service personnel, the number of states presidents have visited, the number of golf outings they take—all are regularly subject to journalistic scrutiny.[4] Academics have concentrated some attention on this subject, tending to emphasize the connections between travel and public opinion.[5] The places in which speeches are delivered, however, and the strategic considerations that might guide the choice of locations, have been comparatively neglected.[6]

A small but growing body of scholarship has sought to address these deficiencies. Brendan Doherty, for example, looked at modern presidents beginning with Jimmy Carter, using travel as a window into the "permanent campaign"—where presidents increasingly orient their activities towards the goal of re-election.[7] Similarly, Kathryn Tenpas, James McCann, and I have considered how campaign considerations have influenced first-term presidential travel since Eisenhower—showing that recent presidents have traveled outside of the nation's capital much more frequently and more purposefully than in the past.[8] In terms of frequency, the increases have been dramatic—with President George W. Bush undertaking approximately eight times the number of trips taken by Eisenhower, for example.[9] In terms of purpose, the geographic pattern of domestic travel in a president's first term suggests a strategic focus on re-election. That is, recent presidents have disproportionately visited large (in terms of population) "swing" states which they won or lost narrowly, while neglecting smaller, less competitive states. This was particularly apparent in their fourth year of office—election year—but increasingly so across the first term.[10]

This is not to say, however, that all first-term presidential travel is electorally strategic. There are numerous reasons why a president might visit a specific location. Some travel is reflective of the president's symbolic role as head of state—visiting areas struck by natural disasters, for example, or representing the United States overseas. As Commander in Chief, the president might visit military bases, or meet with injured service members. At the same time, the president may have political but not immediately electoral objectives when visiting a particular location. Travel can showcase policies, for example. Why speak on education reform in the Rose Garden, when you can illustrate its purposes in an inner-city school? Why sign an environmental bill in the East Room when you can do it in a national park? The "optics" of such locations can augment the president's message. Even travel that is electorally motivated may not be designed to aid the president's prospects alone. The president may campaign for his party's senators or representatives in Congress. And finally, some travel is electorally motivated but guided by financial rather than voting imperatives—holding fundraisers in wealthy cities and states irrespective of their population size (i.e. their number of voters) or competitive status.

Considering a president's second term, moreover, complicates the idea of electorally motivated travel—since the president no longer has an electoral imperative of his own. How does this change in the strategic context affect presidential travel? One possibility is that the president simply continues to "campaign"—only this time for a potential successor rather than himself. The evidence suggests, however, looking at re-elected presidents from Eisenhower to George W. Bush, that they travel somewhat less in their second terms, and the overarching geographic pattern of travel is less electorally strategic (that is, they do not prioritize large swing states to the same extent as in their first terms).[11] While these findings do not entirely discount the relevance of electoral considerations in the second term, they do indicate the importance of other motivations for re-elected presidents when planning their public activities.[12] This chapter builds on the suggestion that legacy considerations become more relevant as presidents reflect on their achievements and how they wish to be perceived in the longer term. It thus extends the earlier analysis of second-term presidents since Eisenhower, looking in greater depth at the substance and purposes of their travel, focusing primarily on the final year in office.

Conceiving of "legacy" in terms of three dimensions—international, electoral, and policy-related—the chapter provides both quantitative and qualitative analysis of five second-term presidents, considering how their public appearances outside of Washington, DC presented a vision of their presidencies—one they hoped would prove enduring.

Patterns of second-term travel

INTERNATIONAL TRAVEL

One crude indication of a greater concern with legacy than elections in the second term is international travel. Overseas travel places the president in the guise of "statesman," highlights his claims to global leadership, and surrounds him with formal symbols of power and prestige.[13] Achievements on the international stage—as warrior, negotiator, or peacemaker—can provide an entrée into the pantheon of presidential "greatness," and travel can highlight a president's case for such an accolade.[14] Indeed, data gathered from the *Public Papers of the Presidents* suggests that presidents tend to take more international trips in their second terms, despite generally traveling somewhat less compared to their first terms, as shown in Table 1.[15] While domestic travel still dominates, the relative emphasis on international travel is substantially higher in the second term—especially so for Presidents Eisenhower, Clinton, and Obama. Only President Reagan showed little difference in international travel across his two terms.

Table 1. Comparing first-term and second-term travel

President	Total term 1 trips	% International	Total term 2 trips	% International
Eisenhower	100	5%	101	38%
Reagan	274	11%	215	12%
Clinton	589	12%	561	27%
Bush II	805	9%	684	19%
Obama	667	11%	404	25%

Source: Compiled from information in the *Public Papers of the Presidents* (US Government Printing Office).

Table 2. Examining final-year travel

President	Total final year trips	% International
Eisenhower	47	34%
Reagan	71	8%
Clinton	163	20%
Bush II	151	34%
Obama	93	27%

Note: "Final year" includes travel in subsequent calendar year prior to the inauguration of a successor.
Source: Compiled from information in the *Public Papers of the Presidents* (US Government Printing Office).

Similarly, Reagan proves to be the exception when looking solely at the final year in office. As shown in Table 2, international trips account for at least 20 percent of all other presidents' travel schedules that year, and only 8 percent for Reagan.

Of course, enhancing a president's stature might not be the only reason to head overseas. Foreign travel might also serve to garner attention when the media—and likely the public—is distracted by the search for a presidential successor. There is risk involved too, since it does not always enhance stature, depending on the international climate. Whatever the motivations, while international trips appear important for most presidents, the majority of trips—in both their final years and their second terms overall—remain in the domestic sphere.

ELECTION-RELATED TRAVEL

The search for a successor, even if it takes the spotlight off the incumbent to some extent, might well play into his second-term travel considerations. A "third term" for the president's party is a powerful symbol of success—with implications for a president's personal prestige and the survival of his legislative or administrative achievements. As such, even if less strategic in orientation, and less consuming in emphasis, a president may still travel to aid a hoped-for successor and other co-partisans who can help secure his substantive legacy in the long term.

In fact, a basic quantitative analysis of final-year domestic travel suggests that electorally motivated travel does have an important place in most presidents' schedules—though with some notable exceptions. Coding domestic trips according to the activities undertaken in locations outside of Washington, DC (headlining a rally or attending a fundraiser in a public location, for example), or the content of remarks delivered (urging support for a particular party

Table 3. Election-related travel in final year

President	Total domestic trips	# Election-related trips	% Election (of domestic)	% Election (of total trips)
Eisenhower	31	12	39%	26%
Reagan	65	34	52%	48%
Clinton	130	54	42%	33%
Bush II	99	3	3%	2%
Obama	68	23	34%	25%

Note: "Final year" includes travel in subsequent calendar year prior to the inauguration of a successor.
Source: Compiled from information in the *Public Papers of the Presidents* (US Government Printing Office).

or candidate), reveals that election-related trips generally accounted for a quarter to a third of final-year travel overall.[16] In the case of Ronald Reagan, it accounted for as much as 48 percent, compared to as little as 2 percent in the case of George W. Bush. If the focus is narrowed to final year *domestic* travel, then Reagan's proportion reaches 52 percent, while Bush's only rises to 3 percent. This divergence suggests that wider factors—presidential popularity, for example, or connections to a potential successor—can influence the extent of election-related travel undertaken by outgoing presidents.

Policy-related Travel

Cultivating international prestige or helping to elect a successor are not the only ways outgoing presidents might seek to bolster their legacy. Arguably the most important dimension on which their presidencies will be judged is the extent, impact, and popularity of their domestic policy initiatives. Presidents can certainly "barnstorm" the country to urge passage of their legislative proposals, as much as promote their own candidacies. While radio, television, and now internet technologies provide ways for presidents to "go public" (that is, to pressure Congress through appeals to the wider public without leaving the comforts of the White House), travel outside of Washington can often dramatize and amplify such channels—through local media coverage, for example.[17] Presidents might still try to "sell" policies to the public in their second terms, though the sense that they become "lame ducks" after the midterms might affect their prospects of achieving new objectives. One might expect, therefore, that they would place a limited emphasis on policy-related travel in their final year of office, especially compared to election-related or international travel.

A preliminary analysis suggests that policy-related travel accounts for a substantial amount of final-year presidential trips—just under a third in most cases, and as high as 44 percent in the case of George W. Bush, as shown in Table 4.

Comparable data across presidential administrations is not yet available, thus the relative emphasis on policy-related travel across years or terms cannot be ascertained at this point. Nonetheless,

Table 4. Policy-related travel in final year

President	Total domestic trips (final year)	# Policy-related trips	% Policy (of domestic)	% Policy (of total trips)
Eisenhower	31	13	42%	28%
Reagan	65	22	34%	31%
Clinton	130	56	43%	34%
Bush II	99	66	67%	44%
Obama	68	29	43%	31%

Note: "Final year" includes travel in subsequent calendar year prior to the inauguration of a successor.
Source: Compiled from information in the *Public Papers of the Presidents* (US Government Printing Office).

the extent of policy-related travel in the final year suggests a different kind of presidential "salesmanship" may be of relevance for outgoing presidents—less advocating for new policies, and more highlighting those they have already accomplished.

The three categories reviewed here—international, election-related, and policy-related travel—account for at least 80 percent of the trips undertaken by these second-term presidents in their final year in office. Basic quantitative analysis suggests some patterns—a relatively greater emphasis on international travel in a president's second term, for example—and some intriguing variations across presidents in terms of election- or policy-related travel. But numbers can only tell part of the story. To elaborate these patterns and explore variation in greater detail, the rest of this chapter will take a qualitative approach—considering each president's itinerary and public activities in their final year of office, and the portrait of their presidencies that emerges.[18]

Second-term presidents—case studies

DWIGHT D. EISENHOWER (1960–61)

Eisenhower is famous for the Farewell Address he gave just before leaving office in January 1961, warning of a growing "military-industrial complex" that threatened to imperil American liberties at home. But he also stressed the importance of America's international role, and his travels in his last year as president reflected this emphasis on the international sphere. Foreign destinations accounted for 34 percent of his 1960–61 trips. Indeed, 38 percent of his second-term travel was international, compared to just 5 percent in his first term.

Cold War considerations underpinned much of Eisenhower's foreign travel. He undertook three international tours in his final year—to Latin America in the early spring, to western Europe in May, and then to Southeast Asia in June—all of which connected to the superpower struggle. The Latin America tour, for example, which included trips to Brazil, Argentina, Chile, and Uruguay, was designed to counter Soviet charges "that the United States has held Latin America in a colonial relationship to ourselves," as Eisenhower explained in a television address to the American people.[19] He traveled to France in May for long-awaited talks with Soviet premier Nikita Khrushchev, though the Paris summit quickly fell apart due to the capture of US pilot Gary Powers just two weeks before.[20] Finally, traveling to the Philippines, Taiwan, Japan, and Korea in June, Eisenhower emphasized the importance of US guaranteed security as part of the "Free World's" stand against "international communism."[21]

These international tours were not so much about clothing Eisenhower in the symbols and trappings of the presidency, but about the kind of international legacy he wished to leave. As Eisenhower explained in a speech after returning from Asia, his visit had been "planned as one of a series which have, in toto, taken me nearly around the world," visiting twenty-seven nations over the previous year (in 1959, Eisenhower had also visited parts of North America, western Europe, North Africa, the Middle East, and the Indian subcontinent on what he termed a "goodwill" tour).[22] These trips were designed to bolster American policy declarations (of peaceful intent, desire to improve common security, and to raise living standards around the world), he explained, and even signal US respect for international social etiquette—with Eisenhower personally accepting return invitations from foreign leaders who had visited the United States. "Overseas visits by me, all of us felt, would be a strong support of other successful programs."[23] This was a diplomatic initiative, therefore, but with an eye on his international legacy. It was only at the end of his presidency that Eisenhower personally took up these invitations, having sent representatives such as the Secretary of State in previous years. Prior to 1959, Eisenhower had never visited more than two countries per year, and then primarily in the western hemisphere.[24]

Eisenhower also undertook a substantial number of election-oriented trips in his final year—nearly 40 percent of his domestic trips had an electoral dimension (and about a quarter of his final-year travel overall), including Republican fundraising, addressing the GOP convention in Chicago, and aiding the presidential campaign of his vice president, Richard Nixon. This seems understandable when we consider that Ike was immensely popular—with a second-term average Gallup approval rating of over 60 percent, making him a perceived asset to the Nixon campaign (despite the occasional embarrassing comment about the VP).[25] It is interesting to note, however, that while he attended a number of Republican Party rallies and events around the country, Eisenhower only made a personal appearance for one Republican congressional candidate, Representative Katharine St. George of New York.[26]

Nonetheless, some of Eisenhower's domestic trips had a distinctly non-political thrust—reviewing the troops as Commander in Chief, addressing charitable groups, and making commencement speeches with civic themes, for example.[27] But policy-related trips made up a significant amount of his travel, more so than election-related trips—42 percent of Eisenhower's domestic trips, and 28 percent of his overall travel in the final year, showcased his policy achievements as president. Some promoted major domestic changes he had supported but not initiated—statehood for Alaska and Hawaii, for example, which he marked with personal visits in 1960. Other trips related to initiatives with which he was more personally involved: the National Aeronautics and Space Administration (NASA), for example, and the Interstate Highway System—two of Eisenhower's most notable policy legacies.[28] Thus in October, Eisenhower left a Republican rally in St. Paul, Minnesota to visit nearby Red Wing, to dedicate the new Hiawatha Bridge spanning the Mississippi River (built with federal funds).

Yet Eisenhower used much of his dedication speech to sound internationalist rather than domestic themes. "Hiawatha was a founder of a United Nations organization in America," Eisenhower told the crowd, in a somewhat bewildering rhetorical shift away from highways—likening the Iroquois Confederation to the UN.[29] Indeed, a majority of Eisenhower's policy-related trips touched on foreign policy or a combination of foreign and domestic issues, rather than domestic initiatives alone.[30] This points once more to international affairs as Eisenhower's prime consideration as he left the presidency, and something heavily reflected in his second-term and final-year travel.

Ronald Reagan (1988–89)

Ronald Reagan offers several exceptions to the general patterns detailed here. This is primarily because Reagan placed less of an emphasis on physical travel than he did on his ability to communicate and connect with people via television, from the relative comfort of the West Wing or the Rose Garden. He still traveled quite a bit more than Nixon or Eisenhower, but less than his immediate predecessor, Jimmy Carter. And this may have related not simply to his gifts of communication, as much as his age, his health—including recovery from an assassination attempt in 1981—and his personal inclinations, having expressed little enthusiasm for the discomforts of the road while governor of California.[31] But Reagan's final year of presidential travel in 1988 does provide some insight into his personal vision of his presidency, his priorities, and what he thought he had achieved.

Reagan took only six international trips in 1988–89, out of 71 in his final year in office—comprising just 8 percent of his travel. As noted above, this proportion is much lower than that of other presidents considered here, and Reagan is the only president not to show a relative increase in international travel in his second term. His personal preferences and physical considerations, therefore, seem to have impacted his international as well as domestic travel—understandable since foreign travel involves longer distances and more extensive itineraries. Still, he covered all the major bases in terms of his foreign policy. He visited Mexico and Canada, highlighting ties with America's closest hemispheric neighbors. He attended a North Atlantic Treaty Organization (NATO) summit in Brussels, Belgium; visited London and stressed the "special relationship" with the UK; and most importantly, he went to Moscow in May, for a summit meeting with Soviet premier Mikhail Gorbachev which finalized an important nuclear arms limitation treaty. This was Reagan's first visit to the USSR, in the last year of his administration, and suggests the importance he accorded his evolving relationship with the Soviets for his legacy. Asked by reporters why he was visiting what he had once dubbed "an evil empire," Reagan replied that he had spoken in "another time, another era"—a powerful statement delivered in the heart of the Kremlin.[32]

Reagan's first international trip in 1988, however, which was to Mexico, also connected to a domestic policy priority—one that involved the First Lady too. Alongside discussing immigration and border issues with the Mexican president, Reagan stressed his commitment to the so-called "war on drugs."[33] Complementing this federal policy, First Lady Nancy Reagan had made the "just say no" anti-drugs campaign central to her personal platform during her husband's presidency. Back on American soil, Reagan talked about the war on drugs in his Commencement address at the Coast Guard academy and in a trip to North Carolina where he addressed a seminar on workplace drug abuse.[34] In one of his last trips as President, moreover—in January 1989—Reagan addressed a fundraiser in Los Angeles for the Nancy Reagan Drug Abuse Center.[35]

Other domestic trips highlighted the economic achievements of the Reagan administration—with the president touring various businesses in 1988, touting economic recovery and growth.[36] He also made a series of visits to schools across the country. "I've taken to visiting schools lately to find out first hand what's going on," he told an audience at Oakton High School in Vienna, Virginia in March.[37] But these visits were as much about showcasing as fact-finding, highlighting Reagan's preferred education reforms such as magnet schools, accountability, and "parental choice"—policies that were not to be imposed from the federal level but encouraged by presidential commissions and reports.[38]

Surprisingly, one of the key domestic policy legacies often attributed to the Reagan administration—the withdrawal of budgetary support from federal welfare programs—received little emphasis in Reagan's final-year travel. There were no trips highlighting "success stories" of people moving from welfare into the workplace in the booming Reagan economy. Nonetheless, Reagan's final trip as president touched on this issue indirectly. In early 1989 he visited New York, where he addressed the Knights of Malta—a lay Catholic religious order—on themes of faith and charity, and its superiority to government aid in winning the war on poverty.[39]

It was electoral politics, not policy, which accounted for more of Reagan's final-year travel. Almost 50 percent of his trips were concerned with the electoral prospects of fellow Republicans in the November 1988 election. Reagan headlined numerous rallies and fundraisers, addressed the Republican National Convention, and urged support for his vice president and Republican nominee, George H.W. Bush. He also campaigned for congressional Republicans, primarily for senators, perhaps recognizing the greater chance of recapturing control of the Senate in 1988, which Republicans had lost just two years prior (unlike the House, which had been under Democratic control since 1954). Like Eisenhower, Reagan also enjoyed relatively decent approval rates in his second term, after rebounding from the Iran-Contra affair—with a second-term average of 55.3 percent. His presence on the campaign trail could therefore be viewed as beneficial. Indeed, Reagan is the only president considered here whose preferred successor—in this case, Bush—actually won. That he dedicated more of his travel to electoral purposes—both proportionally and, with the exception of Bill Clinton, in absolute terms—is thus potentially significant.

Finally, Reagan took a number of trips in 1988–89 which had a distinctly personal and retrospective flavor, trips which showcased aspects of his journey to the presidency. He returned to Davenport, Iowa, for example, for a dedication ceremony at the radio station where he began his career as a sportscaster.[40] And few trips are as imbued with personal symbolism as Reagan's visit to the University of Notre Dame in March 1988, where he went not to deliver a commencement address or offer remarks on higher education, but to unveil a new Post Office stamp commemorating Knute Rockne: Notre Dame's most famous American football coach, and the subject of Reagan's most famous film. It was in *Knute Rockne, All American* (1940) that Reagan played George Gipp, the star Notre Dame football player who, struck with a fatal illness before the big game, tells his teammates to go out "and win one for the Gipper."[41] Reagan's use of "the Gipper" persona in his public life is worthy of its own study, but this appearance suggests his desire to project it into his legacy. His remarks themselves had a retrospective quality, too, centered on a previous visit to Notre Dame early in 1981, where he had given one of his first major addresses as president. In the twilight of his presidency, Reagan's 1988 speech at Notre Dame emphasized how far the US had come, highlighting his two key achievements: economic prosperity and a nascent ideological victory over Communism.[42]

Bill Clinton (2000–01)

Over the course of both his terms in office, Bill Clinton traveled much more extensively than either Eisenhower or Reagan. This might reflect an increasing demand for presidential accessibility, or a growing recognition within the White House that locations outside the Beltway could provide useful media visuals and variety. The fact that Clinton had a dedicated "director of production for presidential events" suggests the extent to which staging, at home and abroad, had become an essential aspect of the public presidency.[43]

The larger number of trips necessitates a broader sweep through Clinton's travels, highlighting those visits which appear most significant. Thus, of Clinton's international trips in 2000 and 2001—which made up 20 percent of his travel—some showcased important aspects of his administration's foreign policy. He visited India and Pakistan, for example, as part of a post-USSR strategic reset in South Asia.[44] He also visited both western and eastern Europe, encouraging European stability and integration in the wake of the Soviet collapse and the Balkan wars, in which the US—via NATO—had played a major role. In contrast, there was relatively little emphasis on the western hemisphere, which is interesting in light of Clinton's signing the North American Free Trade Agreement (NAFTA) in 1993, and the retrospective significance it is normally accorded in Clinton's policy accomplishments.[45]

Clinton also made state visits to Nigeria and Tanzania, to highlight a new emphasis on African relations he had pushed in his second term, and in the case of Tanzania, to mark the two-year anniversary of the bombing of the US embassy in Dar es Salaam.[46] That bombing had taken place in 1998, just a few months after Clinton returned from a major African tour, including a visit to Rwanda, where he had apologized for the US failure to intervene in that nation's bloody civil war.[47] His Tanzanian visit in 2000 involved peace talks aimed at ending ethnic conflict in nearby Burundi, suggesting Clinton's effort to transcend his foreign policy failures in Rwanda (and also Somalia) as his term drew to a close, to try and close this painful chapter and, in a sense, bind up his own nation's wounds.[48] Similarly, Clinton visited Vietnam in November 2000, the first US president to do so since the end of the Vietnam War, marking the normalization of relations his administration had engineered.[49]

Peace talks, of course, lay at the heart of one of Clinton's signature international achievements—aiding the peace process in Northern Ireland, via the appointment of US Special Envoy for Northern Ireland, former Senator George Mitchell, and culminating in the Good Friday Agreement of 1998. It is perhaps no surprise, therefore, that Clinton paid a visit to Northern Ireland (his third) as his presidency drew to a close.[50] There he could adopt the mantle of the great international peacemaker, a powerful image with enduring resonance for evaluations of presidential "greatness."[51] Yet Clinton was not resting on his laurels in 2000. Rather, he looked to resolve another seemingly intractable struggle: the Israeli-Palestinian conflict. Clinton devoted extensive time in his final year to bringing about an agreement. This involved a major summit in Egypt, but also talks between Israeli and Palestinian representatives at Camp David in Maryland, and between Israeli and Syrian negotiators in Shepherdstown, West Virginia. Both of those locations were chosen for symbolic reasons (as well as the practical reasons of proximity to DC)—Camp David for its associations with the historic 1978 agreement between Israel and Egypt negotiated by President

Carter, and Shepherdstown for its connection to the American Civil War, which Clinton hoped might focus the delegates' minds upon peace.[52] Indeed, in several speeches within the US at this time, Clinton stressed the importance of the Middle East peace process and his hopes for its success.[53]

In this aim Clinton was to be disappointed, but the attempt demonstrates his efforts to achieve new objectives in his final year of office—on the international stage, but also on the domestic front, as other aspects of his travel illustrate. Clinton's domestic trips did not simply hit a reflective note and showcase the major policy achievements of his administration. He took only one trip highlighting welfare reform, for example, visiting a jobs access program in Denver, Colorado.[54] In contrast, he took a number of trips in the wake of his final State of the Union address in January 2000, highlighting several new policy proposals. He visited elementary and high schools to talk about federal investment in public school infrastructure, educational reforms, and the charter school movement.[55] He dropped by senior centers to highlight a proposed Medicare prescription drug benefit.[56] He pushed a federal Patients' Bill of Rights, too—in a speech in Missouri, for example, where a state-level version had passed.[57] And he went to a Minnesota farm to stress the benefits to US agriculture of permanent normal trading relations with China.[58] Clinton also made several appearances urging gun control legislation at the state and federal level—a long-standing priority he pushed with renewed intensity after the Columbine High School shootings in April 1999.[59] On and off throughout the year, moreover, he undertook what he called a "New Markets" tour, promoting legislation designed to help economically deprived communities—both urban and rural—to develop new markets and stimulate growth through public-private partnerships.[60] Connecting these communities to the internet was a big theme, bridging a "digital divide" that Clinton felt was holding them back.[61] Clinton even told an interviewer that he wanted "to be remembered as the President that led America from the industrial era into the information age," and also "tried to empower poor people," among other things.[62]

Few of these initiatives passed, while those that did—the New Markets legislation and normalized trade with China—have not figured as prominently as NAFTA or welfare reform in early readings of Clinton's presidency.[63] Nonetheless, these policy-oriented trips suggest that Clinton was still setting new directions and seeking legislative victories during the "lame duck" phase of his presidency, despite Republican control of Congress—perhaps making up for time consumed by the Monica Lewinsky scandal early in his second term. "I want to get everything done I can possibly do while I'm here [in office]," he told a reporter in late November, which was notably *after* the election to determine his successor.[64] Even trips intended to showcase major achievements—highlighting economic growth and technological achievement in the 1990s, for example—had something of a prospective flavor. He stressed how his administration had helped created the conditions for economic success, but also what must be done with that prosperity to ensure the security of all Americans in the future.[65]

Clinton linked that theme, of properly using the fruits of his administration, to the election of those closely involved with it—both Vice President Al Gore and First Lady Hillary Clinton. Indeed, election-oriented trips accounted for 44 percent of his domestic travel in 2000, including a large number of trips to New York to aid his wife's Senate bid. Otherwise, from a congressional perspective, Clinton campaigned mostly for House rather than Senate candidates—perhaps prioritizing Hillary's campaign for the upper chamber, or perhaps believing Democrats had a better chance of recapturing the House (ultimately, it was the Senate that would go 50:50 in the 2000 election).[66] Clinton addressed the Democratic National Convention in Los Angeles in August, and tried to aid Gore's presidential bid more generally, though the dynamics between the two were somewhat prickly. Clinton's approval rating averaged over 60 percent in his second term, which made him a welcome campaigner for most Democrats.[67] At the same time, there was a concern that Gore might be outshone by his charismatic predecessor. Thus, the series of rallies Clinton headlined just before the election had a broader "Get out the Vote" message, designed to draw on Clinton's appeal to help down-ballot Democrats, rather than compete with Gore at the top. As the *New York Times* remarked: "The buddy movie that began when these two young Southern centrists started off on a high-energy bus tour across America in the 1992 campaign wasn't supposed to end like this."[68] Though the ending went further awry with Gore's narrow loss to Republican George W. Bush, the reference to the bus tour suggests how important travel had been to the Clinton presidency from the start.

In January 2001, as the dust was settling on a contentious election and he prepared to leave office, Clinton undertook something of a personal retrospective tour—visiting places that had been important to him and to his political career. He went to Illinois, Michigan, and New Hampshire, states that had been critical to his securing the Democratic nomination in 1992. "I came here one last time as President to New Hampshire to thank you for making me the Comeback Kid," he told the crowd in Dover, "but more, and far more important, to thank you for making America the Comeback Country."[69] Then he went to Boston, where he invoked the legacy of John F. Kennedy, and spoke about the progressive presidents who had inspired him: Franklin Roosevelt and Theodore Roosevelt.[70] Finally, a few days later, just before the inauguration of his successor, Clinton went home to Little Rock, Arkansas—where he had begun his political career—and addressed a Joint Session of the State Legislature, offering a sweeping overview of what his administration had done for Arkansas and for America.[71] Here, at last, with no time left to push new initiatives, Clinton made the retrospective case for his legacy.

George W. Bush (2008–09)

Though George W. Bush had campaigned on a largely domestic platform in 2000, international affairs came to define his presidency. It is hardly surprising, therefore, that he placed a particular emphasis on international travel in his final year of office: 34 percent overall, the same high proportion as Eisenhower (though amounting to four times as many international trips).

Much of his international travel can be seen through the lens of the War on Terror—shoring up alliances and urging support for this US strategy around the world. Like Clinton, Bush also made a major push to resolve the Israeli-Palestinian conflict in his final year in office—trying to bring some stability to a region rocked by US military interventions in the wake of 9/11. Thus in January 2008 he made his first presidential trip to Israel, and visited the Palestinian West Bank for the first time. Afterward he traveled to Kuwait, the United Arab Emirates, Saudi Arabia, and Egypt, where he promoted his "freedom agenda," stressing the need to combat extremism and spread democracy in the Middle East, and sought support for the Israeli-Palestinian peace process.[72] Bush returned to Israel in May to mark the sixtieth anniversary of its statehood, and spoke of his hopes for transformation in the wider region.[73] Again, as in Clinton's case, the peace process stalled, while the democratic transformation of the Middle East remains elusive, with Bush's legacy in the region widely criticized at home—by voices across the political spectrum.

In his last international trips as president, in December 2008, Bush visited Iraq and Afghanistan, recognizing the two wars at the center of his controversial foreign policy. He visited military bases, expressed appreciation for the troops, and stressed the progress that was being made in both countries.[74] These were far from "Mission Accomplished" moments despite Bush's notorious staged appearance in 2003, when he stood on the deck of the USS *Abraham Lincoln* declaring an end to major combat operations in Iraq.[75] Bush used these later, more muted appearances to claim the corner had been turned in these conflicts, and to try and shape the conversation about his accomplishments moving forward, placing an emphasis on the "surge" of 2007, for example, rather than the initial intervention in Iraq.

Another major international trip highlighted work for which Bush has gained more positive recognition in retirement—suggesting that travel can illuminate presidential priorities that may otherwise gain little attention. In February, Bush visited Benin, Tanzania, Rwanda, Ghana, and Liberia to promote his Africa initiatives: the President's Emergency Plan for AIDS Relief, or "PEPFAR"; malaria prevention and treatment programs; the Millennium Challenge Corporation (which tied US economic development grants to efforts to reduce government corruption); and various educational initiatives. The impact of these programs, particularly those combating AIDS and Malaria, has begun to factor in to assessments of Bush's presidency, though in part through his continued advocacy of these causes in retirement.[76] As the example of Jimmy Carter also shows, post-presidential reputation can be somewhat rehabilitated through international humanitarian work.[77]

Indeed, when in 2013 Gallup asked Americans how they felt about former presidents, Bush gained a 47 percent approval rating, compared to 34 percent when he left office.[78] Just before the November 2008 elections, in fact, Bush's approval rating had fallen to its lowest ever point: just 25 percent. Perhaps unsurprisingly, then, Bush appears to have been unwelcome on the campaign trail—whether stumping for the Republican presidential nominee, Senator John McCain of Arizona, for congressional Republicans, or for other candidates. Just three of his domestic trips in 2008 involved a public expression of support for GOP candidates, and he did not address the Republican National Convention in person. Rather, the incumbent president was kept at a distance, making his remarks via satellite. In other ways, Bush was something of a distant presence in the campaign. He did attend a number of private fundraisers for congressional candidates and the party, reflecting a stark divergence in partisan attitudes towards the president. Even at his lowest point, 61 percent of self-described Republicans still approved of the job Bush was doing as president, compared to 20 percent of independents and just 5 percent of Democrats.[79] Still, for the purposes of aiding the party without hurting their candidates' broader appeal, Bush's appearances were kept behind closed doors.[80]

Bush's perceived public toxicity suggests an element of "getting out of Dodge" to Bush's international travels in 2008: removing him from the domestic political scene and utilizing the scenery and ceremony of foreign trips to convey a statesmanlike aura back to domestic audiences (though the international climate of opinion did not always ensure a positive reception).[81] Yet international issues also infused many of the non-electoral domestic trips Bush undertook in 2008. He talked about his Africa initiatives in several US appearances, and gave numerous addresses around the country on the War on Terror.[82] Many more of Bush's appearances had a military theme: visiting West Point, the Air Force Academy, and various Army and Air Force bases, as well as attending military appreciation parades and participating in commissioning ceremonies. All presidents engage in some events which showcase their Commander in Chief role, but these appear to have had particular significance for Bush.[83]

So too did another category of "typical" presidential trips: visiting communities struck by natural disasters or other traumatic events. The specter of Hurricane Katrina, which hit the Gulf Coast in 2005, still loomed over Bush's second term—when the response of his administration, and the president personally, had been widely denounced. A photograph of Bush taken during an aerial tour of the damage had sparked a firestorm of criticism, with many questioning his initial absence from New Orleans and failure to show solidarity with the community. Bush even admitted in retrospect that it was a "huge mistake," acknowledging how the photo made him look "detached and uncaring."[84] Thus, if anything, he responded more actively, more publicly, and more personally to subsequent natural disasters, including several in his final year. In 2008 he visited tornado-struck regions in Tennessee, flood-ravaged parts of Iowa, and fire-scorched areas in California. He gave a high school commencement address in Kansas, one year on from a major tornado that had struck the town.[85] And when, in September, Hurricanes Gustav and Ike looked set to strike communities still reeling from Katrina, he sprang into action with a series of public appearances and briefings conveying his personal involvement and concern (and stressing the superior federal response this time around).[86] More than this, Bush did symbolic penance in New Orleans itself—hosting a major NAFTA summit in April to show the strides the city was making, and returning in August to highlight reconstruction efforts along the Gulf Coast.[87] Bush could not escape the shadow of the storm over his presidency, but he used these later appearances—as with those in Iraq and Afghanistan—to try and alter the larger narrative.

In other respects, Bush sought to emphasize the substantive achievements of his administration. In January of both 2008 and 2009, just before he left office, Bush visited elementary schools (in Chicago and Philadelphia respectively) to mark the anniversary of his signature education initiative: the No Child Left Behind Act.[88] He went to Maryland and North Carolina, moreover, to highlight projects launched under the auspices of his White House Office of

Faith-Based Initiatives.[89] Both reflected elements of the "compassionate conservative" agenda Bush had brought into office. But there was little hint in his final-year travels of a late push on any unmet domestic policy goals—such as immigration reform, for example, which Bush had unsuccessfully pushed in 2007.[90] Unlike Clinton, then, Bush's domestic trips in his final year had a largely retrospective quality.[91]

There was one front, however, on which Bush did urge new measures in his last year as president: the economy, though this was largely down to circumstances. As the US economy slowed in late 2007 and early 2008, Bush urged Congress to pass a major economic stimulus package.[92] He visited small businesses to highlight its various tax breaks and rebates, and plugged the stimulus in similar appearances after it was approved.[93] He also made appearances highlighting a mortgage counseling program created in 2007, to help homeowners struggling with foreclosure as the subprime mortgage crisis began to take hold.[94] After the financial crisis began in earnest in September, Bush again went out on the road to explain the Troubled Asset Relief Program (TARP) he had signed into law on October 3.[95] He had talked about the steps being taken to address the financial crisis in major televised addresses and other remarks from the White House.[96] But his meetings with small business owners added the folksy, personal quality for which Bush was famed, using travel as a tool to reassure and explain—though given the scale and timing of the crisis, there was little opportunity for Bush to reframe the narrative more positively.

Barack Obama (2016–17)

Barack Obama's second-term travel challenges previous patterns in some respects. While he traveled less in the second than the first term, as expected, he challenged the upward trajectory of trips in both terms overall. In his first term, for example, Obama traveled substantially less than Bush, but still somewhat more than Clinton, as shown in Table 1. In his second term, however, Obama took far fewer trips than both: 280 less than Bush and over 150 less than Clinton. A number of factors might account for this. Firstly, Bush's schedule may have reached a saturation point beyond which further trips provide little additional value, whether in terms of media coverage or public response. A fatigue factor may be relevant too, even with younger presidents such as Clinton, Bush, and Obama. Still, Obama did not simply maintain the pace set by his predecessors, but actively reduced it. Family considerations may be relevant here, since, unlike his two immediate predecessors, Obama had two young daughters who still lived in the White House throughout his second term.[97] But another factor may have facilitated this lighter schedule: new technology.

While jet aircraft helped propel presidential travel in the post-Eisenhower era, communications technologies like television played a somewhat contradictory role, at once enabling the president to reach a wider public without leaving the confines of the White House, and simultaneously encouraging the use of new backdrops to stage the "optics" of presidential activity.[98] Obama's reduced itinerary may reflect the impact of new internet technology through web and social media platforms which allow the imagery of travel to live on and still seem dynamic. White House communicators can recycle and re-post old images of the president in significant locations, coordinating this imagery with the legislative calendar, significant anniversaries or other news "hooks."[99] They no longer need to stage a constant flow of new events to ensure coverage from local and national media outlets. Instead, they can get more mileage out of fewer events, pushing images and messages through social media accounts that they themselves control.

Nonetheless, some patterns remained the same. International travel, for example, featured more prominently in Obama's second term than his first, as with all other presidents considered here except Reagan. Approximately one quarter of Obama's second-term travel was international, with a similar proportion when looking at final-year travel alone (27 percent). This international emphasis in the final year was slightly lower than Bush's but higher than Clinton's. Like his predecessors, though, some of Obama's international trips had particular significance—in this case, signaling his desired redirection of US foreign policy. His trip to Cuba in March 2016, for example, marked a major shift in US policy towards normalized relations with that nation, as noted at the outset. He also made a brief stop in the UK in April during the run-up to the Brexit referendum, highlighting his support for the European Union as a political and trading partner, while seemingly downplaying the so-called "special relationship" with Britain.[100] It was Obama's "pivot to Asia," however—a larger strategic reorientation of US foreign policy— that was most prominently reflected in his itinerary.

In late May 2016, Obama visited Vietnam, touring both Hanoi and Saigon, and emphasizing the productive relationship forged since the normalization of relations under Clinton.[101] He then headed to Japan for the G-7 meeting. The location itself was pre-determined, but Obama added a layer of significance by choosing to visit Hiroshima, becoming the first US president to do so. Numerous conservative commentators critiqued what they saw as an "apology tour," a theme first sounded by former Bush administration official Karl Rove back in 2009.[102] Journalist Jacob Weisberg offered a different framing, seeing Obama's visit to this nuclear shrine, along with the Cuba visit, as part of a "reconciliation" theme animating Obama's final year.[103] This continued in September, when Obama became the first incumbent president to visit Laos, acknowledging the devastation caused by secret CIA operations there during the Vietnam War.[104] These trips were, however, just as much about geopolitics as guilt, reflecting Obama's new international vision—centered on Asia rather than western Europe or the Middle East.

Perhaps unsurprisingly, Obama's itinerary did not draw attention to ongoing US involvement in Middle Eastern conflicts— from which he had hoped to fully withdraw.[105] His only trips to the region included a brief stop in Saudi Arabia in April, and a short visit to Israel in September (for the funeral of former Israeli president Shimon Peres). There was no grand effort to resolve the Israel-Palestine question as his presidency wound down. Still, Obama enjoyed greater international prestige than his immediate predecessor: polls of both Asian and western European nations showed significantly higher confidence in Obama's leadership than that of Bush (though there were more mixed results in the Middle East).[106] Obama had even tapped into this potential as a candidate in 2008, making an unprecedented overseas campaign trip to Germany, and casting himself in Berlin as a "citizen of the world."[107] His second-term and final-year travel, especially, seemed designed to cement that legacy.

Electoral politics still comes calling in a president's final year of office, and with an average second-term approval rating of 46.7 percent, Obama was a more welcome campaign surrogate than George W. Bush had been—though his rating falls below that of most re-elected presidents considered here.[108] Obama addressed the Democratic National Convention in person, and dedicated about a quarter of his final-year travel to electoral aims—far more than Bush (2 percent) but somewhat less than Bill Clinton (33 percent), as shown above in Table 3. Unlike Clinton's emphasis on down-ballot Democrats, however, most of Obama's 2016 election-related travel involved appearances to promote the Democratic nominee—this time, former First Lady and Secretary of State Hillary Clinton.[109] Concerns about overshadowing were perhaps lessened in the combative atmosphere of the 2016 campaign, but Obama proved no more successful in helping elect a successor than Bill Clinton had been.[110]

On the domestic front, Obama undertook two trips showcasing his major legislative success: healthcare reform. In March, Obama went to Milwaukee, Wisconsin to mark the sixth anniversary of the Patient Protection and Affordable Care Act. He met first with local citizens who had written to him describing how the law had saved their lives, and then delivered a major speech, highlighting some of these personal stories while outlining the achievements of "Obamacare." (Milwaukee was chosen as the backdrop, the President explained, because it had done the most to expand its coverage of uninsured citizens).[111] Then, in October, Obama traveled to Miami, Florida, where he offered a lengthy defence of the healthcare law and its positive impact. With the general election less than a month away, this Miami backdrop reflected at least some electoral considerations: Florida was a large swing state, after all. It was also one of nineteen states which had not yet expanded its Medicaid program, the President noted, leaving 700,000 eligible Floridians uninsured. When the crowd conveyed their disapproval, Obama offered a clear electoral message:

"Don't boo, vote."[112] That night, in fact, Obama also headlined a campaign rally for Hillary Clinton in Miami.[113]

Beyond healthcare, however, Obama had few concrete legislative achievements to showcase. Facing a difficult congressional environment, particularly in his second term, he had relied instead on executive action to promote various priorities, such as immigration reform and gun control.[114] Yet Obama did not undertake any trips in his final year specifically designed to highlight these areas—perhaps due to controversy over the means he had used to advance them (and perhaps the fragility of the ends: the Supreme Court blocked much of Obama's immigration action in a June 2016 decision).[115] He did, however, emphasize one policy area in which executive action had featured prominently: the environment. Throughout the summer of 2016, Obama took several trips highlighting conservation and environmental protection. The US national parks formed an important backdrop for both. He visited Carlsbad Caverns in New Mexico in June, followed by a trip to Yosemite National Park in California the next day—tying together the centenary of the National Park Service with the issue of climate change.[116] At Yosemite, he warned of rising temperatures and sea levels threatening America's parks, monuments, and natural beauty—"And that's not the America I want to pass on to the next generation," Obama said, "[t]hat's not the legacy, I think, any of us want to leave behind."[117] Observers noted that these visits would "become part of Mr. Obama's legacy on conservation," as a *New York Times* article put it, noting that Obama had protected more acres of public land than any president except Carter.[118] If public waters were included, then Obama outstripped them all.

Obama continued the environmental theme later in the summer, addressing conservation conferences in Lake Tahoe, California, and Honolulu, Hawaii, where he discussed the protection of public lands and the Paris climate agreement (negotiated under executive auspices).[119] Then he flew on to Midway Island in the North Pacific Ocean, visiting the Papahānaumokuākea Marine National Monument, which he had recently quadrupled in size by executive proclamation, making it the largest protected marine area in the world.[120] From there, he flew to Hangzhou, China, for the G-20 meeting of nations, where he formally announced US entry into the Paris agreement.[121] In this itinerary itself, Obama demonstrated that environmental protection was both a "domestic" and a global issue.

Obama also found time for a series of trips designed to highlight his personal and political journey. In February, he returned to the Illinois state capitol—where his political career began, and where in 2007 he launched his presidential campaign—to deliver a speech on partisanship and the state of the US political system.[122] Then, in April, he returned to the University of Chicago's Law school—where he had once taught—to give a lecture on the Supreme Court. These trips reflected key stages in Obama's life and key motifs of his presidency: his legal training and academic background, and the "post-partisan" message that had so energized his supporters in 2008.[123] "[O]ne of my few regrets," Obama told the lawmakers in Springfield, had been his "inability to reduce the polarization and meanness in our politics."[124] This, he told them, was something he would continue to work for in his final year in office and afterward as a private citizen. In this sense, Obama's personal reminiscences blended with a prospective agenda—advocating campaign finance reforms, redistricting reform, and measures making it easier for citizens to vote.[125] Yet he did not so much push specific legislative proposals (as Clinton had in his last year as president) as outline an agenda and an advocacy role that could stretch beyond the presidency. Indeed, Obama laid tangible groundwork for this prior to leaving office, transforming his campaign organization, "Obama for America," into a grassroots advocacy network, "Organizing for Action," which might assist his efforts.[126]

Perhaps surprisingly, Obama did not take any trips in 2016–17 overtly emphasizing another crucial part of his personal story: his historic status as the first African American to hold the nation's highest office. (He did deliver the Commencement Address at Howard University, the nation's premier historically black university, but this was located within Washington, DC and thus does not appear in the data.)[127] Nonetheless, Obama emphasized the issue of race substantively, if not symbolically, during his final year in office. In July, for example, Obama spoke at a memorial service in Dallas, Texas—following the shooting of several police officers, where he drew attention to the racial divides in American society and articulated concerns expressed by the Black Lives Matter movement.[128] In his final public event as president, moreover—an address to the nation delivered from his hometown of Chicago—Obama rejected the notion of a "postracial" society, which some thought his election had augured, and called on all Americans to work for racial justice.[129] At the same time, he framed ongoing racial division as one of a series of threats to American democracy—including political polarization and apathy—and urged action to address them all.

The optics and oratory of this Farewell Address struck an oddly discordant note. On the one hand, it took place amid political defeat for the Democrats. Despite his efforts on behalf of Hillary Clinton and other co-partisans, Republican nominee Donald Trump had won election as Obama's successor, and Republicans retained control of the Congress. Obama's warnings of threats to American democracy perhaps channeled the fears of his more despondent supporters. Yet the setting in which he spoke had something of a triumphal quality. Unlike Eisenhower's famous Farewell Address—a short speech delivered straight to camera and broadcast from the White House—Obama's was a staged event at a Chicago convention center, where he delivered a lengthy speech to a large crowd.[130] In this, it was more reminiscent of a campaign rally—the crowd loudly registering its disapproval of the threats Obama identified, and cheering as he switched gears to recount the achievements of his administration. In some ways, this last act of the Obama administration reflected a longer-term trend in presidential travel: an emphasis on staging and showmanship that has reached new levels under President Donald Trump.

Conclusion

Eliot Cohen, a State Department counsellor during the George W. Bush administration, recently reflected that "[a]n administration in its last year resembles a small woodland creature reaching the end of its life, seeking only a quiet burrow in which to meet its demise."[131] It would "exhibit pointless twitches of frantic activity before the very end," he said, which "mostly involve extensive foreign travel to nice or particularly interesting places . . . But sooner or later you return to Washington, and there realize that your unglamorous duty consists chiefly in leaving the dog's breakfast of a policy in the least-desperate shape you can for the next team."[132] This disheartening description may capture something of the outgoing president's experience, but this chapter suggests there is a greater purpose to the "twitches of frantic activity" in which presidents engage as their terms draw to a close. In their travels at home and abroad, they do more than just gaze at the scenery—they offer a vision of their presidency and try to build their legacy, through rhetoric and imagery enhanced by each locale. Future research might consider how *effective* these efforts are—that is, the extent to which a president's own vision of their presidency, as constructed through travel, impacts immediate and enduring assessments of their legacy. But as suggested in this chapter, they engage in purposeful activity intended to bolster their prestige through international engagement, aiding their co-partisans in future elections, and highlighting the issues and achievements they hold most dear.

Notes

1. Charles Krauthammer, "While Obama Fiddles . . ." *Washington Post*, February 25, 2016.
2. Ibid. Krauthammer was referring to the January 2015 attack on the "Charlie Hebdo" offices in Paris, and the attack on the Bataclan nightclub in November of that year. Obama did lay a wreath outside the Bataclan later in November, while visiting Paris for UN talks on a climate change agreement. See "Paris Attacks: Obama Pays Respects at Bataclan Theatre," *BBC News*, November 30, 2015, <https://www.bbc.co.uk/news/world-europe-34960730> (accessed June 13, 2018).
3. Ibid.
4. An illustrative but by no means systematic sampling includes: Jennifer Loven, "Taxpayers Pay for Bush's Campaign Travel," *Washington Post*, August 30, 2006; D'Angelo Gore, "The Traveling President," *FactCheck.Org*, July 8, 2011, <https://www.factcheck.org/2011/07/the-traveling-president/> (accessed June 13, 2018); Jose A. DelReal, "Only Three Presidents Have Visited all 50 States in Office. Until

Now," *Washington Post*, May 7, 2015; Philip Bump, "Air Force One is a Heck of an Expensive Perk—for Taxpayers," *Washington Post*, July 5, 2016; Sarah Wheaton, "Secret Service Faces Massive Bill for Protecting Trump," *Politico*, December 3, 2016 <https://www.politico.com/story/2016/12/secret-service-faces-massive-bill-for-protecting-trump-232153> (accessed June 13, 2018); Karen Yourish and K.K. Rebecca Lai, "Trump Tops Obama, Bush and Clinton in Golfing and Private Getaways So Far," *New York Times*, April 28, 2017; Dan Merica, "Trump On Pace to Surpass 8 Years of Obama's Travel Spending in 1 Year," *CNN Politics*, April 11, 2017, <https://edition.cnn.com/2017/04/10/politics/donald-trump-obama-travel-costs/index.html> (accessed June 13, 2018). President Trump's penchant for visiting his own hotels and golf clubs has prompted extensive journalistic coverage, with the potential for self-enrichment adding an additional accountability dimension to tracking costs. See, for example, Jeremy Venook, "Why the Trumps' Travel Expenses Matter," *The Atlantic*, February 7, 2017.

5. Lammers (1982) and Kernell (1986/2007), for example, described public appearances outside of Washington, DC as an aspect of modern presidential communications strategies. King and Ragsdale (1988), Ragsdale (1994/2014), and Brace and Hinckley (1992, 1993) subsequently compiled and analyzed some quantitative data on twentieth-century presidential travel at home and abroad. These scholars tended to count days of travel, or number of presidential appearances, however, rather than the number of distinct locations visited, and to provide overall totals rather than more nuanced geographic analysis. See William Lammers, "Presidential Attention-Focusing Activities," in Doris A. Graber (ed.), *The President and the American Public* (Philadelphia: Institute for the Study of Human Issues, 1982), 145–71; Samuel Kernell, *Going Public: New Strategies of Presidential Leadership* (Washington, DC: CQ Press, 2007); Gary King and Lyn Ragsdale, *The Elusive Executive* (Washington, DC: CQ Press, 1988); Lyn Ragsdale, *Vital Statistics on the Presidency* (Washington, DC: CQ Press, 2014); Paul Brace and Barbara Hinckley, *Follow the Leader* (New York: Basic Books, 1992); Paul Brace and Barbara Hinckley, "Presidential Activities from Truman through Reagan: Timing and Impact," *The Journal of Politics* 55, no. 2 (May 1993): 382–98. See also Robert E. Darcy and Alvin Richman, "Presidential Travel and Public Opinion," *Presidential Studies Quarterly* 18, no. 1 (Winter 1988): 85–90; Jeffrey E. Cohen and Richard J. Powell, "Building Public

Support from the Grassroots Up: The Impact of Presidential Travel on State-Level Approval," *Presidential Studies Quarterly* 35, no. 1 (March 2005): 11–27. Some studies examine the impact of presidential travel on other concrete measures beyond public opinion, such as voting or the fortunes of co-partisans. See, for example, Jeffrey M. Jones, "Does Bringing out the Candidate Bring out the Votes? The Effects of Nominee Campaigning in Presidential Elections," *American Politics Research* 26, no. 4 (1998): 395–419; Patrick J. Sellers and Laura M. Denton, "Presidential Visits and Midterm Senate Elections," *Presidential Studies Quarterly* 36, no.3 (Summer 2006): 410–32. For a historical overview of presidential travel, see Ellis (2008), who traces its contours from the early Republic up to the second Bush administration. Richard J. Ellis, *Presidential Travel: The Journey from George Washington to George W. Bush* (Lawrence: University Press of Kansas, 2008).

6. There are a handful of strategic assessments touching on presidential travel, but they tend to examine limited timeframes (usually the last three months before an election), exclude more recent presidents, and use time-based rather than location-based measures. See, for example, Steven J. Brams and Morton D. Davis, "The 3/2's Rule in Presidential Campaigning," *The American Political Science Review* 68 no.1 (1974): 113–34; Claude S. Colantoni, Terrence J. Levesque, and Peter C. Ordeshook, "Campaign Resource Allocations Under the Electoral College," *The American Political Science Review* 69 no. 1 (1975): 141–54; Scott L. Althaus, Peter F. Nardulli, and Daron R. Shaw, "Candidate Appearances in Presidential Elections, 1972–2000," *Political Communication* 19 no. 1 (2002): 49–72; and Matthew Hoddie and Stephen R. Routh, "Predicting the Presidential Presence: Explaining Presidential Midterm Elections Campaign Behavior," *Political Research Quarterly* 57 No. 2 (2004): 257–65.

7. Brendan J. Doherty, "The Politics of the Permanent Campaign: Presidential Travel and the Electoral College, 1977–2004," *Presidential Studies Quarterly* 37, no. 4 (December 2007): 749–73; Brendan J. Doherty, *The Rise of the President's Permanent Campaign* (Lawrence: University Press of Kansas, 2012), Chapter 4, "Strategic Travel and the Permanent Campaign." Doherty counts days of travel and the number of individual events held in each state (including fundraisers), compiling this information from the *Public Papers of the Presidents*, published by the Government Printing Office.

8. Emily Jane Charnock, James A. McCann, and Kathryn Dunn Tenpas, "Presidential Travel from Eisenhower to George W. Bush:

An 'Electoral College' Strategy," *Political Science Quarterly* 124, no. 2 (Summer 2009): 323–39. Rather than counting "days" of travel or individual presidential appearances, individual locations were used as the basic unit of measurement here. Using the *Public Papers of the Presidents*, the authors tracked significant public activity by presidents in locations outside of Washington, DC. Typically this involved a speech or brief remarks to an audience, which are transcribed and appear in the Public Papers, but occasionally other activities were deemed sufficiently "public" or significant to be counted, such as throwing out the first pitch at a baseball game or awarding medals to injured service members. These activities are noted in the President's daily schedule, which is also included in the Public Papers (since the Carter administration, it has formed part of a weekly "Digest of Other White House Announcements"). Private activities such as a presidential vacation, or even a political fundraiser—if held at a private residence—were not counted. Further, since it functions much like a secondary White House (and activities there are not strategically related to the locale), trips to Camp David, MD, and other presidential retreats are also excluded from the data. This methodology counts multiple appearances in the same location as one "trip," unless the president engages in significant activity elsewhere between such appearances.

9. Ibid. 327.
10. Ibid. 336–37.
11. Emily J. Charnock, James A. McCann, and Kathryn Dunn Tenpas, "What to Expect in the Second Term: Presidential Travel and the Rise of Legacy-Building, 1957–2009," *Issues in Governance Studies* 54 (December 2012): 1–11. Doherty (2012) did also compile some second-term data (for Reagan, Clinton, and Bush), but he does not analyze the data separately, and due to publication dates, does not include the second term of Barack Obama.
12. Charnock et al. (2012) use electoral data from the previous election to determine "swing states"—defined as those a president won or lost by three percentage points or less. The electoral map may look different for a prospective successor, whether due to shifts in the political climate (indicated by polling), or particular geographic strengths or weaknesses they may have. As such, presidential travel might still reflect an electorally strategic dimension on behalf of a prospective successor that is not fully captured in the analysis.
13. Darcy and Richman (1988) noted that presidential visits overseas were widely believed to promote domestic support for the president.

14. Robert K. Murray and Tim H. Blessing, *Greatness in the White House: Rating the Presidents, from Washington through Ronald Reagan* (University Park: The Pennsylvania State University Press, 1994), 62.
15. A "trip" means a presidential visit to a distinct location, outside of Washington, DC, where the president engaged in one or more public activities. Following the methodology described in footnote 8 above, the trips discussed in this chapter all appear in the *Public Papers of the Presidents*—a compilation of presidential documents regularly published by the Government Printing Office (GPO). *Public Papers* from 1992 onward are available online through the GPO website, <https://www.gpo.gov> (accessed June 13, 2018). Earlier *Public Papers* have been compiled and made available online by Gerhard Peters and John T. Woolley, *The American Presidency Project*, <http://www.presidency.ucsb.edu> (accessed June 13, 2018). The travel data referenced in this chapter was compiled from the original *Public Papers*, either in hard copy or through the GPO website. For convenience, "American Presidency Project" links are often used when referencing presidential speeches or other remarks.
16. Since the overall figures include trips undertaken *after* Election Day, the emphasis on political travel before Election Day is likely higher.
17. On "going public" as a presidential communication strategy, see Kernell (2007).
18. These case studies are necessarily partial rather than comprehensive accounts of final-year travel, highlighting the most relevant trips from the perspective of the categories of analysis outlined above, and other notable activities.
19. Dwight D. Eisenhower, "Radio and Television Address to the American People on the Eve of South American Trip," February 21, 1960, *The American Presidency Project*, <http://www.presidency.ucsb.edu/ws/index.php?pid=12084> (accessed June 13, 2018).
20. "U-2 Incident Wrecks Paris Summit Meeting," *CQ Almanac* (Washington, DC: Congressional Quarterly, 1960). Eisenhower also made a brief visit to Portugal on this European trip.
21. Dwight D. Eisenhower, "Radio and Television Report to the American People on the Trip to the far East," June 27, 1960, *The American Presidency Project*, <http://www.presidency.ucsb.edu/ws/?pid=11850> (accessed June 13, 2018).
22. Ibid. Eisenhower suggested he had visited "twenty-seven nations of Europe, the Middle East, South Asia, North Africa, the Americas, and the far East . . . during the last ten months." Based on public activities,

the number within that period (from August, 1959) actually appears to be twenty-four (counting France on multiple occasions). If all of Eisenhower's foreign travel from the beginning of 1959 is included (when he visited Canada and Mexico), the total reaches twenty-six. The US Department of State's Office of the Historian, which provides some descriptive information on Eisenhower's foreign travels, adds a rest stop in the UK in September 1959, which would bring the total to twenty-seven (counting multiple trips to the UK and France separately). See "Dwight D. Eisenhower" (Presidential Travel Abroad), US Department of State—Office of the Historian, <https://history.state.gov/departmenthistory/travels/president/eisenhower-dwight-d> (accessed June 13, 2018).

23. Ibid.
24. In 1953, Eisenhower visited Canada and Bermuda. In 1954 he made no trips abroad. In 1955 he visited Iceland and Switzerland. In 1956 he traveled to Panama. In 1957 he visited Bermuda again and also France. In 1958 he returned to Canada, and in 1959 he visited Mexico and Canada once again.
25. Eisenhower was famously asked during a news conference if he could "give us an example of a major idea" of Nixon's that he had adopted as president. "If you give me a week, I might think of one. I don't remember," Eisenhower replied. Dwight D. Eisenhower, "The President's News Conference," August 24, 1960, *The American Presidency Project*, <http://www.presidency.ucsb.edu/ws/index.php?pid=11915> (accessed June 13, 2018).
26. Dwight D. Eisenhower, "Remarks at a Testimonial Dinner in Honor of Representative St. George, Bear Mountain State Park, New York," June 4, 1960, *The American Presidency Project*, <http://www.presidency.ucsb.edu/ws/index.php?pid=11810> (accessed June 13, 2018).
27. See Dwight D. Eisenhower, "Address 'Beyond the Campus' Delivered at the Commencement Exercises of the University of Notre Dame," June 5, 1960, *The American Presidency Project*, <http://www.presidency.ucsb.edu/ws/index.php?pid=11811> (accessed June 13, 2018).
28. Eisenhower signed the National Interstate and Defense Highways Act—creating the interstate system—on June 29, 1956, and on July 29, 1958 he signed legislation establishing NASA. On September 8, 1960, Eisenhower dedicated the George C. Marshall Space Flight Center in Huntsville, Alabama, and on October 18, 1960, he visited a new highway bridge in Red Wing, Minnesota. Eisenhower's legacy

was visibly stamped upon US interstate highways in 1993, when commemorative signs were introduced informing motorists they were traveling on the "Eisenhower Interstate System." Legislation in 1990 had officially renamed the highway system the "Dwight D. Eisenhower National System of Interstate and Defense Highways." See US Department of Transportation, Federal Highway Administration, "Interstate Frequently Asked Questions," <https://www.fhwa.dot.gov/interstate/faq.cfm#question23> (accessed June 13, 2018).

29. Dwight D. Eisenhower, "Remarks at the Dedication of the Hiawatha Bridge, Red Wing, Minnesota," October 18, 1960, *The American Presidency Project*, <http://www.presidency.ucsb.edu/ws/index.php?pid=11985> (accessed June 13, 2018).

30. Of the thirteen "policy-related" trips Eisenhower undertook in 1960–61, four highlighted foreign policy, five domestic policy, and four a combination of the two with an emphasis on foreign policy.

31. As Sidney Blumenthal explains, Reagan's campaign manager for his 1966 California gubernatorial bid "cut out many needless personal appearances at shopping malls and banquets, partly because Reagan tired and got irritable under a stressful schedule," but also because "[he] recognized that television could replace shaking voters' hands." Sidney Blumenthal, *The Permanent Campaign* (New York: Touchstone, 1982), 173. Similarly, in the 1980 campaign, "Reagan's handlers knew that their elderly candidate tired easily and that his performances were badly affected by fatigue," as Grossback, Peterson, and Stimson note. While the pace increased somewhat during the election year, they initially "sought to keep him fresh by running a long-distance media campaign and keeping the candidate rested for the later fray." Lawrence J. Grossback, David A.M. Peterson, and James A. Stimson, *Mandate Politics* (Cambridge University Press, 2006), n. 35.

32. Stanley Meisler, "Reagan Recants 'Evil Empire' Description," *Los Angeles Times*, June 1, 1988.

33. Ronald Reagan, "Radio Address to the Nation on the President's Trip to Mexico," February 13, 1988, *The American Presidency Project*, <http://www.presidency.ucsb.edu/ws/index.php?pid=35397> (accessed June 13, 2018).

34. Ronald Reagan, "Remarks at the United States Coast Guard Academy Commencement Ceremony in New London, Connecticut," May 18, 1988; "Remarks at a Seminar on Substance Abuse in the Workplace in Durham, North Carolina," February 8, 1988, *The American Presidency Project*, <http://www.presidency.ucsb.edu> (accessed June 13, 2018).

35. Ronald Reagan, "Remarks at the Nancy Reagan Drug Abuse Center Benefit Dinner in Los Angeles, California," January 4, 1989, *The American Presidency Project*, <http://www.presidency.ucsb.edu/ws/index.php?pid=35324> (accessed June 13, 2018).
36. For example, on March 28, 1988, Reagan visited Reynolds Aluminum Co. in Richmond, Virginia, where he discussed the business climate, job creation, and US economic success. He also emphasized the economy on August 8, 1988, in remarks at United States Precision Lens, Inc., in Cincinnati, Ohio.
37. Ronald Reagan, "Remarks and a Question-and-Answer Session with Students and Faculty at Oakton High School in Vienna, Virginia," March 24, 1988, *The American Presidency Project*, <http://www.presidency.ucsb.edu/ws/?pid=35597> (accessed June 13, 2018). In late January 1988, Reagan had visited Suitland High School in Maryland, a once underachieving school that had made a turnaround which he hoped to see replicated elsewhere. Two months later, he visited Oakton High School in Vienna, Virginia—a school nestled in the outer rim of Washington, DC's exurbs—and sounded similar themes. In October, he also visited high schools in Sterling Heights, Michigan, and Upper Darby, Pennsylvania, though his appearances here sounded more political themes relating to the upcoming election.
38. Ibid. Reagan's speech at Oakton mentioned the National Commission on Excellence in Education he had established during his first term, which published an influential report in 1983: "A Nation at Risk: The Imperative for Educational Reform." He referred also to a five-year progress report that would soon be published.
39. Ronald Reagan, "Remarks at the Annual Dinner of the Knights of Malta in New York, New York," January 13, 1989, *The American Presidency Project*, <http://www.presidency.ucsb.edu/ws/index.php?pid=35379> (accessed June 13, 2018).
40. Ronald Reagan, "Remarks at the WOC Radio Station Dedication Ceremony in Davenport, Iowa," July 14, 1988, *The American Presidency Project*, <http://www.presidency.ucsb.edu/ws/?pid=36120> (accessed June 13, 2018).
41. Rob Nixon, "Knute Rockne, All American," *TCM Film Article*, <http://www.tcm.com/this-month/article/102726%7C0/Knute-Rockne-All-American.html>.
42. Ronald Reagan, "Remarks at the Unveiling of the Knute Rockne Commemorative Stamp at the University of Notre Dame in Indiana," March 9, 1988, *The American Presidency Project*, <http://www.presidency.ucsb.edu/ws/?pid=35527> (accessed June 13, 2018).

43. Clinton's director of production was Josh King, who detailed his experiences in *Off Script: An Advance Man's Guide to White House Stagecraft, Campaign Spectacle, and Political Suicide* (St. Martin's Press, 2016).
44. Jane Perlez, "Clinton Begins Visit to India, But First Comes Bangladesh," *New York Times*, March 20, 2000.
45. Clinton only made one brief visit to a western hemisphere country in 2000–2001—Colombia, on August 30, 2000, where he highlighted US military assistance for its efforts to stop drug trafficking. He did not visit either of the NAFTA signatory countries—Canada or Mexico—in his final year. See Richard Chacon, "Colombia's Drug War Gets Boost from Clinton," *Boston Globe*, August 31, 2000.
46. William J. Clinton, "Remarks Following Discussions with President Olusegun Obasanjo of Nigeria and an Exchange with Reporters in Abuja, Nigeria," August 26, 2000; "Remarks at the Signing Ceremony for the Tanzania-United States Open Skies Agreement in Arusha, Tanzania," August 28, 2000, *The American Presidency Project*, <http://www.presidency.ucsb.edu> (accessed June 13, 2018).
47. Russell L. Riley, "Bill Clinton: Foreign Affairs," *University of Virginia Miller Center*, <https://millercenter.org/president/clinton/foreign-affairs> (accessed June 13, 2018).
48. Marc Lacey, "Clinton, Visiting Tanzania, Calls for Peace in Burundi," *New York Times*, August 29, 2000.
49. Clinton visited Vietnam following a trip to Brunei for the Asia-Pacific Economic Cooperation organization meeting. See William J. Clinton, "Interview with John King of CNN in Ho Chi Minh City," November 19, 2000, and "The President's Radio Address," November 18, 2000, *The American Presidency Project*, <http://www.presidency.ucsb.edu> (accessed June 13, 2018).
50. William J. Clinton, "Remarks to the People of Northern Ireland in Belfast," December 13, 2000, *The American Presidency Project*, <http://www.presidency.ucsb.edu/ws/index.php?pid=65345&st=&st1=> (accessed June 13, 2018). Clinton also visited Ireland and the mainland UK as part of this visit.
51. Clinton himself told reporters on board Air Force One that the trip was designed to have a positive psychological impact on the people of Northern Ireland, to give them a sense of the permanency of the peace process. See William J. Clinton, "Exchange with Reporters aboard Air Force One," December 14, 2000, *The American Presidency Project*, <http://www.presidency.ucsb.edu/ws/index.php?pid=942&st=&st1=> (accessed June 13, 2018).

52. Shepherdstown had "historical associations" which Clinton hoped "might focus Israeli and Syrian minds," a BBC correspondent explained. "It is in an area which was at the center of hostilities during the bloody American civil war in the 1860s." Richard Lister, "Peace Talks Town in the Spotlight," *BBC News*, January 7, 2000 <http://news.bbc.co.uk/1/hi/world/americas/594019.stm> (accessed June 13, 2018). Following the Shepherdstown talks in January, Clinton held a summit with Palestinian and Israeli representatives at Camp David in July. While of relevance to the discussion here, this trip is not included in the quantitative data, since (as mentioned in footnote 8), Camp David is an official presidential retreat which functions much like the White House. In October, Clinton convened a wider Middle East summit at Sharm al-Sheikh in Egypt.
53. For example, William J. Clinton, "Remarks at the Partners in History Dinner in New York City," September 11, 2000; "Remarks at an Israel Policy Forum Dinner in New York City," January 7, 2001, *The American Presidency Project*, <http://www.presidency.ucsb.edu> (accessed June 13, 2018).
54. William J. Clinton, "Remarks on the Job Access Initiative in Denver, Colorado," October 14, 2000, *The American Presidency Project*, <http://www.presidency.ucsb.edu/ws/?pid=1206> (accessed June 13, 2018).
55. William J. Clinton, "Remarks at Audubon Elementary School in Owensboro, Kentucky," May 3, 2000; "Remarks at Central High School in Davenport, Iowa," May 3, 2000; "Remarks at the City Academy in St. Paul, Minnesota," May 4, 2000; "Remarks in a Roundtable Discussion on Reforming America's Schools in Columbus, Ohio," May 4, 2000,*The American Presidency Project*, <http://www.presidency.ucsb.edu> (accessed June 13, 2018).
56. William J. Clinton, "Remarks at the Selfhelp Austin Street Senior Center in New York City," March 30, 2000; "Remarks at the David Barksdale Senior Center in Tampa," July 31, 2000, *The American Presidency Project*, <http://www.presidency.ucsb.edu> (accessed June 13, 2018).
57. William J. Clinton, "Remarks at the University of Missouri in Columbia, Missouri," July 6, 2000, *The American Presidency Project*, <http://www.presidency.ucsb.edu/ws/index.php?pid=1633&st=&st1=> (accessed June 13, 2018).
58. William J. Clinton, "Opening Remarks at Roundtable Discussion in Akron on Permanent Normal Trade Relations with China," May 12, 2000, *The American Presidency Project*, <http://www.presidency.ucsb.edu/ws/index.php?pid=58140&st=&st1=> (accessed June 13, 2018).

59. On April 13, 2000, for example, Clinton traveled to Denver, Colorado, for a gun safety rally—close to the one-year anniversary of the shootings in nearby Columbine. On April 12 he had traveled to Annapolis, Maryland, to attend a bill-signing ceremony for state gun control legislation which had just passed. On May 12 he met with Ohio representatives planning to attend the "Million Mom March," highlighting their push for gun safety. The march took place in Washington, DC on May 14—Mother's Day—and Clinton addressed the crowd. Clinton also touched on gun control in remarks at other appearances outside of Washington, DC in 2000–2001.
60. He visited parts of New York, Illinois, Michigan, North Carolina, Virginia, California, and New Mexico on this tour. The "New Markets" initiative aimed to spur investment in economically blighted areas, both urban and rural, through tax credits and other incentives. The idea was that economic growth and job creation went hand in hand, through the creation of new consumer markets: "the only way to keep the [economic] growth going without inflation is to find both new businesses and new employees and new customers at the same time." William J. Clinton, "Remarks at the Wall Street Project Conference in New York City," January 13, 2000, *The American Presidency Project*, <http://www.presidency.ucsb.edu/ws/?pid=58365> (accessed June 13, 2018).
61. See, for example, William J. Clinton, "Remarks to the People of the Navajo Nation in Shiprock, New Mexico," April 17, 2000, *The American Presidency Project*, <http://www.presidency.ucsb.edu/ws/?pid=58134> (accessed June 13, 2018).
62. William J. Clinton, "Remarks at a Discussion at the Ministers' Leadership Conference in South Barrington, Illinois," August 10, 2000, *The American Presidency Project*, <http://www.presidency.ucsb.edu/ws/index.php?pid=1485> (accessed June 13, 2018).
63. See, for example, Russell L. Riley, "Bill Clinton: Impact and Legacy," *University of Virginia Miller Center website*, <https://millercenter.org/president/clinton/impact-and-legacy> (accessed June 13, 2018). While NAFTA and welfare reform are featured prominently in this overview, the "new markets" legislation and congressional legislation approving normalized trade with China do not appear (the latter was not fully implemented until 2001).
64. Clinton, "Interview with John King of CNN in Ho Chi Minh City."
65. See, for example, William J. Clinton, "Remarks to the Granoff Forum at the University of Pennsylvania in Philadelphia, Pennsylvania," February 24, 2000. Clinton regularly referred to a "magic moment" of domestic prosperity and international peace, urging

Americans to make the most of this opportunity by supporting long-term investments in education, health, and social security. See Clinton, "Interview with Francine Kiefer and Skip Thurman of the *Christian Science Monitor* in Boston," January 18, 2000, *The American Presidency Project*, <http://www.presidency.ucsb.edu/ws/?pid=58520> (accessed June 13, 2018).

66. Of fifty-four events I classified as election-related in 2000–2001, only two appear to have promoted a senatorial candidate—a July reception and an October rally for Representative Ron Klink of Pennsylvania.
67. "Presidential Approval Ratings—Bill Clinton," *Gallup*, <http://www.gallup.com> (accessed June 13, 2018).
68. Melinda Henneberger and Don Van Natta Jr., "Once Close to Clinton, Gore Keeps a Distance," *New York Times*, October 20, 2000.
69. William J. Clinton, "Remarks to the Community in Dover, New Hampshire," January 11, 2001, *The American Presidency Project*, <http://www.presidency.ucsb.edu/ws/?pid=65045> (accessed June 13, 2018).
70. William J. Clinton, "Remarks at Northeastern University in Boston, Massachusetts," January 11, 2001, *The American Presidency Project*, <http://www.presidency.ucsb.edu/ws/?pid=63147> (accessed June 13, 2018).
71. William J. Clinton, "Remarks to a Joint Session of the Arkansas State Legislature in Little Rock, Arkansas," January 17, 2001, *The American Presidency Project*, <http://www.presidency.ucsb.edu/ws/?pid=73512> (accessed June 13, 2018).
72. See, for example, "Remarks Prior to a Discussion on Democracy and Development with Kuwaiti Women in Kuwait City, Kuwait," January 12, 2008. In Abu Dhabi, Bush delivered a major address on the advance of freedom in the Middle East, the need to combat extremism, the Israeli-Palestinian peace process, as well as Iraq and Iran. George W. Bush, "Remarks in Abu Dhabi, United Arab Emirates," January 13, 2008, *The American Presidency Project*, <http://www.presidency.ucsb.edu/ws/index.php?pid=76296&st=&st1=> (accessed June 13, 2018).
73. George W. Bush, "Address to Members of the Knesset in Jerusalem," May 15, 2008, *The American Presidency Project*, <http://www.presidency.ucsb.edu/ws/index.php?pid=77330&st=&st1=> (accessed June 13, 2018).
74. George W. Bush, "Remarks to Military Personnel at Camp Victory in Baghdad," December 14, 2008; "Remarks to Military Personnel at Bagram Air Base, Afghanistan," December 15, 2008; "The President's

News Conference With President Hamid Karzai of Afghanistan in Kabul, Afghanistan," December 15, 2008, *The American Presidency Project*, <http://www.presidency.ucsb.edu> (accessed June 13, 2018).

75. Bush delivered this speech on May 1, 2003. The USS *Abraham Lincoln* was docked off San Diego, and Bush had arrived by plane to land on the aircraft carrier. He delivered his remarks with a large banner in the background, emblazoned with "Mission Accomplished." In an interview late in his administration, Bush acknowledged that this banner had "conveyed the wrong message." Alexander Mooney, "Bush: 'Mission Accomplished' A Mistake," *CNN Politics*, November 12, 2008, <http://edition.cnn.com/2008/POLITICS/11/12/bush.regrets/index.html> (accessed June 13, 2018).

76. Eugene Robinson, "George W. Bush's Greatest Legacy—His Battle against AIDS," *Washington Post*, July 26, 2012.

77. See, for example, Stephen Collinson, "Jimmy Carter's Rewarding Post-Presidency," *CNN Politics*, August 20, 2015 <http://edition.cnn.com> (accessed June 13, 2018).

78. Jeffrey M. Jones, "History Usually Kinder to Ex-Presidents," *Gallup*, April 25, 2013 <http://news.gallup.com/poll/162044/history-usually-kinder-presidents.aspx> (accessed June 13, 2018).

79. "Presidential Approval Ratings—George W. Bush," *Gallup*, <http://www.gallup.com> (accessed June 13, 2018).

80. As mentioned in footnote 8, these fundraisers do not appear in the quantitative data since they took place in private homes.

81. See "Global Public Opinion in the Bush Years (2001–2008)," *Pew Research Center*, December 18, 2008, <http://www.pewglobal.org> (accessed June 13, 2018).

82. See, for example, George W. Bush, "Remarks on Malaria Awareness Day in Hartford," April 25, 2008; "Remarks on the War on Terror in Las Vegas, Nevada," January 31, 2008, *The American Presidency Project*, <http://www.presidency.ucsb.edu> (accessed June 13, 2018).

83. Much of Bush's post-election travel in late 2008 and early 2009 related directly or indirectly to the military and the War on Terror. Trips highlighting his role as Commander in Chief included a Military Appreciation Parade in Virginia, and a ceremony commissioning a new naval aircraft carrier: the USS *George H.W. Bush*, named for the president's father.

84. Alexander Mooney, "Bush Calls Katrina Photo 'Huge Mistake,'" *CNN Politics*, November 6, 2010 <http://politicalticker.blogs.cnn.com/2010/11/06/bush-calls-katrina-photo-huge-mistake/> (accessed June 13, 2018). Hurricane Katrina made landfall in the US on

August 29, 2005. The photograph was taken on August 31 as Air Force One flew over the Gulf Coast. Bush toured the city of New Orleans in person on September 12 and made several subsequent visits to the area.

85. George W. Bush, "Commencement Address at Greensburg High School in Greensburg, Kansas," May 4, 2008, *The American Presidency Project*, <http://www.presidency.ucsb.edu/ws/index.php?pid=77292> (accessed June 13, 2018).

86. On September 1, for example, he was briefed at the Emergency Operations Center in Austin, Texas, and then again on September 3 in Baton Rouge, Louisiana. On September 16 he returned to Texas, and was briefed on recovery efforts from Hurricane Ike. In all cases he made public remarks following the briefings.

87. Bush visited both New Orleans and Gulfport, Mississippi, on August 20 to highlight reconstruction efforts.

88. Bush signed the No Child Left Behind Act into law on January 8, 2002. For remarks during these visits, see George W. Bush, "Remarks at Horace Greeley Elementary School in Chicago, Illinois," January 7, 2008; "Remarks on the No Child Left Behind Act in Philadelphia, Pennsylvania," January 8, 2009, *The American Presidency Project*, <http://www.presidency.ucsb.edu> (accessed June 13, 2018).

89. These projects were the "Jericho Program" in Baltimore, which he visited in January 2008, and the "Mentoring Children of Prisoners Initiative," in Greensboro, North Carolina, which he visited in December 2008.

90. Bush called for a temporary worker program in 2004, and made a comprehensive immigration reform bill the centerpiece of his State of the Union Address in 2007. Both initiatives failed to pass in Congress. See Camille J. Bosworth, "Note: Guest Worker Policy: A Critical Analysis of President Bush's Proposed Reform," *Hastings Law Journal* 56, no. 5 (May 2005): 1095–1120; Donna Smith, "Senate Kills Bush Immigration Reform Bill," *Reuters*, June 29, 2007.

91. A minor exception here is energy policy, where Bush urged Congress to lift a ban on oil exploration in the "Outer Continental Shelf" and potentially expand domestic oil exploration, and also cut regulation surrounding the building of refineries. He did this in two speeches, though this initiative did not appear as concrete or extensive as those pushed by Clinton in his final year. See George W. Bush, "Remarks at Lincoln Electric Company in Euclid, Ohio," July 29, 2008; "Remarks to the West Virginia Coal Association in White Sulphur Springs, West Virginia," July 31, 2008, *The American Presidency Project*, <http://www.presidency.ucsb.edu> (accessed June 13, 2018).

92. As finally passed by Congress, and signed by President Bush on February 13, the stimulus package was worth $168 billion over two years, with most earmarked for 2008. Jeremy Pelofsky, "Bush Signs Stimulus Bill and Cites Economic Resilience," *Reuters*, February 13, 2008.
93. Prior to passage of the Economic Stimulus Act in 2008, for example, Bush visited the Robinson Helicopter Company in Torrance, California and Hallmark Cards, Inc. in Kansas City, Missouri, as well as making a major speech urging action in Chicago (January 30, February 1, and January 7, 2008 respectively). After its passage in early February, Bush made a speech to the Economic Club of New York, and participated in a question-and-answer session (March 14). He then visited two small businesses to highlight the impact of the stimulus: ColorCraft in Sterling, Virginia and the Silverado Cable Company in Mesa, Arizona (March 26 and May 27, respectively). On May 27, he also made remarks on the national economy and participated in a question-and-answer session in Maryland Heights, Missouri.
94. The HOPE NOW alliance was created in 2007, as the subprime mortgage crisis took hold. See George W. Bush, "Remarks Following a Tour of Novadebt in Freehold, New Jersey," March 28, 2008; "Remarks Following a Roundtable Discussion on Housing Counseling in North Little Rock, Arkansas," July 1, 2008, *The American Presidency Project*, <http://www.presidency.ucsb.edu> (accessed June 13, 2018).
95. The acute phase of the financial crisis began with the placement of Fannie Mae and Freddie Mac—the government-sponsored mortgage companies—into federal conservatorship on September 6, and the collapse of Lehman Brothers on September 15. After signing the Troubled Asset Relief Program (TARP) into law on October 3, Bush went to San Antonio and talked with small-business owners about the effects of the credit crunch, and how the TARP would begin to help soon. On October 7, he made extensive remarks on the national economy and participated in a question-and-answer session at a small business in Chantilly, Virginia (Guernsey Office Products). Also in October, Bush met with business leaders in Ada, Michigan, and spoke with reporters afterward about his message—that the economic rescue plan was sufficient, temporary, and helpful to small-business owners. A few days later, Bush met with business leaders in Alexandria, Louisiana, and conveyed similar themes—that despite being a

"market-oriented president" he had urged government action because the crisis *was not* confined to Wall Street. He emphasized that the program was temporary, would not waste taxpayer's money, and would provide assistance to small businesses. See George W. Bush, "Remarks Following a Meeting With Business Leaders and an Exchange With Reporters in Ada, Michigan," October 15, 2008; "Remarks Following a Meeting With Business Leaders in Alexandria, Louisiana," October 20, 2008, *The American Presidency Project*, <http://www.presidency.ucsb.edu> (accessed June 13, 2018).

96. Bush delivered an address to the nation from the White House on September 24, just before signing the TARP on October 3. He also discussed the law in remarks from the Rose Garden on October 10 and 14, among other appearances.
97. In contrast, Bill Clinton's daughter Chelsea left for college in 1997, early in her father's second term, while Jenna and Barbara Bush were already in college when their father, George W. Bush, took office in early 2001.
98. While Eisenhower had access to a jet aircraft in the last year of his presidency, John F. Kennedy was the first to enjoy exclusive use of a dedicated jet especially designed for the president.
99. On August 20, 2016, for example, the White House Instagram account reposted a 2015 picture of Obama with explorer Bear Grylls in Alaska, to mark "World Photo Day." It was originally posted on September 2, 2015 (and was reposted previously on December 18, 2015). On August 29 they posted a picture of Obama at Yosemite National Park, taken back in June, side by side with a picture of President Theodore Roosevelt visiting the park in 1903. The post marked the centenary of the National Park Service. On August 30, 2016, also to mark the centenary, the White House Instagram posted a 2009 picture of Obama at the Grand Canyon, urging followers to visit a Medium.com link which featured a montage of "POTUS in Parks" photographs. An archive of the Obama White House Instagram account is maintained by the US National Archives and Records Administration (NARA), available at <https://www.instagram.com/obamawhitehouse> (accessed June 13, 2018).
100. In a rare foray by a US president into the domestic politics of another country, Obama warned that the UK would find itself at the "back of the queue" for a trade deal with the US, if it left the European Union. "Barack Obama: Brexit Would Put UK 'Back of the Queue' for Trade Talks," *Guardian*, April 22, 2016.

101. See, for example, Barack Obama, "Remarks in Hanoi, Vietnam," May 24, 2016, *The American Presidency Project*, <http://www.presidency.ucsb.edu/ws/?pid=117720> (accessed June 13, 2018).
102. See, for example, John Bolton, "Obama's Shameful Apology Tour Lands in Hiroshima," *New York Post*, May 26, 2016; Karl Rove, "The President's Apology Tour," *Wall Street Journal*, April 23, 2009. For overviews of this narrative see Callum Borchers, "Obama's Trip to Hiroshima, and the Looming 'Apology Tour' Narrative," *Washington Post*, May 10, 2016; Edward-Isaac Dovere, "Obama's 'Apology' Complex," *Politico*, May 22, 2016; Amanda Marcotte, "Conservatives Return to the 'Obama Apology Tour' Myth," *Salon*, May 31, 2016.
103. Jacob Weisberg, "Why Obama Is Going to Hiroshima," *Slate*, May 16, 2016.
104. Mark Landler, "Obama Acknowledges Scars of America's Shadow War in Laos," *New York Times*, September 6, 2016.
105. Mark Landler, "For Obama, an Unexpected Legacy of Two Full Terms at War," *New York Times*, May 14, 2016.
106. Richard Wike, Jacob Poushter, Hani Zainulbhai, "As Obama Years Draw to Close, President and US Seen Favorably in Europe and Asia," *Pew Research Center*, June 29, 2016 <http://www.pewglobal.org> (accessed June 13, 2018).
107. "Obama's Speech in Berlin," *New York Times*, July 24, 2008.
108. Jeffrey M. Jones, "Obama Averages 47.9% Job Approval as President," *Gallup*, January 20, 2017 <http://www.gallup.com> (accessed June 13, 2018).
109. Seventeen of Obama's twenty-three election-related trips in 2016–17 involved rallies for (and on one occasion a fundraiser for) Hillary Clinton.
110. Of course, both the 2000 and 2016 presidential elections produced popular vote victories for Democratic candidates, but losses in the Electoral College.
111. Barack Obama, "Remarks on the Patient Protection and Affordable Care Act in Milwaukee, Wisconsin," March 3, 2016 <https://www.gpo.gov/fdsys/pkg/DCPD-201600121/content-detail.html> (accessed June 13, 2018).
112. Barack Obama, "Remarks on the Patient Protection and Affordable Care Act in Miami, Florida," October 20, 2016 <http://www.presidency.ucsb.edu/ws/?pid=119525> (accessed June 13, 2018).
113. Barack Obama, "Remarks at a Campaign Rally for Democratic Presidential Nominee Hillary Rodham Clinton in Miami Gardens,

Florida," October 20, 2016. <https://www.gpo.gov/fdsys/pkg/DCPD-201600713/content-detail.html> (accessed June 13, 2018).

114. In June 2012, for example, Obama issued an executive directive establishing the "Deferred Action for Childhood Arrivals" (DACA) program. Following the failure of congressional legislation, it provided some protection against deportation and temporary work authorization for undocumented immigrants brought to the US as children. In November 2014, Obama expanded this program as part of a wider set of "executive actions" on immigration, which also granted protections to the undocumented parents of US citizens and permanent residents. In January 2016, Obama also signed a set of "executive actions" which tightened certain types of gun sale and expanded background checks. These "executive actions" were not legally binding "executive orders," but operational directives to the executive branch. See Max Ehrenfreund, "Your Complete Guide to Obama's Immigration Executive Action," *Washington Post*, November 20, 2014; Eric Bradner and Gregory Krieg, "Emotional Obama Calls for 'Sense of Urgency' to Fight Gun Violence," *CNN Politics*, January 6, 2016 <https://edition.cnn.com/2016/01/05/politics/obama-executive-action-gun-control/index.html> (accessed June 13, 2018).

115. On June 16, 2016, Obama did briefly mention gun control in his remarks in Orlando, Florida, following the attack on the Pulse nightclub, but highlighting his executive actions was not the main purpose of this visit. Barack Obama, "Remarks on the Shootings in Orlando, Florida," June 12, 2016. On the fate of Obama's immigration plans, see Adam Liptak and Michael D. Shear, "Supreme Court Tie Blocks Obama Immigration Plan," *New York Times*, June 23, 2016.

116. Gardiner Harris, "President Obama and Family Tour 'Cool' Carlsbad Caverns," *New York Times*, June 17, 2016; Sammy Roth, "Why Obama is visiting Yosemite and Carlsbad Caverns," *The Desert Sun*, June 16, 2016.

117. Barack Obama, "Remarks at Yosemite National Park, California," June 18, 2016, <https://www.gpo.gov> (accessed June 13, 2018).

118. Harris, "President Obama and Family Tour 'Cool' Carlsbad Caverns."

119. Obama addressed the Lake Tahoe Summit on August 31 and the World Conservation Congress in Honolulu later that same day. He visited Midway Island on September 1. In the environmental policy areas noted here there is a more established role for executive

discretion: according to various statutes in the case of public lands, and the Constitution in regard to foreign relations. Nonetheless, the Paris accord was negotiated as an "executive agreement" rather than a treaty, which would have required Senate approval, and thus ventured into more unilateral territory. See Noah Feldman, "The Paris Accord and the Reality of Presidential Power," *Bloomberg News*, June 2, 2017, <https://www.bloomberg.com> (accessed June 13, 2018). In addition, Obama sought to pursue some of his climate change objectives through executive orders, on emissions standards for example. See "Regulation Database—Executive Orders," *Columbia Law School—Sabin Center for Climate Change Law*, <http://columbiaclimatelaw.com> (accessed June 13, 2018).

120. Indeed, it was this expansion that underpinned Obama's claim to have protected more land *and water* than any other president. Barack Obama, "Remarks on the Expansion of the Papahānaumokuākea Marine National Monument on Midway Atoll," September 1, 2016, <https://www.gpo.gov/fdsys/pkg/DCPD-201600548/pdf/DCPD-201600548.pdf> (accessed June 13, 2018); "Fact Sheet: President Obama to Create the World's Largest Marine Protected Area," Obama White House press release, August 26, 2016.

121. Barack Obama, "Remarks Announcing the United States Formal Entry into the United Nations Framework Convention on Climate Change Paris Agreement in Hangzhou, China," September 3, 2016, <https://www.gpo.gov/fdsys/pkg/DCPD-201600556/content-detail.html> (accessed June 13, 2018).

122. Barack Obama, "Remarks to the Illinois General Assembly in Springfield, Illinois," February 10, 2016 <https://www.gpo.gov/fdsys/pkg/DCPD-201600062/content-detail.html> (accessed June 13, 2018).

123. On the "post-partisan" dimension of Obama's appeal, see Sidney M. Milkis, Jesse H. Rhodes, and Emily J. Charnock, "What Happened to Post-Partisanship? Barack Obama and the New American Party System," *Perspectives on Politics* 10, no. 1 (March 2012): 57–76.

124. Obama, "Remarks to the Illinois General Assembly in Springfield, Illinois."

125. Ibid.

126. At time of writing, Obama has not deployed OFA as a personal advocacy vehicle, and has not yet fully embraced the political post-presidency he outlined, though he has spoken out on some issues. See Sidney M. Milkis and John W. York, "If the Obama

Presidency is Winding Down, Why is His Group Organizing for Action Ramping Up?" *Washington Post*, July 29, 2015; Krissah Thompson and Juliet Eilperin, "Two Months Out of Office, Barack Obama is Having a Post-Presidency Like No Other," *Washington Post*, March 26, 2017; Edward-Isaac Dovere, "Obama's Carefully Political Post-Presidency," *Politico*, May 4, 2017; Edward-Isaac Dovere, "Obama's Army Takes on Trump," *Politico*, August 6, 2017.

127. Barack Obama, "Commencement Address at Howard University," May 7, 2016 <https://www.gpo.gov/fdsys/pkg/DCPD-201600304/pdf/DCPD-201600304.pdf> (accessed June 13, 2018).

128. Barack Obama, "Remarks at a Memorial Service for Victims of the Shootings in Dallas, Texas," July 12, 2016 <https://www.gpo.gov/fdsys/pkg/DCPD-201600461/content-detail.html> (accessed June 13, 2018). Obama's relationship with the "Black Lives Matter" movement was complex, with some activists frustrated by his emphasis on political engagement rather than protest. Obama had faced criticism early in his presidency for appearing reluctant to publicly address questions of race in American society—as he had so powerfully in his Philadelphia speech during the 2008 campaign. His 2015 eulogy in Charleston, South Carolina—following the shooting of several African Americans by a white nationalist gunman—has been seen as a turning point, where Obama increasingly "led a national conversation on race." Michael D. Shear and Yamiche Alcindor, "Jolted by Deaths, Obama Found His Voice on Race," *New York Times*, January 14, 2017.

129. Barack Obama, "Farewell Address to the Nation from Chicago, Illinois," January 10, 2017 <https://www.gpo.gov/fdsys/pkg/DCPD-201700008/pdf/DCPD-201700008.pdf> (accessed June 13, 2018).

130. For word count comparisons, see Gerhard Peters, "Presidential Farewell Addresses," *The American Presidency Project*, <http://www.presidency.ucsb.edu/farewell_addresses.php> (accessed June 13, 2018).

131. Eliot Cohen, "They Won't Miss You When You're Gone," *The American Interest*, January 5, 2016.

132. Ibid.

8

Reflecting or reshaping?: Landmark anniversaries and presidential legacy

Mark McLay

On February 7, 1909, the *Chicago Tribune* printed what they deemed the "The Great Issue of the World's Greatest Paper." Weighing in at a mighty 3¼ pounds, this Sunday edition of the *Tribune* composed 194 pages, and placed prominently on the front page a cartoon depicting a young boy in a rocking chair excitedly reading "The Story of Lincoln." Underneath the drawing, the *Tribune* mused that "Somewhere in this country today there is an unknown boy who will be the country's greatest living man forty years from now."[1] Undoubtedly, with the 100th anniversary celebrations of Lincoln's birth fast approaching, the editors were making it clear where the newspaper proudly stood on the "Great Emancipator's" legacy. Two days later, the nation (parts of the white South excepted) followed suit. In Chicago, businesses shut down to enable the public to attend special centennial events, including a speech by the president of Princeton University, Woodrow Wilson.[2] In New York, one million people took part in Lincoln celebrations, while in Kentucky, President Theodore Roosevelt gave a moving speech before laying the cornerstone of a new Lincoln Memorial. Beyond American shores, the Brazilian navy ordered a 21-gun salute to "that noble martyr of moral and neighborly love."[3] Caught up in the Lincoln haze, scholars also churned out Lincoln books and poets penned odes to a great man. And perhaps most significantly, the National Association for the Advancement of Colored People (NAACP) was officially formed on February 12, 1909—exactly one hundred years since Honest

Abe's birth.[4] The Lincoln Centenary, it is fair to say, was not a small affair.

Presidential anniversaries, and the way American society chooses to mark them, reveal a great deal about presidential legacy. Nevertheless, the scholar Merrill D. Peterson observes that "The commemoration of the one hundredth anniversary of Lincoln's birth was one of those events that took up more space in the actual observance than it would in the historical record."[5] Indeed, while historians have lavished attention on the popular outpouring of grief that trailed Lincoln's body as it made its winding journey from Washington, DC to Springfield, Illinois in 1865, they have not given similar consideration to the Lincoln Centenary. Yet both events reveal much about Lincoln's legacy during the time in which they took place. The former unearthed a surprising swell of affection for a leader whose popular mandate had appeared in question only a few months earlier, while the latter confirmed that this emotional attachment had only continued to grow in the decades since the sixteenth president's final journey home. Lincoln's legacy, the centennial celebrations confirmed, had only been enhanced by the passage of time and for many Americans he was without doubt their greatest president.

Just as he was an exceptional president, Lincoln is also an exceptional case. Most presidents have not, and never will, enjoy such reverence on similar anniversaries. One million New Yorkers did not pause to commemorate William Howard Taft's centennial and it is unlikely that the Brazilian navy will be on standby to celebrate Rutherford B. Hayes's upcoming 200th birthday. Still, even those presidents who do not enjoy substantial veneration often provoke smaller-scale remembrance activities during landmark anniversaries. For example, plans are afoot in Warren Harding's hometown of Marion, Ohio to build a Harding Presidential Center as part of the Harding 2020 project to mark one hundred years since his ascension to the nation's highest office.[6] It is doubtful, however, that many beyond Marion's confines will flock to commemorate a president best remembered for an array of scandals and his romantic dalliances. Even so, those presidential anniversaries that are muted affairs reveal much about presidential legacy. The nation, by failing to remember significant anniversaries, is often saying just as much as the *Chicago Tribune* was when it printed 194 pages in memory of Lincoln.

For those that are remembered intensely, this article will argue that such anniversaries can trigger a reassessment of a president's legacy or they can simply confirm that the original legacy remains firmly in place. In most cases, it is the latter—celebrations that *reflect* a presidential legacy, but do little to alter it. Nevertheless, in some rare cases, presidential anniversaries can *reshape* a presidential legacy. Lyndon B. Johnson's recent reassessment following a spate of landmark anniversaries is one such example of this phenomenon and will be discussed extensively as a case study below. In addition to Johnson, this article will briefly examine the most prominent anniversary celebrations, including those relating to George Washington, Thomas Jefferson, Franklin D. Roosevelt, and Ronald Reagan, as well as the myriad of anniversaries devoted to John F. Kennedy. Of all these anniversaries, it is clear that only Jefferson and Johnson—and perhaps Reagan—had their legacy reshaped in some way during anniversary activities, but the anniversaries of Washington, Franklin Roosevelt, and Kennedy provide an insight into their legacies as well as contemporary political divides and the evolving state of the media in the United States. Presidential landmark anniversaries therefore, in reflecting or reshaping presidential legacies, are illustrative of larger trends in American politics and society.

Celebrating landmark anniversaries

Presidents are remembered and reassessed through various anniversary landmarks, most obviously those occasions associated with a president's birth or death. More tangential, but no less frequent, are anniversaries that mark the passage of significant legislation or the outbreak of a war with which a president is associated. Sometimes these celebrations are not even related to events that occurred during the individual's presidency. For instance, George Washington was minted on a coin in 1876 during the nation's centennial, while one scholar argues that celebrations to mark the War of 1812's centennial did much to cement Andrew Jackson's legacy as a heroic figure in American history. Both of those events took place before either man had ascended to the nation's highest office, however.[7] Some commemorations make bizarre use of anniversaries, like the decision to release a 100th anniversary special edition "Teddy bear" which, upon squeezing its paw, told "T.R.'s" story.[8]

Beyond simply offering an insight into a president's legacy, presidential anniversaries offer a window into contemporary political divides. This was especially true of the nation's first president, George Washington. In 1832, preparations for the centennial of Washington's birth exposed sectional tensions that were already rife in the young nation. As the anniversary approached, Senator Henry Clay suggested that Congress mark the occasion by disinterring Washington's body from its resting place in Mount Vernon, Virginia, and moving it into the Capitol building. Southerners, rather than critiquing Clay's plan for being a bit odd, instead charged Clay and those supporting the resolution with attempting a Northern power grab by the federal government against Virginia and the South. Future president and proud Virginian John Tyler argued—in what was meant as a compliment—that Washington's body was a "state relic."[9] Thankfully, common sense prevailed and the fierce debate was cut short when Washington's ancestors refused the federal application. Despite the controversy, it was widely reported that Washington's centennial was celebrated by Americans in the spirit of national unity and patriotism for which it was intended.[10] While Washington's anniversary exposed the frailties in the nation he helped build, ultimately his centennial reflected the esteem in which he continued to be held by most Americans.

Washington's fellow Founding Father, Thomas Jefferson, however, had not been so universally appreciated in the years following his death. Nonetheless, his bicentennial offered the perfect moment to rehabilitate the third president. As Francis Cogliano outlines, Jefferson's legacy had been damaged by both the Civil War and the process of industrialization in the United States. The former event had brought to the forefront Jefferson's slave ownership and his views on states' rights, while the latter had undermined his vision of an agrarian America—instead boosting the legacy of his great rival, Alexander Hamilton.[11] Jefferson's 200th birthday would bring with it the chance to reshape this damaged legacy.

In 1943, with the United States embroiled in World War II, Jefferson became an avatar of American values of freedom and democracy. Fresh from having his faced carved onto Mount Rushmore, the 1940s would prove the "age of Jefferson monuments" as America's Enlightenment man resurfaced to aid the battle against the darkness of the Third Reich and Japanese militarism.[12] During his bicentennial year, the Jefferson Memorial was opened in Washington, DC and was quickly followed by a six-volume biography that cemented Jefferson's reputation as an American icon for the age.[13] In this instance, Jefferson's anniversary had coincided with the ideal moment for his legacy to enjoy a resurgence in popular and academic opinion. Of course, in Jefferson's case, the hagiographic reshaping of his legacy proved temporary, and his legacy would evolve again in the 1960s towards a more critical view.[14] Still, the Jefferson Memorial in Washington, DC is a permanent reminder of how the nation chose to celebrate his bicentennial. As President Franklin Roosevelt noted in his remarks at the opening of the memorial: "To Thomas Jefferson, Apostle of Freedom, we are paying a debt long overdue . . . for our generation of Americans can understand much in Jefferson's life which intervening generations could not see as well as we."[15] Roosevelt's comments once again emphasized the importance of the bicentennial's context to the reshaping of Jefferson's legacy.

In 1982, Roosevelt himself was subject to a contentious centennial celebration. Far from coming together in a spirit of harmony to remember FDR, the occasion proved an outlet for contemporary political disputes. Gathering at Roosevelt's old Hudson River estate, the Governor of New York, Hugh Carey, used the occasion to take a swipe at President Ronald Reagan's slashing of social welfare programs. Declaring "we need [FDR] now more than ever," Carey caustically noted, "Franklin Roosevelt gave us the New Deal, but now we are getting the fast shuffle."[16] Meanwhile, Franklin Roosevelt Jr. refused to attend a White House ceremony honoring his father's centennial in protest that Reagan was whittling away FDR's programs.[17] Speaking at those celebrations, Reagan protested, "This is not a political gathering. It's a celebration of a great man who led our nation through historic times." Moreover, Reagan—an avowed admirer of FDR—sought to create a link between himself and his erstwhile hero. Noting that legendary columnist Walter Lippmann had initially described Roosevelt as "a pleasant man, who, without any important qualifications for the office, would very much like to be President," Reagan, the former actor, joked that "Forgive me but now and then I think I've been hearing an echo."[18]

Reagan did, however, attempt to use FDR's centennial to justify his own actions, just as Roosevelt had looked to Jefferson in the 1940s. Having used his inaugural address to declare that government—which Roosevelt had done much to expand—was no longer the solution to American problems, Reagan suggested that FDR would have acted similarly if he had been in the Oval Office in the 1980s. "[Americans are] a practical people with an inborn sense of proportion," Reagan told his audience. "We sense when things have gone too far, when the time has come to make fundamental changes. Franklin Roosevelt was that kind of a person, too." Moreover, the 40th president had no doubt that the 32nd president would have supported increased pressure on the Soviet Union's "evil empire." Reagan asserted that "Like Franklin Roosevelt we know that for free men hope will always be a stronger force than fear, that we only fail when we allow ourselves to be boxed in by the limitations and errors of the past."[19] Later that year, Reagan signed a bill authorizing the creation of a Roosevelt memorial in the Tidal Basin, although the legislation included no government funding to begin construction. As historian William Leuchtenburg wryly notes, "No expression of the baffling, labyrinthine relationship of Ronald Reagan and Franklin Roosevelt could have been more fitting."[20]

Still, Reagan's attempt to wrap himself in FDR's legacy during the centennial celebrations stood in stark contrast to his conservative colleagues, many of whom were repulsed by the very idea of celebrating the president who gave rise to the American welfare state. Despite a Democratic Congress appropriating $7 million for former president Herbert Hoover's centenary in 1974, a more conservative Congress restricted funding for his more illustrious successor to $25,000. The *National Review* even lampooned proposed FDR celebrations, speculating that if the organizers truly sought to remember Roosevelt then the centennial would be "bureaucratic . . . unconstitutional, more expensive than any before, and perpetual so that our children's children can help pay for it a hundred years from now."[21] All things considered, the Roosevelt Centennial showed that FDR continued to inspire either adoration or loathing among Americans—albeit with more of the former than the latter—just as his presidency had when it began fifty years previously. The centennial celebrations merely reflected this legacy, rather than offering a reassessment or appreciation of America's longest-serving president.

In 2011, Ronald Reagan's centennial took place in a media landscape that had shifted dramatically over the three decades since the "Gipper" had honored Roosevelt. The *Washington Post*, for instance, devoted an entire section of their website to evaluating Reagan's life and legacy. Little effort was spared in a climate where content was king and the *Post*'s coverage included everything from opinion columns to a live Q&A with Reagan historians, an online quiz, and articles which asked "Is Obama like Reagan?" and "How 2012 [Republican presidential candidate] hopefuls can claim the Reagan mantle," or the helpful, "What's named after Reagan where you live?"[22] *LIFE* magazine compiled two separate online galleries of photographs to mark Reagan's life and released them as special collections to purchase on Amazon.[23] Meanwhile, a vastly increased range of television channels meant that there were more biographical documentaries to mark a president's centennial than ever before. While Roosevelt's centenary received one documentary, Reagan's centennial was marked with separate documentaries on HBO, the History Channel, and PBS. Over on the twenty-four-hour news channels, Reagan's centennial was also a goldmine for news directors. Reflecting the esteem in which conservatives continued to hold Reagan, Fox News entitled one segment: "A Truly Beautiful Human Being."[24] For a media consumer in February 2011, it would have been quite the accomplishment to avoid Reagan centennial coverage.

While Congress had dragged its heels over FDR's centennial, it showed no reluctance for Reagan. In 2009, a Democratic-controlled Congress passed an act, then signed by President Barack Obama, that created a twelve-member bipartisan Centennial Commission—containing members running the ideological gambit from liberal senator Dianne Feinstein to conservative commentator Peggy Noonan—to develop plans to celebrate the anniversary.[25]

LANDMARK ANNIVERSARIES AND PRESIDENTIAL LEGACY

The Ronald Reagan Foundation was also able to raise substantial sums of money for the celebration, including a $15 million donation from Reagan's old employers, General Electric.[26] Out of these efforts sprung a new Ronald Reagan stamp, a rock concert, and even a Reagan Centennial NASCAR show car. More traditionally, an extravagant gala to celebrate Reagan's life also took place in Washington, DC.[27] Beyond such official events, Americans in Pasadena, California had already led a 55-foot float featuring black-and-white photographs of Reagan, while in Eastern Europe, cities hoisted statues to commemorate Reagan's contribution to bringing about the Cold War's end. To top it all off, Reagan received a video homage during America's most watched event—the Super Bowl.[28]

For all the noise made around Reagan's centennial, what did it actually mean for his legacy? Perhaps given the recent nature of Reagan's passing (he died in 2004 after a long battle with Alzheimer's), and with his widow Nancy Reagan heavily involved in events, there was less of the rancour on display that had been seen in FDR's centennial. If anything, there was a hint that Reagan's legacy was undergoing a change among his former Democratic opponents. Following the Republican Party's lurching to the right during the 2010 midterm elections, Democrats were especially keen to portray the new Grand Old Party (GOP) as being too extreme, even for Ronald Reagan. While this did not involve embracing all aspects of the Gipper's legacy, it meant a softening towards their old nemesis. Indeed, during the lead up to the centennial celebrations, Obama's staff let it be known that the current president was reading a sympathetic Reagan biography.[29] Meanwhile, for Republicans, the centennial celebrations saw GOP presidential candidates jostle for the position of Reagan Admirer-in-Chief. Former Speaker Newt Gingrich ultimately took the prize when, during the centennial, he toured with a hagiographic documentary, *Ronald Reagan: Rendezvous with Destiny*, hosted and narrated by Gingrich and his wife.[30] Ultimately, Reagan's legacy was not fundamentally reshaped, especially for conservatives who continued to adore him, although it was not entirely unaltered by his centennial.

John F. Kennedy represents an oddity when it comes to how his anniversaries have unfolded. For a presidency that achieved comparatively little, Kennedy's legacy has been boosted by consistent bursts of anniversary remembrance since his tragic death.

Historian Mark White's analysis of JFK's cultural legacy (published fifty years after Kennedy's assassination itself) reveals the spurts of media and scholarly output that coincide with ten-year intervals from Kennedy's short presidency.[31] For instance, the *Kennedy* television miniseries starring Martin Sheen as JFK first aired on November 20, 1983, almost exactly twenty years since his assassination. Fifty years on from his inauguration, *The Kennedys* (2011) cast a more critical eye over JFK on the small screen. Beyond television, waves of JFK scholarship appeared at the beginning of the 1980s and 1990s, while Oliver Stone's controversial *JFK* (1992) appeared in such a timeframe.[32] JFK was also honored with his own GI Joe Doll on the fortieth anniversary of his election victory—proving that Theodore Roosevelt was not the only president to inspire bizarre ephemera. Finally, the fiftieth anniversary of Kennedy's election moved President Obama to publish an article on JFK's inspirational qualities, *USA Today* to publish a special edition of their newspaper, and the New York Mint to issue a new coin in his honor.[33]

Meanwhile, another round of JFK-commemorative frenzy unfolded amid the fiftieth anniversary of events in Dallas, including novelist Stephen King's *11.22.63*, which sought to imagine a world where Lee Harvey Oswald's plot was foiled and JFK lived. By the time Kennedy's centennial arrived in 2017—despite the Kennedy Foundation's best efforts—it was a somewhat muted affair, as Americans had little left to learn. Even content-hungry news outlets devoted far less time to the centennial than they had to the fiftieth anniversary of his assassination. Still, the seemingly endless sequence of JFK-related landmark anniversaries have undeniably contributed to what White calls the "extraordinarily potent" image of Kennedy.[34] Indeed, it is an image that has seen him remain the most fondly remembered post-World War II president among Americans.[35] While Kennedy's presidency was not without accomplishments, such omnipresence in American culture and memory remains excessive if judged against his time in the Oval Office. Perhaps, then, Kennedy's legacy will start to recede without such obvious anniversary landmarks on the horizon.

While this chapter cannot assess every presidential anniversary, the examples of Lincoln, Washington, Jefferson, Roosevelt,

Reagan, and Kennedy offer an insight into how presidents have been remembered on landmark occasions. Clearly, it is a process that is greatly affected by the context in which the anniversary takes place; the level of celebration affected by how highly Americans value a president's successes or failures from the platform of hindsight on which the contemporary public, media, and scholars stand. Nevertheless, it is only on rare occasions that a true reassessment is proffered during anniversary remembrance. Perhaps the most recent example of this infrequent phenomenon has taken place in recent years with regard to one of the nation's previously most forgotten presidents, Lyndon B. Johnson.

Lyndon Johnson reassessed

Presidential biographer Robert Dallek concluded his nuanced portrait of Lyndon Johnson by arguing that, with regards to LBJ's legacy, "Only one thing seems certain: Lyndon Johnson will not join the many obscure—almost nameless, faceless—Presidents whose terms of office register on most Americans as blank slates. He will not be forgotten."[36] Arguably, Dallek, who was writing in 1998, had already failed to perceive that Johnson was well on his way to becoming one of the United States' many faceless former presidents. Sandwiched between the headline-grabbing presidencies of John Kennedy and Richard Nixon, LBJ was the odd one out in the triumvirate of 1960s presidents who dominated the political landscape during an era which profoundly shaped American society. Historian Bernard von Bothmer, conducting a study into the political legacy of the 1960s, found in 2010 that, "More than anything, Johnson is simply forgotten: when members of the public are asked whether they approve or disapprove of past presidents, Johnson always leads in the category 'unsure.'"[37] By 2015, Dallek was forced to revisit his old assertion, admitting that "LBJ has disappeared."[38] This observation was confirmed by the fact that Dallek's admission appeared in an article for a book entitled *LBJ's Neglected Legacy*. Since this was the president who presided over the passage of the Civil Rights Act, the Voting Rights Act, and a host of Great Society legislation that remade the government's relationship to the American people on a par with Franklin Roosevelt's New Deal, Johnson-amnesia was a puzzling phenomenon.

Perhaps unsurprisingly then, like all trends, the trajectory of Johnson's legacy has reversed—in large part thanks to a host of landmark anniversaries that have brought LBJ back into popular memory. As the editors of *LBJ's Neglected Legacy* began their collection, "The centennial anniversary of the birth of Lyndon B. Johnson and the fiftieth anniversaries of his signal legislative achievements . . . have combined to stimulate renewed interest in the legacies of his extraordinary and controversial presidency."[39] In this assertion, the editors were half right as, in reality, Johnson's centennial passed without much acknowledgment beyond official events. Certainly, LBJ was almost entirely ignored by his own party, when the Democrats failed to recognize Johnson at their 2008 convention. Given the symbolism attached to Barack Obama's nomination as the first African American to head a major party ticket, it was telling that the Democrats chose to shun a video tribute to LBJ—the president most closely identified with civil and voting rights. As Dallek speculates, this decision may well have been partly inspired by the controversial Iraq War serving to revive negative memories of Johnson's Vietnam legacy.[40]

Instead, it was the slew of anniversaries related to his legislative accomplishments that thrust LBJ back into the spotlight between 2013 and 2016. Johnson received voluminous coverage in the news media, reassessment by Hollywood, a new burst of scholarship, and a revival as a figure whose legacy triggered debate amongst contemporary politicians—both Democratic and Republican. While it is likely that anniversaries of his grand accomplishments, such as the civil rights acts, would have increased focus on Johnson anyway, it is the context in which these anniversaries took place that helped spur a greater reassessment of Johnson—largely in a positive fashion for the 34th president. Finally, it is also true that Johnson's legacy was out of kilter with his accomplishments anyway, and therefore his legacy was uniquely placed to benefit from a reassessment triggered by a wave of landmark anniversary celebrations.

Speaking confidently in 2014, Larry Temple, a former Johnson aide and head of the LBJ Foundation, predicted a revival for his former boss. "The next five years will be the 50th anniversary of everything he did," Temple presciently observed. Taken together, Johnson's anniversaries have inspired such vast amounts of spilled ink—be it real or virtual—that it would make the editors of the *Chicago Tribune*'s Lincoln special edition blush. Like Reagan's centennial celebrations, the wave of Johnson anniversaries took place in a new media climate that prized opinion columnists over investigative journalists, and demanded reams of content to fill both web and printed pages. Dissecting Johnson's legislative achievements proved perfect fodder for such a task. For instance, on the fiftieth anniversary of Johnson's announcement that his administration would pursue a Great Society, the *Washington Post* ran a series on how LBJ's major programs evolved and whether they could be deemed successful—it ran to sixty-two pages, and was released as a stand-alone Kindle book.[41] Elsewhere, in most major newspapers, columnists—conservative and liberal alike—battled it out over Johnson's legislative record on healthcare, education, immigration, and consumer regulation and whether it had benefited or harmed American society in the ensuing fifty years. Scholars also chipped in, as Johnson's Great Society legacy was reassessed in popular history books such as those by Julian Zelizer (positive) and Jonathan Darman (negative).[42]

The fiftieth anniversary of the War on Poverty, a controversial element of Johnson's Great Society, sparked such debate that it spilled over into the political arena. In January 2014, five decades on from LBJ's declaration of an "unconditional War on Poverty," Republicans used the occasion to hammer home Ronald Reagan's old damning maxim that, "We fought a War on Poverty, and poverty won."[43] Symbolically speaking in the Senate's Lyndon Baines Johnson Room, Marco Rubio, a young Republican senator preparing to run for president, made a speech calling for the states to take control of those federal poverty programs that remained from Johnson's era.[44] Meanwhile, future House Speaker Paul Ryan used the occasion to release "The War on Poverty: Fifty Years Later"—an unflattering report on Johnson's antipoverty initiatives.[45] On the other side of the aisle, Democratic Leader Nancy Pelosi released a statement that affirmed, "The programs born from the War on Poverty . . . have lifted millions of American families out of destitution and despair." "On the 50th anniversary of the War on Poverty," Pelosi demanded, "we must renew our commitment to rooting out poverty in America."[46] Such partisan commentary reflected the growing polarization that had commenced between the two parties on social welfare issues since the 1960s. Moreover, it demonstrated that, five decades on and despite previous ignorance of his years in office, Johnson's presidential legacy was still relevant to American society.

The Johnson anniversaries also witnessed the entertainment industry take another look at LBJ's larger-than-life character. Prior to 2013, Johnson—if he featured in historical dramas at all—was often depicted in an entirely negative light. For instance, Johnson's portrayal in the aforementioned 1980s *Kennedy* series was almost wholly unflattering, while the HBO film *Path to War* (2002) focused on a misguided Johnson escalating the Vietnam War and the subsequent unraveling of his presidency.[47] By 2014, however, Johnson was the central character in the Broadway phenomenon *All the Way*, in which Bryan Cranston portrayed a dynamic and complex Johnson as he strove to pass the landmark Civil Rights Act of 1964 and win election in his own right.[48] Cranston went on to reprise his role for the successful HBO film of the same name that appeared in 2016.[49] Meanwhile, Hollywood has churned out another film—*LBJ*—due to be released in early 2018, featuring Woody Harrelson as Johnson. The film will examine Johnson's early life, as well as his leadership following Kennedy's assassination, a time that historians almost unanimously agree Johnson handed with immense skill.[50] Finally, Ava DuVernay's film *Selma* (2014), which focused on the struggle for the Voting Rights Act, offered a largely negative portrayal of Johnson.[51] Nonetheless, this kicked off a fierce debate in the media as former Johnson aides and historians jumped to his defence. As such, unintentionally, the film triggered media coverage that portrayed Johnson in a positive light once again.[52]

In April 2014, LBJ's anniversary revival was crowned by a Civil Rights Summit at the LBJ Library in Austin, Texas. With President Obama delivering the keynote address, and former President William J. Clinton also speaking, the event was guaranteed media attention. Obama, in keeping with a long line of previous leading Democrats, had embraced JFK in his rhetoric, eschewing any mention of Johnson. As such, it represented a departure for the incumbent president to speak glowingly of LBJ's contribution to the Civil Rights Movement. Moreover, Obama also saluted Johnson's faith in the power of government to do good, justifying this through his own life story: "Because I have lived out the promise of LBJ's efforts. Because Michelle [Obama] has lived out the legacy of those efforts. Because my daughters have lived out the legacy of those efforts. Because I and millions of my generation were in a position to take the baton that he handed to us."[53] It represented a ringing endorsement of Johnson from the Democratic Party's leader, when only six years earlier, the same party had spurned LBJ during Obama's own nomination.

Ultimately, LBJ's spate of anniversaries triggered a revival of his image for the public to consume. As it was with Reagan's centennial, it would have been quite the feat for public audiences between 2013 and 2016 to avoid hearing or reading about Johnson's achievements. This is without even considering the impact that social media—vastly expanded in years since Reagan's 2011 centennial—likely had in spreading the word beyond traditional outlets. While it is hard to accurately measure how much this led to a broader societal appreciation of Johnson's legacy, it is fair to say that the anniversaries pushed many Americans to learn more about the man who had perhaps previously been the most forgotten of America's unforgettable presidents. It also reshaped his legacy from the man who had escalated the Vietnam War, to the president who had embraced civil rights and sought to improve American society through government action. Nonetheless, as with Jefferson during World War II, the context in which LBJ's landmark anniversaries took place was just as important to the Johnson legacy revival.

While Obama's presence at the Civil Rights Summit boosted the prestige of that occasion, it was his presidency that provided the context to ensure Johnson's anniversaries received the level of attention that they did. Following the 2010 midterm elections, in which Republicans gained control of both houses of Congress and consequently stymied Obama's efforts at passing new liberal legislation, commentators increasingly began to draw comparisons between LBJ's handling of Congress and that of Obama. "Lyndon Johnson has come to look far more formidable today than he did in 1968," historian Sean Wilentz noted in 2014. "Current commentators yearn for a time when a master partisan politician worked the levers of power in Washington and won numerous victories."[54] Despite Obama's glowing tribute to LBJ at the Civil Rights Summit, it was not a comparison that was received well by the White House. By June 2015, Politico's chief Washington correspondent, Edward-Isaac Dovere, observed that, "In the White House, there's no topic that so quickly and consistently makes heads explode as suggesting Obama needs to be more like LBJ."[55] Obama, clearly irked, refuted the comparison himself in an interview—somewhat justifiably claiming that LBJ had the same problems with congressional obstruction following Republican gains in 1966 as Obama experienced after 2010.[56] Nonetheless, Johnson's stature was only increased by the whole episode. In a sense, as Obama struggled to make further gains, LBJ became a lionized liberal icon, a status he was never granted either during his time in office or in the decades that followed.

Other aspects of Obama's presidency ensured that Johnson's anniversaries had a disproportionate impact. Firstly, American race relations—a core element of Johnson's legacy—were once again front and center in American politics following the election of the first African American president and an array of events that brought racial politics to the fore. Indeed, the formation of Black Lives Matter in late 2013 and unrest in Ferguson, Missouri, in 2014, coincided with the fiftieth anniversaries of the Civil Rights Act. While these incidents showed that Johnson's presidency had far from solved racial issues in the United States, they also ensured that his civil rights legacy was discussed.[57]

Obama's final contribution to reviving Johnson's legacy lay in their shared visions for the government's role in the United States. Certainly, Obama was the first president to openly affirm his belief in the federal government's ability to improve Americans' lives since LBJ left the White House. In the decades following Johnson's departure, conservatives were ascendant, and Johnson's embrace of increasingly loathed "big government" was tarnished by many of his successors. Reagan made no secret of his antipathy towards the Great Society, blaming Johnson's programs for the mess that the US economy had gotten itself into in the following years.[58] Meanwhile, even Democratic President Bill Clinton famously declared that "the era of big government is over."[59] With Obama in residence at 1600 Pennsylvania Avenue, those who believed in the Great Society's ethos—its faith in government to solve problems—once more had a spokesman in the White House. Indeed, in passing the Affordable Care Act of 2010, the 43rd president passed the largest social welfare expansion since the Johnson era. All in all, the coinciding of Obama's presidency with the series of Johnson legislative anniversaries proved a potent mix in reviving LBJ's legacy.

Finally, the unique nature of Johnson's legacy meant that, under the right conditions, his presidency was ripe for revisiting and reviving. Simply put, the legislative avalanche unleashed during LBJ's presidency was too significant in its impact on American society for the man who precipitated it to fade into obscurity. For Johnson, salvation ultimately lay within his substantial domestic accomplishments. Indeed, historians had long been preparing for a revival on such grounds. For while the public showed ignorance towards the Texan, LBJ has always been a rich figure for biographers and political historians alike. As Johnson scholar Kent Germany noted in 2009, "writers have produced approximately 250 Ph.D. dissertations, well over one hundred books, and countless articles regarding specific aspects of Johnson's career and his policies."[60] Part of this phenomenon, Germany notes, stemmed from the wealth of sources Johnson left behind, whether it was his presidential tape recordings or Johnson's insistence that the LBJ Library be an institution that let scholars have access to everything—good and bad—in his presidency. Still more important is Germany's observation that "Johnson was more than just a president during a momentous era. He was a historical whirlwind unto himself."[61] Moreover, in recent decades, scholars have observed that LBJ's Great Society "bequeathed an era" in American politics and society, thus underlining the significance of his presidency.[62]

As such, Johnson's forgotten legacy was purely a public phenomenon rather than a scholarly one. LBJ's legacy ultimately lay dormant, bubbling away intensely in academia, until the eruption of public and media interest was unleashed by his landmark anniversaries. Attempting to understand the previous lack of public interest, Dallek believes it can be explained by a combination of the Vietnam War and the ascendancy of conservatism's anti-government message.[63] In addition, there was the small aforementioned issue of Johnson being sandwiched between the martyred JFK and the dastardly Richard Nixon in the public memory. Perhaps also, Johnson, due to his dour appearance on television, was not remembered as a particularly charismatic personality. As such, it is unsurprising that the centennial of his birth, with its obvious focus on Johnson "the man," made such a small splash in comparison to the anniversaries of his legislative achievements. When time came to revive Johnson's legacy, a wealth of scholarship existed for media outlets and Hollywood to draw upon.

Of course, for Johnson—as happened to Jefferson—his legacy may well evolve again. For while his domestic accomplishments have been the focus of recent years, it is likely that the upcoming anniversary of the Tet Offensive—the Vietnam War's most pivotal event—in 2018 will turn attention back onto Johnson's folly in Southeast Asia. Nevertheless, even if his legacy is tarnished by another reassessment, perhaps Dallek's assertion that LBJ will not join the nameless or faceless presidents in American history is finally true.

Conclusion

Presidential legacies, as this volume demonstrates, are complicated tapestries, woven together with many different materials and by many different artisans. For even the best artisans—in this case, historians, presidential foundations, the media, Hollywood, literary figures, and the public—can only produce something truly remarkable if the raw materials—vision, foreign and domestic leadership, moral authority, and a positive effect on future society—are there in the first place. Landmark anniversaries can either see this tapestry brought out and given a prominent position in the national gallery to receive appreciation from the American people, or it can simply be left to gather dust in the attic—deemed unremarkable and unworthy of attention. Occasionally, however, the tapestry can acquire a new design and thus a new appreciation.

As such, landmark anniversaries often reflect a presidential legacy, but on rare occasions they can reshape one. Beyond their relevance to presidential legacy, landmark anniversaries can also reveal much about American society at the time in which they take place; whether it be sectional tensions during Washington's centennial, a spirit of national unity during Lincoln's centennial and Jefferson's bicentennial, political polarization during Franklin Roosevelt and Ronald Reagan's one hundredth birthdays, or even a nation still mourning a lost leader in the consistent remembrance of John F. Kennedy. In the case of Lyndon Johnson, the desire for a politician bestowed with near-mythical deal-making powers spoke volumes about the frustrations felt at the contemporary Washington gridlock. With one eye on the horizon, the upcoming fiftieth anniversary of Richard Nixon's Watergate scandal will surely offer a similarly fascinating reveal of American society. Historians would do well to observe the occasion with keen interest.

Notes

1. *Chicago Tribune*, February 7, 1909.
2. "This is Lincoln Centennial Day," *Chicago Tribune*, February 12, 1909.
3. "Lincoln's Contested Legacy," *Smithsonian Magazine*, February 2009, <https://www.smithsonianmag.com/history/lincolns-contested-legacy-44978351/> (accessed June 13, 2018).
4. Ibid.
5. Merrill D. Peterson, *Lincoln in American Memory* (New York: Oxford University Press, 1994), 175.
6. "Harding 2020," *Ohio Historical Society*, <https://www.ohiohistory.org/give/harding-2020> (accessed June 13, 2018).
7. Tom Kanon, "Forging the 'Hero of New Orleans': Tennessee Looks at the Centennial of the War of 1812," *Tennessee Historical Quarterly* 71, no. 2 (Summer 2012): 128–61.
8. "Teddy Bear Celebrates 100th Birthday," *BBC News*, <http://news.bbc.co.uk/1/hi/england/2537943.stm> (accessed June 13, 2018).
9. John Tyler quoted in Matthew Costello, "Centennial of Washington's Birthday," *George Washington's Mount Vernon*, <https://www.mountvernon.org/library/digitalhistory/digital-encyclopedia/article/centennial-of-washingtons-birthday/> (accessed June 13, 2018).
10. Ibid.

11. Francis Cogliano, *Thomas Jefferson: Reputation and Legacy* (Edinburgh: Edinburgh University Press, 2013), 5.
12. Ibid. 6.
13. Ibid.
14. Ibid. 7.
15. Franklin D. Roosevelt, "Address at the Dedication of the Thomas Jefferson Memorial," April 13, 1943, *The American Presidency Project*, <http://www.presidency.ucsb.edu/ws/index.php?pid=16383> (accessed June 13, 2018).
16. "Roosevelt's Centennial Celebrated at Hyde Park; He is Needed 'Now More Than Ever,' Carey Says," *New York Times*, January 31, 1982.
17. Ibid.
18. Ronald W. Reagan, "Remarks at a White House Luncheon Celebrating the Centennial of the Birth of Franklin Delano Roosevelt," January 28, 1982, *The American Presidency Project*, <http://www.presidency.ucsb.edu/ws/index.php?pid=42798&st=&st1=> (accessed June 13, 2018).
19. Ibid.
20. William E. Leuchtenburg, *In the Shadow of FDR: From Harry Truman to Barack Obama* (New York: Cornell University Press, 2009), 291.
21. Ibid.
22. "Ronald Reagan Centennial," *Washington Post*, <http://www.washingtonpost.com/wp-srv/special/politics/reagan-centennial> (accessed June 13, 2018).
23. "Ronald Reagan at 100," *LIFE*, February 1, 2011.
24. "Ronald Reagan Centennial: 'A Truly Beautiful Human Being,'" *Fox News*, January 31, 2011.
25. Press Statement, "Inaugural Meeting of the Ronald Reagan Centennial Commission at US Capitol," July 29, 2010, <https://www.archives.gov/files/reagan-centennial-commission/press/rrcc-pr-01.pdf> (accessed June 13, 2018).
26. "GE Announces $15 Million Contribution to Ronald Reagan Centennial Celebration," *Philanthropy News Digest*, March 28, 2010.
27. "Reagan Centennial Celebration Events," *Reagan Foundation*, <https://www.reaganfoundation.org> (accessed June 13, 2018).
28. Lisa Rein, "Exhibits, Festivities to Mark 100th Anniversary of Reagan's Birth," *Washington Post*, January 6, 2011.
29. "Obama Reading about Reagan," *ABC News*, December 23, 2010.
30. *Ronald Reagan: Rendezvous with Destiny*, film, dir. Kevin Knoblock (USA: Gingrich Productions, 2009).

31. Mark White, *Kennedy: A Cultural History of an American Icon* (London: Bloomsbury, 2013).
32. *Kennedy*, television drama, dir. Jim Goddard (UK/USA: NBC, 1983); *The Kennedys*, television drama, dir. Jon Cassar (USA/Canada: Reelz, 2011); *JFK*, film, dir. Oliver Stone (USA: Warner Brothers, 1991).
33. White, *Kennedy*, 116–39.
34. White, *Kennedy*, 1.
35. Andrew Dugan and Frank Newport, "Americans Rate JFK as Top Modern President," *Gallup*, November 15, 2013, <http://news.gallup.com/poll/165902/americans-rate-jfk-top-modern-president.aspx> (accessed June 13, 2018).
36. Robert Dallek, *Flawed Giant: Lyndon Johnson and His Times, 1961–1973* (New York: Oxford University Press, 1998), 628.
37. Bernard von Bothmer, *Framing the Sixties: The Use and Abuse of a Decade from Ronald Reagan to George W. Bush* (Amherst: University of Massachusetts Press, 2010), 142.
38. Robert Dallek, "Remembering LBJ: One Historian's Thoughts on Johnson's Place in the Pantheon of Presidents," in Robert H. Wilson, Norman J. Glickman, and Laurence E. Lynn Jr. (eds.), *LBJ's Neglected Legacy: How Lyndon Johnson Reshaped Domestic Policy and Government* (Austin: University of Texas Press, 2015), 21.
39. Wilson et al., "Preface," in *LBJ's Neglected Legacy*, 2.
40. Dallek, "Remembering LBJ," 21.
41. "The Great Society: 50 Years Later," *Washington Post*, May 2014.
42. Julian E. Zelizer, *The Fierce Urgency of Now: Lyndon Johnson, Congress and the Battle for the Great Society* (New York: Penguin Press, 2015); Jonathan Darman, *Landslide: LBJ, Reagan, and New America* (New York: Random House, 2014).
43. Reagan quoted in James T. Patterson, *America's Struggle against Poverty, 1900-1980* (Cambridge, MA: Harvard University Press, 1981), 224.
44. Jackie Kucinich, "Rubio: War on Poverty Has Been Lost," *Washington Post*, January 8, 2014.
45. "The War on Poverty: 50 Years Later," House Budget Committee, 2014.
46. Press Statement, "Pelosi Statement on 50th Anniversary of War on Poverty," January 8, 2014, <http://www.democraticleader.gov> (accessed June 13, 2018).
47. *Path to War*, film, dir. John Frankenheimer (USA: HBO Films, 2002).
48. Peter Osnos, "How Pop Culture is Re-Evaluating Lyndon B. Johnson's Legacy," *The Atlantic*, April 1, 2014.

49. *All the Way*, film, dir. Jay Roach (USA: HBO Films, 2016).
50. *LBJ*, film, dir. Rob Reiner (USA: Castle Rock Entertainment/Electric Entertainment, 2016); Robert A. Caro, *The Years of Lyndon Johnson: The Passage of Power* (New York: Knopf, 2012).
51. *Selma*, film, dir. Ava DuVernay (USA/UK: Pathe/Paramount Pictures, 2014).
52. Mark McLay, "The Meat in the Coconut: Lyndon Johnson and the Voting Rights Act of 1965," in Joe Street and Henry Knight Lozano (eds.), *The Shadow of Selma* (Florida: University of Florida, 2018)
53. Barack Obama, "Remarks by the President at LBJ Presidential Library Civil Rights Summit," April 10, 2014, <https://obamawhitehouse.archives.gov/the-press-office/2014/04/10/remarks-president-lbj-presidential-library-civil-rights-summit> (accessed June 13, 2018).
54. Sean Wilentz, "'Landslide: LBJ and Ronald Reagan at the Dawn of a New America,' by Jonathan Darman," *New York Times*, October 17, 2014.
55. Edward-Isaac Dovere, "Obama v. LBJ on Display at Congressional Picnic," *Politico*, June 17, 2015.
56. Obama quoted in George E. Condon, "The One Piece of Advice Obama Aides Hate Hearing," *The Atlantic*, April 2014.
57. Michael W. Flamm, "From Harlem to Ferguson: LBJ's War on Crime and America's Prison Crisis," *Origins* 8, no. 7 (April 2015); Elizabeth Hinton, "Why We Should Reconsider the War on Crime," *TIME*, March 20, 2015.
58. Ronald Reagan, *The Reagan Diaries*, ed. Douglas Brinkley (New York: HarperCollins, 2007), 65.
59. William J. Clinton, "Address Before a Joint Session of the Congress on the State of the Union," January 23, 1996, *The American Presidency Project*, <http://www.presidency.ucsb.edu/ws/?pid=53091> (accessed June 13, 2018).
60. Kent B. Germany, "Historians and the Many Lyndon Johnsons: A Review Essay," *Journal of Southern History* 75, no. 4 (November 2009): 1002.
61. Ibid. 1003–04.
62. Gareth Davies, *See Government Grow: Education Politics from Johnson to Reagan* (Lawrence: University Press of Kansas, 2007), 287.
63. Dallek, "Remembering LBJ," 22.

9

From a "new paradigm" to "memorial sprawl": The Dwight D. Eisenhower Presidential Memorial

Patrick Hagopian

Whenever a society creates a memorial, it communicates across time: it speaks to the future about the past. It offers lessons and admonitions about examples to emulate and to avoid. In United States presidential monuments, America speaks not just about a particular historical personage but also about itself. Although the US Constitution makes the executive a co-equal branch of government, the president is the pre-eminent representative of the nation. Accordingly, when Americans debate the design of presidential memorials, they usually demand monuments possessing qualities commensurate with the esteem that they believe the nation deserves in the eyes of its citizens and of the world. Of all genres of public art, presidential memorials charge their creators with the responsibility to evoke dignity and promote respect.

A judgment about the design of a presidential memorial always involves a dual evaluation. It requires an assessment of the record and reputation of the remembered president; it also demands an evaluation of the proposed form of the monument: how adequate is it to the general demands of presidential commemoration and to the particular remembered figure? These problems have haunted the debates about the design for the Dwight D. Eisenhower Memorial in the nation's capital, for which ground breaking took place in November 2017 after years of wrangling about the qualities of the design.

The designer of a memorial to Eisenhower faced particular challenges. Unlike Franklin Delano Roosevelt and Ronald Reagan, whose legacies define the poles of national policy debates decades after they left office, Dwight D. Eisenhower does not stand for a philosophy of government that remains salient to contemporary political parties, especially not to the contemporary Republican Party. Advocates of an Eisenhower memorial said that he had saved the world for freedom and presided over eight years of peace and prosperity; he combined personal qualities of humility, determination, and toughness; he chose the middle way between extremes. In our time of partisan conflict and tribal polarization, however, Eisenhower's vaunted virtues seemed to belong to an imperfectly remembered realm of bipartisanship far from the realities of politics today. No one, anyway, came up with a convincing idea of how to represent his qualities and achievements in a memorial.

That task fell to Frank Gehry, the superstar architect of his day.[1] Gehry produced exactly the kind of path-breaking design that was consistent with his record and reputation as an innovator. Traditionalist commentators on architecture and members of the Eisenhower family objected to its principal features, and legislators intervened to force changes. When Republicans won a majority of seats in the House of Representatives in 2010, the party members who assumed the chairs of crucial House committees threatened to de-fund the memorial in order to put pressure on the Eisenhower Memorial Commission (EMC) and the designer. Politicians had little idea of what to put in its place beyond advocating a portrait statue; nevertheless, despite their lack of expertise in art and architecture, they began to tinker with the design. In the end, the statutory review process became unhinged and the commissions with authority over memorials in the nation's capital were rendered spectators in the power play that determined the final outcome. By then, Gehry had altered the design by adding realistic statuary in order to appease the critics; the perceived need for racial inclusiveness in the statues then collided with the historical realities underlying the depicted scenes that current politics demand.

The arguments about the design were particularly fraught because of the lack of consensus about what kind of memorial is appropriate today, an uncertainty that began with shifts in conceptions of "the monumental" that have their roots in the nineteenth century, reached a high pitch in the mid-twentieth century and have never been resolved. In the last century, the design features of modern architecture and art came into conflict with concepts of the monumental to the extent that monumentality and modernism were seen to be contradictory.

In Washington's landscape of commemoration, both grandeur and monumentality have often seemed to equate with neoclassicism or its stripped-down variants. Hard to pin down, the traditional qualities of monuments—solidity, grandeur, classicism, and magnificence—seemed out of step with modernity's élan. To many commentators, they seemed incompatible. Lewis Mumford wrote, "The notion of a modern monument is veritably a contradiction in terms . . . If it is a monument it is not modern, and if it is modern, it cannot be a monument."[2] (One can only guess at how Mumford would have assessed the compatibility of monumentalism and post-modernity.) If one tried to reconcile architectural innovation and monumentalism, questions abounded: should monumental grandeur be achieved through mass and proportion alone, without ornament?[3] How might new materials be incorporated? Glass, steel, chrome, aluminum, and concrete created impressive, at times magnificent modern residential and commercial buildings, but was commemorative architecture and design an intrinsically tradition-bound form that would reject such innovations?

In 1982, commemorative Washington seemed to provide an answer in the form of the minimalist, abstract design of Maya Lin's Vietnam Veterans Memorial, and in the public's overwhelming acceptance of that unprecedented yet magnificent monument. That design may prove to be the exception, rather than an indication of a trend line. Its innovative features responded to the problem of creating a memorial in a nation fissured by the Vietnam War: a unique response to a crisis of representation that could not be answered in the traditional language of memorial design. Moreover, Maya Lin's design was beset by political and aesthetic criticisms, and compromised by the addition of statuary and a flag.[4] Gehry's design for the Eisenhower memorial would be the most formally non-traditional proposal for a Washington memorial since Lin's black granite wall. If one needed a fresh cautionary tale about the hostility that can greet such designs, the story of the Eisenhower Memorial provides it.

The Department of Defense Appropriations Act of 2000 established the EMC to "consider and formulate plans for ... a permanent memorial to Dwight D. Eisenhower, including its nature, design, construction, and location," and made an initial appropriation of $300,000 to cover its costs.[5] The statute provided that the commission membership would consist of four people appointed by the president, four by the president pro tempore of the Senate, and four by the Speaker of the House of Representatives, all groups being bipartisan in composition. One of the presidential appointees was David Eisenhower, the late president's grandson.[6] The EMC's membership seemed to hedge against objections, since the political establishment and Eisenhower family were represented in its number.

In 2002, Congress affirmed the memorial's authorization and appropriated $2.6 million to assist with construction.[7] After several years of study, a piece of federal land in Washington, DC was selected from among twenty-six possibilities.[8] The site is a seven-and-a-half acre urban plaza, of which the memorial precinct would occupy about four acres. The piece of ground is wedged between Independence Avenue to the north, the Lyndon B. Johnson Building (which houses the Department of Education) to the south, and to the east and west 4th and 6th Streets, SW. This rectangle is bisected by the diagonal of Maryland Avenue. On the other side of Independence Avenue is the National Air and Space Museum. The location has its complications. The paved area in front of the Lyndon B. Johnson Building is rather neglected; the memorial must accommodate a sunken courtyard which serves as a light well for and means of egress from the building's basement level. The area is surrounded by multi-storey mid-rise office buildings, and the predominant aesthetic is of mid-twentieth-century modern architecture. A member of Congress who played an influential role in design development called the surrounding architecture "Stalinistic."[9]

In 2006, the National Capital Planning Commission (NCPC) recommended design principles that included the requirement that the memorial harmonize with its site, respect the surrounding buildings and trees, and reflect Pierre Charles L'Enfant's plan for Washington, DC, which had included the creation of broad diagonal avenues giving onto important landmarks.[10] In line with various plans for Washington's commemorative core approved by the NCPC and its partner commissions, the most important axis at the designated location produced reciprocal views to and from the US Capitol along Maryland Avenue.[11]

The EMC held a design competition, which emphasized the credentials and portfolio of the entrants and therefore tended to draw in established architects and designers. The EMC positively invited a non-traditional design. The competition brief said that the commission wanted a "new vision" and a "new paradigm": "The National Eisenhower Memorial at Eisenhower Square will be the first national presidential memorial of the new century. No language currently exists for a twenty-first-century memorial. Eisenhower Square is an opportunity to explore new avenues in memorialization. The competitive designer and design team selection process will embrace the widest possible range of innovative concepts and ideas. It is intended that the physical memorial will have a very significant electronic component. Thus there can be a strong visual statement about Eisenhower and also allow for a depth of information as wanted. The result will be a new vision of memorialization: a new paradigm for memorials."[12] The competition attracted some forty-four entrants, from which an evaluation board, including David Eisenhower, selected four as semi-finalists.[13] A jury of design professionals and David Eisenhower then gathered to make the final selection.[14] They granted the commission to Gehry. The selection of an architect known for using titanium to create sinuous, asymmetrical, sometimes crumpled shapes in landmark buildings, with a prior history of adapting vernacular materials to unexpected purposes, seemed to bear out that the EMC wanted to create a memorial with a "wow" factor—one that would help reinvent the language of memorialization and make the Eisenhower memorial stand out.[15]

Gehry's cause was championed by Rocco Siciliano, a former aide to Eisenhower who chaired the memorial commission.[16] Once the opposition to Gehry's design coalesced, opponents questioned the integrity of the selection process. They said that

Siciliano had a strong and enduring connection with Gehry and had spoken to the architect about designing the Eisenhower Memorial years before the competition took place.[17] They also questioned whether the General Service Administration's (GSA) Design Excellence Program, usually used for the commissioning of government buildings, was the appropriate vehicle for organizing a competition to select a memorial design.[18] Moreover, they said the competition had not observed the steps usually required by the GSA procedure.[19]

In May 2010, Gehry presented three possible designs to the EMC and then to the Commission of Fine Arts (CFA), one of the statutory agencies responsible for approving memorial designs in Washington. The design team preferred the third, featuring massive, limestone-clad columns, eighty feet tall and twelve feet in diameter (later reduced to ten feet). The columns supported large, elevated woven stainless steel "tapestries" representing scenes from Eisenhower's life: perhaps Eisenhower fixing a fence at his home, images from World War II, or Eisenhower in the White House surrounded by his cabinet.[20] There would also be inscriptions from Eisenhower's famous speeches.[21] In the midst of the urban park the memorial created would be trees typical of the landscape of Abilene, Kansas, Eisenhower's hometown. At this stage there were no sculptures or reliefs. Gehry acknowledged that there was a "strong historical tradition" of commemoration with bronze sculptures but he said that modern-day sculptures were "typically not satisfactory."[22] The CFA agreed that the tapestries made sculpture superfluous.[23] Along with these material and visual elements, there would be a so-called E-memorial: some sort of representation of historical and policy research on the life and achievements of the former president. It would involve a website and a downloadable app for the mobile phones of visitors.[24]

In January 2011, the design team of Gehry Partners and the landscape architecture firm AECOM presented the same three alternatives to the CFA, again preferring the third. By this time it had evolved. The Gehry firm had sent the choreographer, theatre designer, and actor Robert Wilson on a mission to Abilene, Kansas, to help identify images for the tapestries. Wilson was inspired by the rural landscape, and he suggested a photograph of Eisenhower's boyhood home and the surrounding countryside for the main tapestry because it would convey Eisenhower's Midwestern background.[25] Images of trees on the woven metal would suggest black-and-white photographs, to evoke "the landscape in Eisenhower's time."[26] They would also provide a backdrop for the living trees of similar species in the memorial precinct. Gehry was enthusiastic. Describing Eisenhower as "a man from the Midwest, from Middle America," Gehry said that he wanted to get away from the Greek temple as a form of commemoration and instead present imagery of the Midwest to Washington, DC, "because a lot of our leaders come from that place and it has not been portrayed in DC."[27] The combination of elements would create a set of symbolic relationships with a narrative component: while the tapestries and plantings would evoke the landscape of the rural Midwest, stone lintels would carry the inscriptions from Eisenhower's speeches, and stone relief sculptures would present scenes of Eisenhower in the White House and Eisenhower as Allied supreme commander. Together, these elements would represent Eisenhower's personal journey from his origins in Abilene, his achievements in rising to a supreme role in the armed forces, and his role as president and, later, world citizen.[28]

Wilson returned from Kansas with another inspiration. The presidential museum in Abilene sells a pamphlet titled "Dreams of a Barefoot Boy."[29] A statue of Eisenhower as a youth exists in downtown Abilene, in "Little Ike Park." Both the pamphlet and the statue recall the homecoming speech Eisenhower had given in June 1945, when he said how proud he was to come from Abilene. The speech begins, "Because no man is really a man who has lost out of himself all of the boy, I want to speak first of the dreams of a barefoot boy."[30] For Wilson, the speech captured the future president's rootedness in the nation's heartland. At a design meeting, he picked up one of the miniature figures populating the architectural model, painted it white, and placed it at the center to represent Eisenhower as a boy. Gehry said, "When Wilson picked up the little figure and put him there, it was a moment of epiphany, somehow."[31]

The result was a new focal point: a small statue of Eisenhower would be placed on a low wall bridging the armed forces and White House scenes.[32] Its presence emphasized the story of Eisenhower the person. This idea had initially come through the symbolism of the landscape, representing the place where Eisenhower was raised.[33] This allusion became vivid with the addition of the young Eisenhower statue. The youth would be caught looking out at what he would become, a general and a statesman, in the relief sculptures.

The proposed design was remarkably successful in adapting to a problematic urban site. The columns and tapestries marked out the perimeter of an urban park in the midst of the built-up area. They created a sense of grandeur from the outside and intimacy inside.[34] Openings among the tapestries, columns, and trees created a view towards the Capitol Building. Unlike other major memorials in Washington, DC, this one would not form a terminal point in the original plan by L'Enfant, or its early-twentieth-century adaptation by the Senate Park Commission. Instead, it occupied an intermediate point on the axis between the Capitol and the Jefferson Memorial. The landscape architect Joe Brown, a member of AECOM, said that this was consistent with L'Enfant's plan of having memorials integrated into the fabric of the city.[35] The design transformed the role of columns, suggestive of a temple's colonnade, in a presidential monument. Since they marked the exterior boundary of the tree-filled precinct, Brown said that instead of creating a temple in a garden, the design created a garden in a temple.[36] A portrait statue at the center of the site would underwhelm; yet a Greek temple would have been overshadowed by its neighbors, the Lyndon B. Johnson Building and the other nearby office buildings, or would have appeared incompatible with them. Gehry's design appeared to have found an ingenious solution to the difficulties of the site.[37]

Some critics and design professionals applauded. Philip Kennicott, the chief art and architecture critic for the *Washington Post*, wrote that Gehry was reinvigorating the language of memorial design. Kennicott said, "Gehry's design, which uses large-scale metal tapestries to memorialize the 34th president, is the first serious innovation in the history of memorial design since the bold and abstract geometries of Maya Lin's Vietnam Veterans Memorial."[38] The architect David Childs, who had chaired both the CFA and the NCPC as well as the prominent architecture firm Skidmore, Owings & Merrill, said that, building on tradition, the design "expresses it within contemporary interpretation." To Childs, it was a humble design, rather than a showy "statement," and he approved of its reliance on architectural and landscape elements rather than statuary groups.[39]

The design team submitted the proposed plan to the statutory review commissions at meetings in 2011, and revised it as a result of their suggestions. The tapestries at the front, which had run parallel to the ones at the rear, were shifted around 90 degrees to create something more like an outdoor "room" rather than a proscenium or a series of layers.[40] The grouping of trees was also configured to draw attention to the vista of the Capitol Building. The precise location and height of the trees were the subject of frequent discussion and tweaking to produce the effect of a park with a perimeter and to produce the desired viewshed. In July 2011 the EMC approved the design and in September 2011, the CFA unanimously gave it conceptual approval.[41]

Gehry had been so focused on the development of the memorial design that he appears to have been caught off guard by the emergence of criticism. In October 2011, Gehry and Wilson spoke at a public conversation at the National Archives. Justin Shubow of the National Civic Art Society, a group that favors traditionalist architecture and monuments, denounced the proposal, saying that it was redolent of chaos and nihilism. He said the memorial rejected the past and tradition, and everything that Eisenhower had stood for.[42] And notably, three of Eisenhower's granddaughters expressed their concerns about the "concept for the memorial," as well as its scope and scale, the first time they had spoken out publicly about the design.[43]

Some Eisenhower family members had been uncomfortable with Gehry's proposal from early on. Soon after the EMC formed, Susan Eisenhower, one of the granddaughters, had reportedly proposed to Siciliano a "living memorial," something like the Woodrow Wilson Center, but she was rebuffed.[44] The family members had a variety of views when they learned of the notion of representing the Kansas landscape through the tapestries, with the young Eisenhower statue in their midst. As the spring of 2011 gave way to summer, the family began to close ranks against the Gehry plan.[45] Initially they expressed their opposition behind the scenes. David Eisenhower had supported another architect during the selection process but remained a member of the commission afterward.[46] His membership in the EMC compromised the family's ability to campaign against the memorial, but also gave them some hope of being able to influence the design development process from within.

Gehry met the Eisenhower granddaughters in New York at the beginning of December 2011. (David Eisenhower did not attend.) Soon after, Anne Eisenhower told Gehry that the family objected to elements of the proposal. David Eisenhower resigned from the commission a week later.[47] This step marked a break between the family and the EMC and freed them to speak out publicly. The president's son, John S.D. Eisenhower, said that the memorial should be "as simple as possible," implicitly distancing himself from a design whose scale and complexity clearly did not fit that description.[48] He advocated an "Eisenhower Square that is a green open space with a simple statue in the middle," a proposal that others later echoed.[49] Precedents for such a statue—which depict Eisenhower as an adult, usually in military uniform—exist in a number of locations, including at the Eisenhower Presidential Library in Abilene and in Grosvenor Square, London. Of course, a simple statue in a park was exactly the sort of traditional memorial concept that the EMC's competition brief had set out to revolutionize.

Susan Eisenhower expressed frustration that the EMC appeared to be forging ahead with the memorial without providing an opportunity to discuss any modifications. This complaint disregarded the existence of a statutory review process where family members, civic groups, and citizens could express their opinions. What Susan Eisenhower seemed to be suggesting, though, was not that the family members be allowed to comment, as anyone else could, but that they had a special right to be heard. Their role had been recognized by the inclusion of one Eisenhower grandchild in the EMC, but he had relinquished his seat. Now they girded themselves to exert pressure from outside.

Susan Eisenhower said that "we do not 'hate' the design, nor do we pass artistic judgment on any of the artists who have been engaged in this process. Appropriateness, however, is absolutely key to the memorialization of Dwight Eisenhower."[50] As family members expressed themselves in various hearings, public fora, and Susan Eisenhower's website, they made clear that they regarded Gehry's design as inappropriate: the memorial was too grandiose in scale; the columns were gargantuan; they disliked the tapestries; and they thought the barefoot boy concept was demeaning. In March 2012, Susan Eisenhower said that the family and the EMC had reached an impasse: as she explained, the "Horatio Alger" narrative implicit in the statue of Eisenhower as a youth was inconsistent with his achievements as president and as liberator of Europe. The president was a great (albeit a modest) man, not a dreamy youth. Controversy about the design, she said, was going to make fundraising impossible, and the memorial would cost considerably more than the amount the design team estimated. It was time to go back to the drawing board.[51]

Raising the issue of fundraising demonstrated the family's willingness to play hardball. The reality to which Susan Eisenhower was drawing attention was that in the face of objections by the family, the EMC was going to find it difficult to raise private funds to pay the costs of the memorial. This issue was critical because Congress had determined that the memorial's costs should be met by a mixture of public and private funding, but the proportions remained undefined.[52] Difficulties in private fundraising would throw the whole responsibility for paying the costs onto Congress. This situation gave legislators reason for concern about the demands on the public purse, but it also gave them leverage. If the opponents of the design could discourage legislators from appropriating funds, they would obtain a stranglehold over the project. In the midterm elections of 2010, political circumstances changed when the Republican Party won a majority in the House of Representatives. One by one, the newly appointed Republican chairmen of House committees with decision-making authority or oversight responsibility over monuments, government operations, and appropriations threw in their lot with the Eisenhower family. Together, the legislators and the family demonstrated that they would prefer to sink the whole project rather than accept a design they disliked.

Susan Eisenhower's positive reference in March 2012 to the design selection process for the Franklin Delano Roosevelt Memorial left no room for doubt about the family's resolve. She saw it not as an obstacle course to be avoided but as an affirmative precedent discouraging haste. As she wrote, "The time is now to get this memorial right. We should not be afraid of delays. The FDR Memorial took three different design competitions before reaching a final plan."[53] This was not strictly true: while the FDR Memorial went through three principal designs, only the first of them was selected as the result of an open competition. Regardless of the historical details, the FDR Memorial might be remembered quite differently, as an unpleasant reminder to the EMC of what could go wrong with a presidential memorial: after Roosevelt family members, some critics, and the CFA rejected the original design by William F. Pedersen and Bradford S. Tilney, a later design by Marcel Breuer also foundered. It took decades before the memorial designed by Lawrence Halprin was dedicated. Advocates of other controversial memorial projects had learned to think of the long delays in the FDR memorial's creation as a warning of how a project could derail, not as an example to emulate.[54] Bruce Cole, an adviser to the National Civic Art Society, a critic of Gehry's design and a late appointee to the EMC, admitted that the FDR memorial was a "bad precedent."[55]

In response to the objections, Gehry considered various modifications: more bas reliefs, a list of Eisenhower's accomplishments, more speeches. He said that, as he researched Eisenhower's life and career, he grew increasingly impressed by Ike's personal characteristics and achievements. When an EMC commissioner asked him how the design embodied these virtues, a floundering Gehry responded that "such qualities and achievements would be represented as emanations from the central idea of Ike's greatness."[56] In the end, Gehry reverted to the most traditional means of celebrating an individual's greatness: he decided to transform the two bas reliefs into three-dimensional bronze statuary groups, one representing Eisenhower as president, flanked by civilian and military advisers in the Oval Office; the other representing Eisenhower as supreme allied commander in World War II, addressing airborne troops on D-Day.[57] Carl W. Reddel, the executive director of the EMC, described them as "heroic-sized."[58]

This change followed a well-trodden path in commemorative Washington. In the nineteenth century, monuments were almost always statues.[59] In one instance after another from the mid-twentieth century to the present, the addition of realistic statuary has been a compromise memorial designers have been pressured to make in trying to get an abstract or non-traditional design built.[60] The acceptance of the need for realistic statuary, which Gehry had once regarded as superfluous, marked a step back towards tradition. Gehry also tried to appease the Eisenhower family by suggesting that the figure of Ike as a young barefoot boy might be replaced by a depiction of Eisenhower in young adulthood, perhaps as a West Point cadet.[61] Had this change been made, it would have tilted the figurative representations towards the military (as, indeed, the design finally approved by the family does, albeit in a different way).

Despite Gehry's expressed willingness to consider modifications, the Eisenhower family were implacably opposed to the design. In October 2012, John Eisenhower wrote to Senator Daniel Inouye (D-Hawaii), a World War II veteran who served as Vice Chairman of the EMC until his death later that year, saying that the scope and scale of the memorial were "too extravagant" and that it tried to do too much.[62] Inouye's death reminded the EMC of the urgent need to complete the memorial while there were members of the "Greatest Generation" alive to see it.[63] Susan Eisenhower, however, asked Congress to defund the current design and to bring together a non-partisan group to reorganize the enterprise.[64]

Congressional leaders, conservative journalists, and others picked up on the cues coming from Eisenhower family members and from a damning report Shubow had issued. The columnist George Will called the memorial "an exhibitionistic triumph of theory over function—more a monument to its creator, Frank Gehry, practitioner of architectural flamboyance, than to the most underrated president."[65] Others agreed that the design drew attention to the architect rather than to Eisenhower. The memorial "is not about Ike. It's about Gehry," the critic Catesby Leigh commented.[66] Rep. Rob Bishop (R-Utah) chimed in that it was not a monument to the president, but "a monument to a designer [Gehry] with a theme about President Eisenhower."[67]

A persistent refrain in the criticisms was the contrast between the architect's supposed egocentrism and the president's exemplary modesty. Rep. Darrell Issa (R-California), who would become the memorial design's nemesis, said that its "immodesty is unbefitting of the humility and plain-spokenness that characterized our 34th President."[68] Military veterans echoed Issa: a navy veteran complained that "the grandiose scope and scale of the memorial do not befit President Eisenhower. He was a general who never bragged, did not wear his medals on his uniform, and requested to be buried in the same $80 casket the Army provides for all of its soldiers."[69] A member of Eisenhower's military staff said that the scale of the design was "out of character for a man who believed so strongly in service and humility." Eisenhower, he said, would want a "simpler, more modest memorial."[70]

The design's innovative quality had become a focal point for attack. Any memorial design that is notable for any reason—for its novelty, grandeur, or impact—brings attention both to the person being commemorated and to the designer. The design team was in a double bind: create a memorial that was innocuous and be accused of diminishing the subject; or produce the sort of path-breaking design that Gehry was presumably selected to create and be accused of abetting the architect's self-promotion. The memorial's detractors said that the tapestries would appear to be a "billboard," an unattractive way of seeing the metallic screens, about which members of the CFA had been critical; worse, the critics said they would be an advertisement not of the president but of the architect himself. Whether or not this "billboard" criticism was fair, it did touch on a problem with which the designers long struggled: how to achieve the right degree of translucency and legibility so that the images in the tapestries could be made out at various distances, and so that the screens would not block too much light from the Lyndon B. Johnson Building behind them.[71]

Members of Congress borrowed a line of attack first mounted by Shubow, the need for a verbal explanation of the symbolic meaning of the tapestries. How, he asked, was anyone supposed to know that the trees depicted in the mesh represented the landscape of the Midwest? It could be anywhere, Kansas or Kazakhstan.

"Monuments," Shubow said, "ought to be clear and unequivocal in their meaning . . . They must be legible without a guide or key, and certainly without a visitor center or iPad. Monuments speak to us even without signage."[72] Legislators critical of the Gehry design extensively quoted Shubow's words. They said the memorial "should be self-explanatory so that ordinary Americans will understand the ideas being conveyed without the need of a visitor center or guide."[73]

The congressional critics took up the complaint about the memorial's mounting costs to the government. Rep. Doc Hastings (R-Washington) was the chairman of the House Natural Resources Committee, and Bishop was the chairman of its Subcommittee on Public Lands and Environmental Regulation. The Natural Resources Committee enjoyed broad jurisdiction over the activities of the National Park Service, the memorial's governmental sponsor. In a joint letter to the GSA, which was in charge of contracts for the project, Hastings and Bishop asked a series of detailed questions that demanded an accounting of expenditures and asked for copies of contracts and other documents.[74] The implication—or warning—was that they were searching for evidence of excessive costs and of impropriety in the awarding of contracts.

By 2014, private fundraising had achieved minimal results. In July of that year, citing objections to the design, the opposition of the family, and fundraising difficulties, Bishop introduced legislation that called for the memorial commission to be reconstituted and for a new design competition to be held. New commission members would be selected with the advice of the Eisenhower Foundation, whose board of directors included the four Eisenhower grandchildren.[75] Opponents of Bishop's bill pointed out that holding a new competition would cost $17 million and hold up the project for years, with no guarantee that the new effort would be any more successful than the old one.[76] Bishop's bill was not enacted, but simultaneously with its introduction, the Natural Resources Committee released a staff report that complained, "The Eisenhower Memorial Commission was established in 1999, and 15 years later there is still no memorial, or approved design for a memorial. Yet the Commission has continued to return each year to Congress to ask for additional funds."[77] Together, Bishop's bill and the committee report registered significant Republican Party opposition to the design.

Amid the rising congressional opposition, the memorial design had been proceeding through the review process in the CFA and the NCPC. Although the CFA had given the design conceptual approval in 2011, the membership of the CFA had changed markedly by 2013, so a recap of the history of the design was needed. New commission members had many reservations about the relationship between landscape and other elements, the content of the tapestries, the plantings, and the configuration of the trees. The CFA approved the design as a whole in July 2013, but the details of the memorial precinct were still subject to review, and hence open to requests for revision.[78]

The review process became entangled with the legislators' objections at the NCPC, of which Rep. Issa was a commissioner. A zealous conservative, he had clear sympathies with the Eisenhower grandchildren. Issa suggested that the designers come back with a revised proposal without the columns and the tapestries.[79] All that would be left would be a park with statues and inscriptions. Had that proposition prevailed, Gehry Partners would have withdrawn from the project.[80] Issa said that he had preferred the tapestries when they depicted scenes from Eisenhower's career—D-Day, the Cold War, desegregation—and he found the trees nondescript.[81] Like Susan Eisenhower and Bishop, Issa used fundraising problems as a form of leverage. "We are running into an incredibly tough time to bring forth [congressional] funds," he said. "The time for endless debate has to be over, [and] the Gehry organization and this Commission [the NCPC] really do have to find a way to find the middle ground."[82] Issa's chairmanship of the House Committee on Oversight and Government Reform, the principal investigating committee of the House of Representatives, gave him authority to delve into the history of the memorial project, and he questioned whether the competition that had selected Gehry had been above board.[83] Issa speculated that if those in authority decided to scrap Gehry's design, they could "just build a park, put in some small statues, take [Gehry's] name off of it and call it a memorial. And it'd be less grand, but, in fact, it would be less blighted too."[84]

In April 2014, with Issa's encouragement, the NCPC determined that the design did not meet all of their seven design principles and had to be revised.[85] The design team and EMC representatives complained in vain that the design did meet the principles and that the NCPC's interpretation of them was "subjective." Whatever the merits of the case, the NCPC had statutory authority to approve or reject a design and the designers were obliged to satisfy the objections. They removed the side tapestry panels, about which the CFA also had long-standing objections, and moved two of the columns further back from Independence Avenue, clearing the view to the Capitol Building.[86] In November, the design team submitted a full proposal, with these revisions, to the CFA. The statuary Gehry had agreed to add would be created by Sergey Eylanbekov and Penelope Jencks, and would stand in front of bas reliefs that acted as a background and stage set.[87] The CFA asked for further refinements in the design, including the transformation of the landscape to one that would be more symbolic than literalistic.[88]

Once the designers introduced the changes, the memorial again came before the CFA and the NCPC, which granted their final approvals in June and July 2015.[89] Normally, that would bring the process of design development and revision to an end. However, the "final approvals" did not end the story. The statutory commissions might be satisfied but the Eisenhower family and the congressional critics were not. A few years earlier, the writer Jeffrey Frank had wittily remarked that the memorial design had managed to achieve something rare in Washington: "in true bipartisan spirit, almost everyone hates it."[90] On the eve of the commissions' final approvals, a *Washingtonian* magazine headline suggested that the remarkable consensus endured: "Everyone Still Hates the Planned Eisenhower Memorial."[91] So long as the Eisenhower family remained resolutely opposed to the memorial, and while the design remained mired in controversy, the chances that it would gain enough private donations and government appropriations to be built were doubtful.

In April 2016, the press reported that private fundraising efforts had raised only $5 million of the expected $150 million the memorial would cost, if it were ever to be constructed. EMC commissioner Cole said, "Americans are simply not opening their wallets to what is essentially a monument to architect Frank Gehry's ego instead of a memorial to Ike."[92] Perhaps just as bad, the government had by then given $66 million of taxpayer money to the memorial, with no certainty it would ever be completed.

Now, the powerful Appropriations Committee lowered the boom. Its chairman, Rep. Hal Rogers (R-KY), was one of those who in 2013 had objected to further federal funding for the memorial.[93] The committee complained about the memorial's "ongoing indifference" to the views of the family, finding it "unacceptable and inconceivable" that a memorial to Eisenhower could go forward without their active support. Taking note of the millions spent on salary costs, consultants, and architect's fees, the committee asked for an accounting of all expenditures and called for a "reset," which would involve a new memorial design competition, with family members involved in the selection of the design, and the appointment of new staff for the EMC. Until Congress authorized "an open, public, and transparent new design process," the committee said that it declined to provide any further capital costs for the construction of the memorial; it would meet only the salary and other costs required to keep the memorial commission alive.[94]

These difficulties induced the EMC and the designers voluntarily to introduce changes in order to win over the opponents. The problem was that any such changes in turn superseded the approvals of the statutory review commissions: each time a new element was introduced, it had to win the support of the NCPC and the CFA all over again. In 2017, the CFA and the NCPC considered three such changes. In a radical transformation of the original concept, the tapestry scene shifted to a portrait of peacetime Normandy instead of the Kansas landscape. The statue of the young Eisenhower moved to an off-center location behind the tapestry, near the Lyndon B. Johnson Building, making it less prominent. Finally, four trees were to be removed. The members of the NCPC approved the revisions, but declared themselves to be "perplexed" and "puzzled" by the changes, and said that they had preferred the Midwestern landscape in the tapestry. Some critics of the previous version of the tapestries were just as unhappy: Shubow, now apparently regretting the changes that his criticisms had helped to prompt, complained that the resulting design was "confused, illegible, and weak."[95] He asked the CFA to reinstate the previous design.[96]

Members of the CFA reluctantly approved the shift in scene from Kansas to peacetime Pointe du Hoc, Normandy, but pointed out the obvious: the transformation of the landscape in the tapestries changed the meaning of the memorial considerably. The design had lost its narrative coherence.[97] The CFA had once described the statue of the young Eisenhower as the "conceptual fulcrum" for the memorial as a whole—linking the aspirations symbolized by the landscape image on the tapestry with the accomplishments of Eisenhower represented in the sculptural tableaux and inscriptions.[98] The removal of the Kansas landscape left the statue of the young Eisenhower bereft of the context in which its presence had once been meaningful. The inscribed wall on which the figure sits will feature an extended passage from the homecoming speech, providing an independent explanatory context for a statue that I suspect will be popular with visitors. There will, however, be no marriage between the depicted landscape of the tapestries and the plantings in the memorial precinct.

Craig Webb, of Gehry Partners, put the best face on things by explaining that the use of the Normandy landscape would "serve as the symbolic bridge between Eisenhower's military and civilian careers," but that statement is unpersuasive.[99] There is no obvious connection between Normandy and Eisenhower's career as president. Supposedly the Normandy coast represents the peacetime world that President Eisenhower strove to achieve, but any tranquil landscape could suggest that. The elephant in the room is that these modifications were being made to appease the opponents of the design, not for any aesthetic reason intelligible to the professional experts on the review commissions. The best, perhaps only, recommendation for the changes was that they had resulted from a compromise accepted by the Eisenhower family. Former Secretary of State James A. Baker III, a member of the EMC's advisory committee, had brokered the agreement. Gehry was said not to have been involved in the discussions.[100] Congress appropriated a further $45 million on top of the $66 million already committed.[101] With the compromise achieved, ground breaking took place at the beginning of November 2017.[102]

Once intended to rewrite the language of monumental commemoration, the memorial instead re-inscribed tradition once realistic statuary and chiseled texts became its central components. By the time the further changes were made, it seemed that there was no longer any reason for anyone to be enthusiastic about the design. The proposal for a presidential memorial that would artistically evoke the Midwestern landscape from which the young Eisenhower sprang at least articulated a meaningful concept, even if some disliked the idea and others believed it would be illegible without an explanatory text. Gehry had emphasized the simplicity of the design in September 2011. "We just don't want it to be three memorials," he said. "We want it to be one essential thing and keep it compact."[103] When the statuary groups and large-scale inscriptions were added, the memorial lost its formal unity. It became a mish-mash of narrative, textual, landscape, architectural, and expressive elements, an instance of what one critic has described as "memorial sprawl": that is, the inability of recent memorial designers to distil people, events, or ideals into formally resonant, non-narrative forms.[104] With the final compromise, the design fell into incoherence.

Issa had spoken presciently at a review meeting of the NCPC when he said that introducing piecemeal changes to answer individual objections "might please everyone individually, [but] you please no one cumulatively."[105] Despite their awareness of such pitfalls, the design's critics seem not to have found a way to avoid them. In 2014 NCPC commissioner Mina Wright said that the memorial was succumbing to "design by committee."[106] Rep. Rush Holt (D-New Jersey) expanded on that charge. Certain that Congress should not interfere with the details of the design, he commented, "The only thing worse than art designed by a Committee is art designed by a Congressional committee."[107] In the end, it was worse even than that: design by a back-room deal.

Few visitors to the memorial, when it is completed, will know about the backstage wrangling from which its final design emerged. They will have still less chance of knowing about a particular decision to alter the design that attracted no attention when it was made and so escaped controversy. In June 2015, Webb said that a change had been introduced in the Oval Office statuary group, which showed Eisenhower flanked by a military adviser and two civilian advisers. The three figures would no longer be portrait statues but would become generic figures. In response to the EMC's advice, one of them would be an African American.[108]

This change follows the trend in recent commemorative statuary, where there has been a felt imperative to produce groups of figures whose ethnic composition "looks like America."[109] The insertion of an African American figure into this statuary group touched on a delicate subject, though. As president, Eisenhower had a decidedly mixed record on Civil Rights; it has been described as "hesitant, cautious, and perhaps even timorous."[110] He signed into law the Civil Rights Act of 1957 and ordered army troops to ensure the desegregation of Central High School in Little Rock, Arkansas, that same year. However, before the Supreme Court's Brown v. Board of Education decision outlawing "separate but equal" educational provision, Eisenhower had expressed sympathy with white Southerners who did not want black students to sit alongside their children.[111] He had been unenthusiastic about the Brown decision and doubted whether legally enforced desegregation would succeed in changing racial attitudes.[112] While there are many photographs of Eisenhower meeting African Americans in the White House, they are usually part of large groups; there was no African American White House aide who would plausibly fit the role of one of Eisenhower's three principal advisers.[113] The scene with generic figures was invented in order to make a point about racial equality that met the political requirements of present times but did not entirely match the historical realities of the Eisenhower White House, except, possibly, in its tokenism.

Webb explains that an African American figure had to be inserted in the White House scene because it was impossible to place any African Americans in the other statuary group, which shows Eisenhower addressing members of the 101st Airborne Division on D-Day. No African Americans served in that unit's combat arms during World War II. Because of that factual position, and because the D-Day scene is based on a historical photograph, it was not considered feasible to change the scene by conjuring any African American soldiers into the group.[114] In contrast, the grouping of figures in the Oval Office scene is imaginary, not based on a photograph, so it was considered acceptable to include an African American figure.[115]

There was another reason that it would have been awkward to include any African American figures in the scene with the 101st Airborne. By the time Eisenhower ordered members of that unit to aid in the desegregation of Central High School, in 1957, the 101st was a racially integrated division. The Eisenhower administration, though, ordered its African American members to be pulled out of the line when the troops took part in the school's desegregation, so as not to offend racist white Southerners.[116] The unit's combat arm was lily white on June 6, 1945 and the troops mustered to confront a racist mob remained so in Little Rock on September 24, 1957. Without delving into the details of the administration's actions, when Issa's proposals for an alternative design came before it, the EMC resolved that Eisenhower's "pragmatic" leadership during the crisis in Little Rock would be a model for its own decision-making.[117]

Visitors to the memorial will have no perception of the hands that always hover above the realized designs of commemorative monuments in Washington, DC, visible only in their effects. The memorial is designed to remember the general, the president, and the person, but it will also recall the work of serial manipulations: the hand that painted a figure white and placed it at the center of an architectural model; the others that, failing to remove that figure altogether, shoved it to a less prominent position; the salute to the South that ensured that no black faces were present in a military unit bent on supporting racial equality; and the later move that, with equal tact, ensured that a black man would be visible to posterity in Eisenhower's Oval Office. The Eisenhower Memorial will help cement the reputation of the figure it honors, but like all memorials in Washington, and perhaps more than most, its carved stone and crafted metal will at once conceal and preserve a story of political pressure, enforced compromise, and tactful euphemism, a story no less redolent of our times than of Eisenhower's own.

Notes

1. For Gehry's career, see Paul Goldberger, *Building Art: The Life and Work of Frank Gehry* (New York: Vintage Books, 2017). The author acknowledges with gratitude the Patricia and Phillip Frost

Senior Fellowship at the Smithsonian American Art Museum, which supported the research on which this chapter is based.
2. Lewis Mumford, *The Culture of Cities*, quoted in Thomas Hawk Creighton, *The Architecture of Monuments: The Franklin Delano Roosevelt Memorial Competition* (New York: Reinhold, 1962), 7. See also the discussion in Kirk Savage, *Monument Wars: Washington, DC, the National Mall, and the Transformation of the Memorial Landscape* (Berkeley: University of California Press, 2009), 18; Bernd Nicolai, "New Monumentalism in Contemporary Architecture," *Anglia* 131, no. 2–3 (2013): 299; Sigfried Giedion, "The Need for a New Monumentality," in Paul Zucker (ed.), *New Architecture and City Planning* (New York: Philosophical Library, 1944), 549–68.
3. Louis Sullivan, "Ornament in Architecture," *The Engineering Magazine*, 1892.
4. Patrick Hagopian, *The Vietnam War in American Memory: Veterans, Memorials, and the Politics of Healing* (Amherst: University of Massachusetts Press, 2009), 118–20, 304.
5. Public Law 106-79, 106th Congress (October 25, 1999).
6. Jennifer Reut, "Ike Memorial Mired in Controversy," *Perspectives on History* (November 2013): 11.
7. Public Law 107-117, 107th Congress (January 10, 2002) amended Public Law 106-79 by providing authority to establish a memorial in compliance with the Commemorative Works Act (CWA), and by authorizing the funds. The National Capital Memorial Commission voted unanimously to recommend a location within Area I at its March 2002 meeting. Transcript of the National Capital Memorial Commission, March 1, 2002. My thanks to Glenn DeMarr for providing me with a copy of the transcript.
8. Carol Ross Joynt, "Tug of War: How a Small Army of VIPs Killed the Eisenhower Memorial," *Washingtonian* (May 2014): 64. The relevant approvals of the location came from the (renamed) National Capital Memorial Advisory Commission on November 8, 2005, the National Capital Planning Commission on September 7, 2006, and the Commission of Fine Arts on September 20, 2006. Congress authorised construction in Area I, into which part of the site falls, by passing Public Law 109-220, 109th Congress (May 5, 2006).
9. Rep. Darrell Issa, Minutes of the National Captial Planning Commission meeting September 4, 2014, 99.
10. National Capital Planning Commission File No. 6694, Dwight D. Eisenhower Memorial, *Approval of Site and Design Principles*,

Staff Recommendation, August 31, 2006. The Design Principles were: 1. Preserve reciprocal views to and from the US Capitol along Maryland Avenue, SW. 2. Enhance the nature of the site as one in a sequence of public spaces embellishing the Maryland Avenue vista. 3. Create a unified memorial site that integrates the disparate parcels into a meaningful and functional public gathering place that also unifies the surrounding precinct. 4. Reflect L'Enfant Plan principles by shaping the Memorial site as a separate and distinct public space that complements the Department of Education Headquarters and other surrounding buildings. 5. Respect and complement the architecture of the surrounding precinct. 6. Respect the building lines of the surrounding rights-of-way and the alignment of trees along Maryland Avenue. 7. Incorporate significant green space into the design of the memorial.

11. NCPC, *Approval of Site and Design Principles, Staff Recommendation*, 15. Part of the site fell into Area II, where the construction of new memorials was encouraged. The relevant planning documents were the National Capital Planning Commission's 1997 *Legacy Plan*, and the 2001 *Museums and Monuments Master Plan*. The *National Capital Framework Plan* of 2006 reaffirmed the principle of moving significant memorials away from the central Mall area.
12. US Gen. Services Administration, EMC-WPC-08-5019, *National Dwight D. Eisenhower Memorial*, August 15, 2008, 1, <https://www.fbo.gov> (accessed June 13, 2018).
13. The board included representatives from the EMC, General Services Administration, the Eisenhower family, and private sector design peers. "A Five-Star Folly: An Investigation into the Cost Increases, Construction Delays, and Design Problems That Have Been a Disservice to the Effort to Memorialize Dwight D. Eisenhower," Majority Staff Report, US Congress, House Committee on Natural Resources, 113th Congress (July 25, 2014), 14.
14. The jury consisted of three architects, two landscape architects, one urban designer, one information designer, one lighting designer, and David Eisenhower. "Five-Star Folly," 18.
15. For an account of the multiple steps in the selection process, see "Five-Star Folly," 14–18, and Carl Reddel's responses to a series of written questions by Rep. Rob Bishop, US House, 112th Congress, 2nd sess., Committee on Natural Resources, Subcommittee on National Parks, Forests and Public Lands, Oversight Hearing, March 20, 2012 (hereafter, March 2012 Hearing), 43–47.

16. Cole, "Monumental Shame." Senator Pat Roberts (R-KS), a commissioner from the inception of the EMC, replaced Siciliano as chairman of the commission in 2015. Siciliano was a fundraiser for the Gehry-designed Walt Disney Concert Hall in Los Angeles. Siciliano and Gehry are honorary life directors of the Los Angeles Philharmonic.
17. March 2012 Hearing, 30–31, 43, 49.
18. See Testimony of Sam Roche, Minutes of the NCPC meeting (October 2, 2014), 73.
19. "Five-Star Folly," 14.
20. Minutes of the CFA meeting May 20, 2010, 5. For the reasons that some of these proposed photographs were rejected, see Philip Kennicott, "The Monument War," *Washington Post Magazine*, May 13, 2012.
21. The speeches on which the EMC eventually settled were Eisenhower's London Guildhall Address of June 12, 1945; his First Inaugural Address; and his Farewell Speech of January 17, 1961. Minutes of the Dwight D. Eisenhower Memorial Commission meeting April 29, 2015.
22. Minutes of the CFA meeting May 20, 2010, 4.
23. Thomas E. Luebke to Margaret O'Dell, Regional Director, NPS National Capital Region, May 28, 2010. In the records of the Commission of Fine Arts.
24. Testimony of Carl Reddel, March 2012 Hearing, 41.
25. Minutes of the CFA meeting January 20, 2011, 3.
26. Gehry Partners/AECOM, *Eisenhower Memorial: Concept Submission to United States Commission of Fine Arts*, January 6, 2011, 74. In the records of the Commission of Fine Arts.
27. Transcript of the discussions at the January 2011 meeting of the CFA, unpaginated [15], in the records of the Commission of Fine Arts. I appreciate the assistance of Kathryn Fanning of the Commission of Fine Arts in obtaining copies of several meeting transcripts.
28. Gehry Partners/AECOM, *Eisenhower Memorial*, January 6, 2011, 72–73.
29. "The Eisenhower Life Series," Eisenhower Presidential Library, Museum, and Boyhood Home, <https://www.eisenhower.archives.gov> (accessed June 13, 2018).
30. Testimony of Carl Reddel, March 2012 Hearing, 35; Gehry Partners/AECOM, *Eisenhower Memorial*, January 6, 2011, 73.
31. CFA Meeting Transcript, January 2011, 13.
32. Minutes of the CFA meeting January 20, 2011, 4.
33. Gehry Partners/AECOM, *Eisenhower Memorial*, January 6, 2011, 73.

34. Ibid. 28–29.
35. Minutes of the CFA meeting May 20, 2010, 3.
36. CFA Meeting Transcript, September 15, 2011, 22.
37. Kennicott, "Monument War," 14.
38. Philip Kennicott, "Review: Frank Gehry's Eisenhower Memorial Reinvigorates the Genre," *Washington Post*, December 15, 2011.
39. David M. Childs to Reps. Rob Bishop and Raul Grijalva, March 2012 Hearing, 6.
40. Remarks of Thomas E. Luebke, CFA Meeting Transcript, September 15, 2011, 9.
41. March 2012 Hearing, 39, 48.
42. Kennicott, "Monument War," 15–16.
43. Philip Kennicott, "Eisenhower Family Calls for Timeout in Approval of Memorial," *Washington Post*, October 6, 2011.
44. Joynt, "Tug of War," 65.
45. Testimony of Susan Eisenhower, March 2012 Hearing, 16; Testimony of Carl Reddel, March 2012 Hearing, 42. David and Anne Eisenhower had spoken favorably about the design before the addition of the young Eisenhower statue. Minutes of the Eisenhower Memorial Commission meeting March 25, 2010, 6–7.
46. Susan Eisenhower, "Let's Engage on the Real Issues with Ike's Memorial," February 3, 2012, <https://susaneisenhower.wordpress.com/2012/02/03/dont-swift-boat-critics-of-the-eisenhower-memorial-design/> (accessed June 13, 2018).
47. Testimony of Carl Reddel, March 2012 Hearing, 42.
48. John S.D. Eisenhower to Anne Eisenhower and Susan Eisenhower, December 11, 2011, <https://susaneisenhower.files.wordpress.com/2012/01/jsde_letter_re_memorial2.pdf> (accessed June 13, 2018).
49. H-Rept 113–705, 3. Judy Scott Feldmann of the National Coalition to Save Our Mall repeated the call for a simple statue on a pedestal. Minutes of the NCPC meeting October 2, 2014, 95.
50. Susan Eisenhower, "The Eisenhower Memorial: Another Front in the Culture Wars?," January 24, 2012, <https://susaneisenhower.wordpress.com/2012/01/24/the-eisenhower-memorial-another-front-in-the-culture-wars/> (accessed June 13, 2018).
51. March 2012 Hearing, 10-17.
52. Testimony of Carl Reddel, March 2012 Hearing, 41.
53. Eisenhower, "The Eisenhower Memorial: Another Front in the Culture Wars?"
54. Jan C. Scruggs and Joel L. Swerdlow, *To Heal a Nation: The Vietnam Veterans Memorial* (New York: Harper and Row, 1985), 73.

55. Minutes of the Eisenhower Memorial Commission meeting September 17, 2014, 9. Cole was appointed as a commissioner of the EMC in August 2013.
56. Minutes of the Eisenhower Memorial Commission meeting July 12, 2011, 7.
57. Testimony of Carl Reddel, US House, 113th Congress, 1st sess., Committee on Natural Resources, Subcommittee on Public Lands and Environmental Regulation, Hearing on HR 1126, Dwight D. Eisenhower Memorial Completion Act (hereafter, March 2013 Hearing), 46; Gehry to Rep. Rob Bishop, March 19, 2012, March 2012 Hearing, 4–5.
58. March 2013 Hearing, 17.
59. Savage, *Monument Wars*, 197.
60. We see this in the Theodore Roosevelt Memorial, where the armillary sphere was replaced by a statue; in the original design for the FDR memorial by Pedersen and Tilney, where a statue was plonked amidst the concrete stele before the whole ensemble was rejected; in the Vietnam Veterans Memorial, where right-wing veterans were appeased by the addition of a statue of infantrymen, leading to the later addition of a women's memorial statue; in the Korean War Veterans Memorial, where the original design called for rough-hewn granite statues forming a symbolic timeline, which were transformed into a realistic cast metal depiction of a platoon in action; and in the Martin Luther King Jr. National Memorial, where the designers added a massive statue in response to a prompt by the memorial commission.
61. Frank Gehry to Commissioners, May 15, 2012, Minutes of the Eisenhower Memorial Commission meeting of May 15, 2012, 3.
62. John S.D. Eisenhower to Sen. Daniel K. Inouye, October 18, 2012, in March 2013 Hearing, 10.
63. Minutes of the Eisenhower Memorial Commission meeting June 19, 2013, 4.
64. March 2013 Hearing, 8.
65. Kennicott, "Monument War," 16.
66. Catesby Leigh, "A Monumental Folly," *National Review*, June 13, 2017.
67. Testimony of Rep. Rob Bishop, March 2013 Hearing, 2.
68. Issa to Preston Bryant Jr., chairman of the NCPC, April 3, 2014, <https://oversight.house.gov> (accessed June 13, 2018).
69. J. William Middendorf II, to L. Preston Bryant Jr., March 23, 2014. In the records of the National Capital Planning Commission. Middendorf served as secretary of the navy from 1974 to 1977.

70. Colonel Ralph Hauenstein, quoted in Rep. Bill Huizinga to L. Preston Bryant Jr., April 3, 2014. In the records of the National Capital Planning Commission. Hauenstein was the former chief of intelligence on General Eisenhower's staff during World War II. See also Blake Seitz, "58 Generals, Admirals Sign Letter Opposing Design of Eisenhower Memorial," *Washington Free Beacon*, September 13, 2016.
71. Leigh, "Monumental Folly."
72. Statement by Justin Shubow, March 2013 Hearing, 35.
73. H-Rpt. 113-705, 4.
74. Reps. Doc Hastings and Rob Bishop to Dan M. Tangherlini, US General Services Administration, May 15, 2013, <https://naturalresources.house.gov/uploadedfiles/05_-15-13_hastingsltractadmintangherlini.pdf> (accessed June 13, 2018).
75. HR 5203, 113th Cong., 2nd sess., Dwight D. Eisenhower Memorial Commission Reform Act, July 25, 2014, <http://www.eisenhowerfoundation.net/160/Foundation> (accessed June 13, 2018).
76. "Dissenting Views," H-Rpt. 113-705, 11. The $17 million sum came from a report by the Congressional Budget Office. Associated Press, "Key Arts Panel Approves Gehry's Eisenhower Memorial Design with Suggested Changes for DC Site," *Washington Post*, July 18, 2013.
77. All Actions H.R.5203, 113th Congress, 2013–2014, <https://www.congress.gov/bill/113th-congress/house-bill/5203/all-actions?overview=closed#tabs> (accessed June 13, 2018); "Five-Star Folly," 10.
78. Minutes of the CFA meeting of July 18, 2013; minutes of the CFA meeting November 21, 2013. Six CFA members had been replaced in the period 2011–13 once their terms expired, and between 2010, when the CFA had responded positively to an informational presentation by the design team, and 2013, the only consistent members of the commission were Chairman Earl A. Powell and Elizabeth Plater-Zyberk.
79. Darrell Issa to Rocco C. Siciliano, http://freebeacon.com/blog/breaking-issa-requests-ike-memorial-commission-to-submit-new-design/, November 14, 2014. Issa was an ex officio member of the NCPC as chairman of the House Committee on Oversight and Government Reform.
80. Minutes of the Eisenhower Memorial Commission meeting of September 17, 2014, 6.
81. Minutes of the NCPC meeting April 3, 2014, 78.

82. Ibid. 75–76.
83. Darrell Issa to Rocco C. Siciliano, February 29, 2012, <http://www.eisenhowermemorial.net/docs/Darrell_Issa_letter_to_Eisenhower_Memorial_Commission.pdf> (accessed June 13, 2018).
84. Minutes of the NCPC meeting September 4, 2014, 123.
85. Minutes of the NCPC meeting April 3, 2014, 51–52. The principal problems were the relationship with nearby buildings, intrusion into their building line, and the reciprocal views to and from the Capitol Building. In the discussion, the commissioners referred to the size and scale of the tapestries as the underlying problem, and also cited the absence of any place for public gatherings.
86. Minutes of the NCPC meeting September 4, 2014, 67, 70.
87. Gehry Partners/AECOM, *Eisenhower Memorial: Commemorative Arts and Landscape Design*, presented to the Commission of Fine Arts, November 20, 2014.
88. Minutes of the CFA meeting November 20, 2014, letter from Thomas E. Luebke, Secretary, Commission of Fine Arts, to Lisa Mendelson-Ielmini, Acting Regional Director, National Park Service, National Capital Region, December 1, 2014. In the records of the Commission of Fine Arts.
89. Minutes of the CFA meeting June 18, 2015, letter from Thomas E. Luebke, Secretary, Commission of Fine Arts, to Robert Fogel, Regional Director, National Park Service, National Capital Region, June 26, 2015. In the records of the Commission of Fine Arts. The National Capital Planning Commission gave final approval for the design at its July 9, 2015 meeting. NCPC, *Dwight D. Eisenhower Memorial: Executive Director's Recommendation*, February 2, 2017, 7.
90. Jeffrey Frank, "Rescuing the Eisenhower Memorial," *The New Yorker*, March 25, 2013.
91. Benjamin Freed, "Everyone Still Hates the Planned Eisenhower Memorial," *Washingtonian*, June 16, 2015.
92. Joe Crowe, "Eisenhower Memorial Raises Just $5 Million of $150 Million Needed," *Newsmax.com*, April 4, 2016, <https://www.newsmax.com/newsfront/eisenhower-memorial-fund/2016/04/27/id/725996/> (accessed June 13, 2018).
93. Sam Roche, "Rogers Aided in Eisenhower Memorial's Fresh Start," *Lexington Herald Leader*, November 8, 2013.
94. US Congress, House, 114th Cong., 1st sess., Committee on Appropriations, Report on Department of the Interior, Environment, and Related Agencies Appropriations Bill, 2016, H-Rpt. 114–170, June 18, 2015, 87–89.

95. Michelle Goldchain, "NCPC 'Puzzled' by Eisenhower Memorial Design Changes, Approves Project Anyway," <https://dc.curbed.com/2017/2/2/14487700/memorial-eisenhower-ncpc> (accessed June 13, 2018).
96. Minutes of the CFA meeting January 23, 2017.
97. Minutes of the CFA meeting May 18, 2017; minutes of the CFA meeting September 20, 2017.
98. Minutes of the CFA meeting May 21, 2015, letter from Thomas Luebke to Robert Vogel, May 29, 2015.
99. Minutes of the CFA meeting January 23, 2017. Gehry had decided around 2012 that his presence in Washington was not helping. Goldberger, *Building Art*, 419. From that point on Gehry Partners was represented in meetings of the EMC by Meaghan Lloyd and John Bowers. From early 2014 onward, Webb was the firm's principal presenter at meetings of the CFA.
100. Dwight D. Eisenhower Memorial Commission, press release, "Senator Pat Roberts Announces Support from the Eisenhower Family for the Eisenhower Memorial Project to Move Forward," September 19, 2016, <http://www.eisenhowermemorial.org/sites/default/files/public/press/Eisenhower%20Family%20Announcement%20Package%209.19.16%20PDF.pdf> (accessed June 13, 2018); Kriston Capps, "Is the Eisenhower Memorial Moving Forward without Frank Gehry?" *CityLab*, September 20, 2016, <https://www.citylab.com/design/2016/09/is-the-eisenhower-memorial-moving-forward-without-frank-gehry/500645/> (accessed June 13, 2018).
101. Rebecca Cooper, "Eisenhower Memorial Gets Go-ahead Funding to Start Construction," *Washington Business Journal*, May 1, 2017.
102. Patrick Lynch, "Construction Begins on Frank Gehry's Eisenhower Memorial in Washington DC," *Arch Daily*, November 2, 2017.
103. CFA Meeting Transcript, September 15, 2011, 18.
104. Remarks of Catesby Leigh, minutes of the CFA meeting May 21, 2017.
105. Minutes of the NCPC meeting September 4, 2014, 110.
106. Ibid. 138, 149–59.
107. Rep. Rush Holt, March 2013 Hearing, 46.
108. Minutes of the CFA meeting June 18, 2015.
109. For a discussion of this trend, see Hagopian, *Vietnam War in American Memory*, 268–72; and Patrick Hagopian, "The Korean War Veterans Memorial and Problems of Representation," *Public Art Dialogue* 2, no. 2 (2012): 232–33.

110. Michael J. Klarman, "Brown, Racial Change, and the Civil Rights Movement," *Virginia Law Review* 80, no. 1 (February 1994): 130.
111. Mark Stern, "Presidential Strategies and Civil Rights: Eisenhower, the Early Years, 1952–54," *Presidential Studies Quarterly* 19, no. 4 (Fall 1989): 788.
112. Michael S. Mayer, "With Much Deliberation and Some Speed: Eisenhower and the Brown Decision," *Journal of Southern History* 52, no. 1 (February 1986): 49.
113. Eisenhower's most prominent African American adviser was E. Frederic Morrow, but he did not occupy the top tier of presidential advisers and his memoir, *Black Man in the White House*, made for uncomfortable reading for anyone invested in the idea of racial egalitarianism in the Eisenhower administration. Wolfgang Saxon, "E. Frederic Morrow, 88, Aide in Eisenhower Administration," *New York Times*, July 21, 1994.
114. "General Dwight D. Eisenhower Gives the Order of the Day, June 6, 1944," by an unknown Army photographer. Library of Congress Prints and Photographs Division. LC-USZ62-25600.
115. Personal communication between the author and Craig Webb at the National Building Museum, June 18, 2015. The Oval Office scene was originally based on "The Elder Statesman," a 1966 photograph by Yousuf Karsh showing Eisenhower with his hand on a globe, but that shows the president alone. In the process of design development, the globe changed to a map in the bas relief that served as a backdrop to the free-standing statuary showing the president with the three advisers.
116. Jean Edward Smith, *Eisenhower in War and Peace* (New York: Random House, 2012), 723; Adam Serwer, "Why Don't We Remember Ike as a Civil Rights Hero?" *MSNBC*, May 18, 2014, <http://www.msnbc.com/msnbc/why-dont-we-ike-civil-rights> (accessed June 13, 2018).
117. Minutes of the Eisenhower Memorial Commission meeting September 17, 2014, 3, 10.

10

Top Trumps: Presidential legacies, new technologies, and a new generation

Sylvia Ellis

In the last two decades presidential campaigning has been transformed by new media technologies. Presidential legacies in the twenty-first century take shape and evolve in cyberspace. The proliferation of websites—from those of presidential libraries to those of conspiracy theorists—provides endless information. Donald Trump's routine tweets show how powerful Twitter can be as a source of information, not to mention Instagram, Snapchat, Facebook, and other social networking sites (SNSs). All kinds of publicity campaigns have taken advantage of the new media landscape, and the gaming industry contributes to our impression of former presidents as well. Bestselling games like Sid Meier's *Civilization* series or the *Call of Duty* franchise (and soon virtual reality) bestow action-hero status on former presidents and demonstrate how chief executives are, and will be, increasingly accessed via digital media. There has never been more information and disinformation on the American presidents readily available to scholars and the public alike.

This chapter focuses on how the memory and legacy of US presidents is mediated for the so-called "digital natives" and "digital immigrants" who are gathering information and reading history in new ways.[1] At this stage in the early history of new media technologies, we can begin to discern some patterns and trends emerging from their use, and to assess how presidents have embraced these innovations. We can also learn more about the impact new media has had on public relations and consider how presidential legacies are changing as digital innovations influence people living in the post-truth world of the Trump presidency. The chapter argues that presidential legacy currently lies in an entirely new paradigm, one in which the lines between fiction and reality have blurred even more than before, and maintains that this is owed to the advent of new media.

The advent of new technology

Recognizing the advantages of speaking directly to the American public, presidents have long embraced new communications technologies, but some occupants of the White House showed varying degrees of enthusiasm. Although patented by Samuel Morse in 1837, antebellum presidents rarely used the telegraph. Abraham Lincoln (1861–65) was the first to use it regularly. In June 1877, just over a year after Alexander Graham Bell patented the telephone, Rutherford B. Hayes spoke to him over the wires while staying at the Rocky Hotel in Warwick, Rhode Island (Bell was thirteen miles away, in Providence). The following October, just months after becoming commercially available, the first White House telephone line was installed. The phone number was "1" and it connected to the Treasury Department across the road.[2] Ironically, in a display of how presidents impact each other's legacies, the degree to which Hayes welcomed this invention was questioned by Barack Obama in 2012. Decrying Republicans who failed to see the benefits of clean energy innovations, Obama said:

> There have always been folks like that. There always have been folks who are the naysayers and don't believe in the future and don't believe in trying to do things differently. One of my predecessors, Rutherford B. Hayes, reportedly said about the telephone, "It's a great invention, but who would ever want to use one?" [*laughter*] That's why he's not on Mount Rushmore [*laughter*] because he's looking backwards. He's not looking forwards. He's explaining why we can't do something, instead of why we can do something.[3]

Obama's appraisal was challenged by historians who pointed out that there is no evidence Hayes ever said such a thing. Biographer

Ari Hoogenboom argues that, to the contrary, Hayes was "hardly hostile to new inventions."[4] But either way, the nineteenth-century president had certainly helped move the nation into a new era of campaigning via telephone.

William McKinley was the first to campaign using film and, in 1901, was the first to have his inauguration filmed.[5] Warren Harding installed the first radio in the White House, and his voice was transmitted to early radio owners on June 14, 1922 as he addressed a crowd in Baltimore at a dedication ceremony for Francis Scott Key. His successor, Calvin Coolidge, took advantage of the rapid growth in radio sales to speak directly from the White House to the people via the airwaves, although curiously enough he refused to use the White House telephone. The day before Coolidge's 1923 State of the Union address, the *New York Times* reported: "The voice of President Coolidge, addressing Congress tomorrow, will be carried over a greater portion of the United States and will be heard by more people than the voice of any man in history."[6] The following day, on December 6, 1923, his address to the joint session of the Senate and the House was listened to by Americans in six cities (New York, Washington, Dallas, Providence, St. Louis, and Kansas City), and reporters eagerly noted that "groups of New Yorkers were drawn together to listen intently to the words of their President, not as embalmed text, but as living things while he was in the very act of speaking to them . . . No competent estimate was obtainable . . . of the number who heard the message broadcast, but there was no discoverable instance of a person equipped with a receiving set who did not use it for that purpose."[7] Franklin D. Roosevelt capitalized on this new means of mass communication with his infamous radio "fireside chats," and he was also the first president to be televised in black and white on an RCA newsreel as he opened the New York World's Fair on April 30, 1939.[8]

Harry S. Truman's inauguration was the first to be televised, and Dwight D. Eisenhower was the first to produce TV campaign advertisements as part of the 1952 presidential election. Running on the slogan "It's Time for a Change," the political announcement paid for by Citizens for Eisenhower ushered in the modern campaign that brandished a celebrity candidate. Advertising executives and movie producers produced jaunty thirty-second ads that emphasized Eisenhower's roots and military experience in "I like Ike" and "The Man from Abilene." John F. Kennedy demonstrated his natural ease in front of the cameras during the first televised presidential debate and embraced the TV era. After narrowly avoiding a nuclear confrontation with the Soviet Union during the Cuban missile crisis, Kennedy took advantage of new technology and installed a direct line to Moscow—the so-called "hot line" telephone—to avoid the dangers of relying on slow, encrypted telegrams and letters. JFK also began to record White House meetings via tape-recording equipment (used originally by FDR from 1940, but massively aided by improved technology in the 1960s); Johnson made even more extensive use of the Dictaphone system, recording thousands of telephone conversations, and also promoted developments in communications satellites. Nixon did the same, although he "lost" a crucial eighteen minutes that probably included incriminating details of the Watergate break-in. Nixon also spoke to astronauts on July 21, 1969 during the first moon landing, as have successive presidents.

Indeed, all the modern presidents have understood the need to use technology to reach out to the American public and the wider world. But it was the presidency of William J. Clinton that saw the leap into the realms of the internet and digital media. The first social interactions via a computer can be traced to the early 1960s and the growth in the ownership of personal computers was a feature of the early to mid-1980s, but it was the creation of the "World Wide Web" by Tim Berners-Lee in 1990 that began to transform access to information and thus change how presidents and their agents communicated. In 1992 Jean A. Polly introduced the term "surfing the internet," and by the mid-1990s use of the web had grown exponentially. In 1996 President Clinton gave a speech in which he recognized this rapid pace of technological change:

> let me say the explosion of information has changed everyone's life, nowhere more than on the Internet. Now, think about the Internet, how rapidly it's become part of our lives ... When I took office [January 1993], only high energy physicists had ever heard of what is called the World Wide Web ... Now even my cat has its own Web page.

Clinton went on to project forward and accurately predicted internet usage numbers:

> the number of people on the Web has been doubling every eight months. Think about that ... Today there are at least 25 million people on the Internet. By 1998 that number will reach 100 million. The day is coming when every home will be connected to it and it will be just as normal a part of our life as a telephone and a television.

According to Clinton, the impact on democracy and everyday life was also becoming evident:

> It is becoming our new town square, changing the way we relate to one another, the way we send mail, the way we hear news, the way we play ... Every citizen can now read the Congressional Record. If you have insomnia, I recommend it. [Laughter and applause] Every citizen can get the text of what's in a new law the very day it passes. Art lovers can go to the Louvre. Baseball fans can pay an on-line visit to Cooperstown. Everyone can find a passage in the Bible or in Shakespeare with the click of a mouse. Most of all, the Internet will be the most profoundly revolutionary tool for educating our children in generations ... but think about the implications for our American democracy. If you want to go into the 21st century with the American Dream alive and well for everyone, everybody has a chance to live up to the fullest of their abilities ... This means for the first time ever in history, children in the most rural schools, children in the poorest inner-city school districts, children in standard, middle-class communities, children in the wealthiest schools, public or private, up and down the line, will have access in real time to the same unlimited store of information. It will revolutionize and democratize education in a way that nothing ever has.[9]

The Clinton administration's Telecommunications Act of 1996 (the first such act in sixty years) included the internet in its definition of media. The Act was passed "to promote competition and reduce regulation in order to secure lower prices and higher quality services for telecommunications consumers and encourage the rapid deployment of new telecommunications technologies."[10] On signing, the President said (and new technologies allow us to see this on the Clinton Digital Library website and YouTube):

> Today, the information revolution is spreading light, the light Jefferson spoke about, all across our land and all across the world ... Americans have always had a genius for communications. The power of our Founding Fathers' words reverberated across the world from the moment they were laid down to the present day. From the Pony Express to the miracle of a human voice over the phone line, American innovation and communications have broken the barriers of time and space to make it easier for us to stay in touch, to learn from each other, to reach for our highest aspirations.[11]

The Clinton administration also understood that new technology could aid public diplomacy campaigns, and as early as 1996 the United States Advisory Commission on Public Diplomacy (part of the United States Information Agency) recommended the White House "make clear through Presidential directives and appointments that information is as important as political, economic, and military power—and that understanding, informing, and influencing foreign publics is a high national priority."[12] Around the globe, politicians had to adapt to changes brought by new technology.

Clinton understood that he, as president, had the opportunity to reach the American public directly and instantaneously while also demonstrating confidence in the latest innovations. Generation X (the post-baby boom generation) and Generation Y (those born between the early 1980s and the 1990s) have gathered and processed information in a fundamentally different way from earlier generations, including the baby boomers. On November 8, 1999 Clinton participated in the "first presidential on-line chat involving audio and video technologies"—the first presidential AMA (ask me anything). Sitting in front of a computer screen at George Washington University, in a recorded session (now available on the Clinton Presidential Library website), he fielded questions from the public (internet users) on a variety of topics. It was widely covered by the mainstream media. The *Washington Post* noted it was an inauspicious start: "While many predict that computer and Web site innovations will play increasingly important roles in US politics, last night's virtual 'town hall chat' showed that these pathways still contain lots of bumps. The 'video streaming' images of Clinton were herky-jerky at best, and technological glitches caused the comments of other participants to be painstakingly delayed at times or difficult to hear." But the Clinton team nevertheless described it as "a great step for a democracy that prizes close links between citizens and elected officials."[13]

But, in the short term, few politicians leapt into this new political space. While many launched their own websites, few were prepared to engage in online chat on a regular basis, although Obama followed Clinton's lead in 2005 by taking part in one.[14] Political scientists thus cast doubt on the hope of greater democratization, especially during the George W. Bush years. Michael Margolis and David Resnick argued that rather than seeing cyberspace as a revolution, it was, as their book title said, *Politics as Usual*.[15] But by embracing new technologies—Clinton was the first president to own an iPod, to have a White House website, and to send emails—he and his wife, Hillary, demonstrated their legitimacy as key communications devices, political tools, and ultimately legacy makers. His successors understood the need to follow his lead, even if they did so in fundamentally different ways.

Obama and the use of new technology

Barack Obama is acknowledged as the "first social media president" and "communicator in chief" because of his engagement with mass communication via new technology.[16] Known for his addiction to his Blackberry (indeed he didn't upgrade to a smartphone until 2016, and then largely for security reasons), his election is partially credited to the internet. By 2008 some 44 percent of American adults and 60 percent of internet users said they went online for news or information about politics or the election (in 1996, just 4 percent of adults and 20 percent of internet users got their news in this way).[17] Obama chose to engage with the American people and the wider world via digital media. As he later recalled, in 2008, his campaign used social media because he "hired a bunch of 25- and 26-year-olds that were all into it," including Chris Hughes, one of the co-founders of Facebook, who left the company to direct the then-senator's social media campaign.[18] The 2008 campaign was dubbed the "Facebook election" due to candidates using social networking sites (MySpace and Facebook) as part of their campaigns and because of Obama's "powerful techno-demographical appeal." He certainly appealed to a younger generation. Early in the campaign, it was clear he was "rocking the youth vote" and final exit polls on his victory confirmed he captured almost 70 percent of the under-25 vote.[19] This generation was indeed "tech savvy" to its core.

Not surprisingly, as president, Obama recognized that politicians were now operating in a "post-party" era and foresaw appeals to the public going through new media technologies. He became the first president to go live on Facebook, share photos on Instagram (231 posts from January 4, 2012 until October 31, 2016), and filter photos on Snapchat (appearing first as a zombie). The First Lady, Michelle Obama, also engaged in similar activity. Obama also began to make judicious use of Twitter. Amongst his most popular messages was his victory tweet after being re-elected in 2012 that said simply: "Four more years," punctuated with a picture of the president hugging Michelle. It was, at that time, the most retweeted tweet in history. At the time of writing, his August 13 tweet following violent white supremacy clashes in Charlottesville is the most liked and the fourth most retweeted in Twitter history.[20] As well as the first African American president, Obama will no doubt go down in the annals of history as being exceptionally good at embracing the power of social media.[21]

During the Clinton and Obama years, the video games industry grew exponentially (it is currently the world's premier entertainment sector by revenue) and 18–35 year olds dominated sales. And, interestingly, many of the most popular products portrayed American presidents. In 1991, Sid Meier's *Civilization* series was launched. A strategy game that covers 6,000 years of history and pits civilizations against each another in a battle of continual self-improvement, it features "Abe" Lincoln as one of the key characters. Established as a strong leader with the tag line "he who makes mortals tremble," Lincoln reappeared in *Civilization II*, *IV*, and *V* along with George Washington. In *Civilization VI*, Theodore Roosevelt appears with the mission of establishing an American Empire: "it is on your broad shoulders . . . to charge forth and lead your people on their great adventure," he beckons. While debates rage about the educational value of such games—they do not profess to be historically accurate—they do, as one commentator said of the *Civilization* series, bring "historical characters to life in a fantastically engaging fashion that a dusty old textbook never could."[22]

Other games make use of former presidents as freely. In February 2011, to coincide with President's Day, two levels of *Call of Duty: Black Ops* were released. In level 5, four important historical figures from the Cold War take center stage: John F. Kennedy, Fidel Castro, Robert McNamara, and Richard Nixon. Gamers play as one of the four characters fighting zombies in the Pentagon. In graphic realism, Kennedy is portrayed as a cool, authoritative leader who is seen somersaulting across rooms after shouting "lock and load" and grabbing a grenade launcher (misleading given his well-known back problems). Nixon is paranoid, fidgety, and gruff, and is armed with a mere shotgun. As Stephany Nunneley, news editor of video game blog *VG24/7*, observed: "Nothing celebrates President's Day like a zombie shooting spree."[23] The following October, video game publisher Ubisoft released *Assassin's Creed III: The Tyranny of King Washington*. The single-player DLC (Downloadable Content) game "explores an alternate reality in which George Washington goes mad with unlimited power, foregoing the presidency to rule as tyrannical king." And the latest *Call of Duty* game focuses on World War II and features audio of Franklin D. Roosevelt's prayer on D-Day, otherwise known as the "mighty endeavor" speech. Interestingly, gaming forums have been replete with enthusiasts bemoaning the fact that FDR is not a playable character. But what the forums also reveal is a certain level of knowledge, for instance about FDR's disability. One wrote: "He could play for the Marines . . . except he wouldn't be able to crouch or go prone . . . or sprint . . . Rocket Powered wheelchair ftw [for the win]."[24] Inevitably, presidential image and presidential legacy are being partially shaped by such ephemera. Not surprisingly, the presidents chosen as "leadership figures" in games are those that feature highly in the public consciousness and are usually ranked highly, namely George Washington, Abraham Lincoln, Theodore Roosevelt, Franklin Roosevelt, and John F. Kennedy.

Trump and media saturation

In the US Presidents edition of the card game *Top Trumps* (available as a traditional pack of cards and digitally) there are several categories through which players educate themselves about the strengths and weaknesses of the men who have occupied the White House. There should be a new category—best use of media. While there would be some impressive candidates for top scorers—Theodore Roosevelt, John F. Kennedy, and Barack Obama—the honor would undoubtedly go to President Donald Trump. If Obama embraced new technology as a way to connect to the American people and the wider world and cement a legacy based on his ideals and achievements, Trump has engaged in governing by social media and appears bent on establishing an entirely different legacy. By the time he took office, social connectivity was the norm. By March 2017, an estimated 88.1 percent of Americans used the internet and almost 50 percent of the world's population were web users.[25] Social networking sites were being described as "the new dinner table."[26] In late 2017, Facebook, the most popular social media platform, could boast over one billion active users worldwide (and over 2.07 billion monthly users), with nearly eight in ten Americans who go online using it.[27] Twitter had 330 million active monthly users.[28] Increasingly, users of social media receive news and information via these sites, and presidents have been and will be able to communicate directly with their public at any time of day or night.

During the campaign, Trump used Facebook and Twitter extensively and boasted of his large number of followers. In the aftermath of the election, he credited the social networks with helping him win: "The fact that I have such power in terms of numbers with Facebook, Twitter, Instagram, etc. . . . I think it helped me win all of these races where they're spending much more money than I spent." He specified that he had more than 28 million followers across various social media platforms, and said that he was getting more each day. "I think I picked up yesterday 100,000 people." He described Twitter and Facebook as "great form[s] of communication" and "a method of fighting back." As he elaborated further: "I'm not saying I love it, but it does get the word out. When you give me a bad story or when you [TV networks] give me an inaccurate story."[29] He indicated that if elected he would be "restrained," if he used SNSs "at all." Indeed, while many assumed his use of Twitter would be minimized and reined in by the practicalities and exigencies of government, and by sensible guidance from key aides and advisers, this proved a misjudgment. Trump has tweeted daily and instead of adopting his predecessor's measured approach to social media, he has instead engaged in unedited streams of consciousness and personal attacks on individuals, institutions, and nations. He has fired government officials via Twitter and has engaged in a running war with the *New York Times* over "fake news."

With the increased numbers of characters now available—280 rather than 140—there is even more scope for chest-beating presidential diatribes, policy announcements, and terse exchanges with heads of state. And, with over 42 million followers and massive media coverage of his tweets and retweets, Trump's demagoguery has found a media channel of unparalleled reach and immediacy. Some have suggested his constant tweets are an attempt to control the news cycles and distract the public from White House scandals and important issues. But others believe that, although his second chief of staff, John Kelly, has attempted to control the information flow to the president, he finds *Fox News* an adequate source of inspiration (the timing and frequency of the Tweets indicates this). In other words, he is "taking his cues from the media."[30]

So, how is all this playing out in terms of current and future presidential legacy? Certainly, Trump's daily, direct, and blunt messages on Twitter have not increased his popularity. Gallup opinion polls indicate that during his first year in office his disapproval ratings started high—as early as the end of January 2017, 52 percent disapproved of the way he was handling the job—and have stayed high but, apart from the occasional increase, have stabilized in the 50s and not over 60 percent.[31] And the impact of new communication technologies on presidential campaigning, presidential profiles, and ultimately presidential legacy may not be as advantageous as many envisaged. The new technologies that quickly connect disparate peoples also allow presidential adversaries to organize effectively. Thus, the women's march on Washington in protest at Trump's election was aided by new media technology; alleged victims of sexual assault rallying together to call for an investigation, alongside mass support for the "Me too" movement and lawsuits and impeachment articles, have all been facilitated by the internet and social media. The "Impeach Trump" Facebook sites with millions of followers have, however, so far been dwarfed by the over 24 million followers on Trump's own pages that celebrate the so-called American Comeback.

Trump has regularly attempted to damage the legacies of previous presidents via social media. Aiming fire at both Bush administrations was part of his presidential campaign. Partly to disparage Jeb Bush by association, he tweeted in February 2016: "Now that George Bush is campaigning for Jeb(!), is he fair game for questions about World Trade Center, Iraq War and eco collapse? Careful!"[32] But most ammunition has been aimed at his immediate predecessor. Negative comments about Obama's record in office have been built upon his early false allegations about Obama's place of birth. Obviously presidents have long been free to criticize each other, but rarely has this been so vociferous, so vicious, and so regular by a sitting president on a previous president. Respect for the office—and for being a member of a small club of living presidents—has, in the main, limited such abuse. Likewise, traditional diplomacy has been conducted, in the main, behind the scenes. Trump has instead posted provocative messages to world leaders on Twitter and attempted to damage the image and credibility of his predecessors. For example, as part of his efforts to deal with apparent North Korean belligerency, he tweeted: "Being nice to Rocket Man hasn't worked in 25 years, why would it work now? Clinton failed, Bush failed, and Obama failed. I won't fail."[33] Presidential politics and, in turn, presidential legacy has entered a new phase. The Trump years will be remembered as a period when the president preferred new media over the old, but also as a time when the democratization of information was under threat. The Federal Communications Commission (FCC) has decided it no longer wants to play a role in guarding net neutrality, something President Trump welcomed. Internet service providers are now free to block content and to slow down access to websites as they see fit for their individual agendas, whatever they may be.

The impact of new technologies

Presidential legacy is now mediated through a much larger range of information sources. In addition to the sources available to previous generations—learning about the presidents in school, television programs, feature films, books, radio—the twenty-first century public (and academics) and especially younger generations are able to follow the latest thoughts of the sitting president as they occur to him; look at presidential memes circulated via social media (mostly funny; sometimes accurate but often incisive); watch YouTube blogs and films, including such favorites as the "60-second Presidents" and the "Epic Rap Battles of History," best described as satire in a rap form to appeal to a modern demographic. The latter does play a part in educating the uninitiated, and reinforcing preconceived ideas, about American political figures. The Donald Trump v. Hillary Clinton Epic Rap Battle condenses their key campaign messages and insults in an accurate fashion but also ends with Lincoln swooping in (delivered by an Eagle) shouting "are you fucking kidding me with this blah blah blah," thus again cementing Lincoln as a "proper" president who would have been angry about the low level of current political debate, and in doing so, it cultivates an updated memory image of one of the most successful and broadly regarded presidents juxtaposed against weaker successors. Such bitesize history—a three-minute music video spoof—is inevitably a natural part of the millennial generation's acquisition of knowledge about the presidency.[34]

But is there any evidence that new technologies are leading to new or revised assessments of the presidents? Certainly they are vital tools in the efforts by former presidents to secure positive legacies. George W. Bush is a telling example here. According to Gallup, on leaving office in January 2009 his presidential approval rates were as low as 34 percent (having reached an all-time low of 25 percent in October 2008), and in public memory he was most associated with his slow response when told of the 9/11 attacks, poor leadership when dealing with Hurricane Katrina, and the foreign policy blunder of invading Iraq.[35] Early historical assessments of Bush Jr.'s time in the White House, the feature film *W* (2008) and YouTube "Bushisms" had also not been kind, often portraying him as inept or idiotic.[36] But in recent years his image has been transformed, so that in March 2017 he was at the top of Reddit, a popular social news site that aims to be "the front page of the internet." As part of a vigorous PR campaign to publicize his book *Portraits of Courage: A Commander in Chief's Tribute to America's Warriors*, Bush appeared on numerous chat shows. Appearing on the Ellen DeGeneres Show, he presented a softer, more amusing "grandpa" figure, and Bush's willingness to add to the public discourse by challenging Trump openly in public speeches and on social media (although these are coded attacks and he does not name the president) has helped redeem him in some quarters, most notably his defending the media on the NBC Today Show as "indispensable to democracy."[37] Likewise photos of Bush painting pictures of his cute dogs and cuddling his new puppy, Freddy, have circulated widely, leading to comments on Twitter such as "Say what you will about George Bush, but could you ever imagine Donald Trump painting a picture? Art is what makes us human, and he ain't." In the past, such images would not have reached as wide an audience. Social media users circulate memes of George W. Bush that are different, too. Earlier memes featured him reading a book upside down (obviously Photoshopped); now the most popular one is a smiling presidential photo of him with the tag line, "Remember when this guy was the scariest person in politics."

Academics are not convinced this change of image will be a lasting one, feeling that history will be less forgiving to his legacy. Bush historian Jean Edward Smith acknowledges that "his behaviour as an ex-president has been exemplary" but does not think "time is causing people to forget" and insists "Bush's decision to invade Iraq is without doubt the worst foreign policy decision ever made by a president."[38] In this sense then, it remains to be seen how far presidential legacy remains connected to the presidential record while in office. But perhaps all the debates about fake news, net neutrality, and information overload are relatively unimportant for most presidents. Some early indications suggest that what occurs during a presidency—positive and negative—is likely to remain the most important factor in defining how much a president is actually remembered. Recent studies by human memory experts have shown that American citizens forget presidents in a predictable pattern. Roediger and DeSoto's work has demonstrated that presidential memory and legacy is partly related to the length of time in office; two-term presidents are often ranked higher.[39] And, naturally, the more recent presidents are often remembered well but are gradually forgotten if they do not resonate across the generations. It is also clear that the importance of the events and policies associated with a president mean that some presidential legacies are more likely to ensure longevity when it comes to presidential legacy. For instance, Abraham Lincoln's association with the Civil War and the abolition of slavery assures this. So, although the Obamas cultivated an image of "being down with the kids" and on leaving office his approval rating remained high (59 percent), in the long term his achievement in securing office as the first black president, his efforts to reform healthcare, and the killing of Osama bin Laden may prove more important in securing his place in history. If remembering a president and his importance historically is linked "to the frequency of mention in popular media," as such memory experts suggest, then we can expect Presidents Obama and Trump will not be forgotten for several generations. And in terms of presidential rankings, Obama is likely to continue to place highly. A 2017 Harris poll put Obama second, behind Abraham Lincoln, as the best president. Among young people (18–34), the largest group using new technologies, Obama was judged best or second best president (gaining 39 percent of their vote; with Lincoln second at 33 percent).[40]

Conclusion

If "memoirs . . . highlight the legacies that top leaders wish to nurture," then presidents and their allies now have to think about the permanent, easily accessible record that is social media as well as how their images might be peddled and discussed on YouTube and via gaming technologies.[41] Historians and the public alike have yet more resources to sift through to study the presidency. In this sense, the work of presidents to construct their legacies has become much harder. It is perhaps too soon to say precisely how this will influence presidential memory and presidential legacy but there is no doubt that it will. Of course, not all people will have their images of American presidents mediated via new technology—there are still 69 million Americans who do not have home-based internet services—but millions more will increasingly use new technologies as additional sources and (hopefully) this will help them triangulate evidence.

New technologies have always been used by presidents and always will be, but the new media age means the cultivation and production of presidential legacy has entered a different, even more challenging phase. Distinguishing between fiction and reality has become even more challenging because of the pervasiveness of new technology and because facts can now be so easily manipulated by those who wish to do so. With the advent of new methods of communication, and those still to come, presidents have diminishing control over creating their own legacy for future generations. Technology assures this.

Notes

1. Marc Prensky, "Digital Natives, Digital Immigrants," *On the Horizon* 9, no. 5 (October 2001): 1–6.
2. Richard T. Loomis, "The Telephone Comes to Washington: George C. Maynard 1839–1919," *Washington History* 12, no. 2 (Fall/Winter 2000–2001): 22–40, 26.
3. Barack Obama, Remarks at Prince George's Community College in Largo, Maryland, March 15, 2012, *The American Presidency Project*, <http://www.presidency.ucsb.edu/ws/index.php?pid=100049> (accessed June 13, 2018).
4. Ari Hoogenboom, *Rutherford B. Hayes: Warrior and President* (Lawrence: University Press of Kansas, 1995).
5. President McKinley's Inauguration Footage, 1901, <https://www.youtube.com/watch?v=AjQqiYq-eTE> (accessed June 13, 2018).
6. "A Million People Will Hear Coolidge's Voice When He Addresses Congress This Afternoon," *New York Times*, December 5, 1923.
7. "Article 1—No Title," *New York Times*, December 7, 1923.
8. C-SPAN, "President Franklin D. Roosevelt Opens the 1939 World Fair," <https://www.c-span.org/video/?319178-1/president-roosevelt-opens-1939-york-worlds-fair> (accessed June 13, 2018).

9. William J. Clinton, "Remarks in Knoxville, Tennessee," October 10, 1996, <http://www.presidency.ucsb.edu/ws/index.php?pid=52079> (accessed June 13, 2018).
10. White House Television (WHTV), "President Clinton Signing Telecommunications Act of 1996," Clinton Digital Library, <https://clinton.presidentiallibraries.us/items/show/15802> (accessed June 13, 2018).
11. William Clinton: "Remarks on Signing the Telecommunications Act of 1996," February 8, 1996, *American Presidency Project*, <http://www.presidency.ucsb.edu/ws/index.php?pid=52278> (accessed June 13, 2018); WHTV, "President Clinton Signing Telecommunications Act of 1996."
12. United States Advisory Commission on Public Diplomacy, "A New Diplomacy for the Information Age," November 1996, <https://1997-2001.state.gov/www/dept/advcom/1996rep.html> (accessed June 13, 2018).
13. "President Goes A Step Further in Online Chat," *Washington Post*, November 9, 1990, A10.
14. Jennifer Stromer-Gailey, "On-Line Interaction and Why Candidates Avoid It," *Journal of Communication* 50, no. 4 (Autumn 2000): 111–32.
15. Michael Margolis and David Resnick, *Politics as Usual: The Cyberspace "Revolution"* (London: Sage Publishers, 2000).
16. James E. Katz, Michael Barris, and Anshul Jain, *The Social Media President: Barack Obama and the Politics of Digital Engagement* (New York: Palgrave Macmillan, 2013); John Allen Hendricks and Robert Denton Jr. (eds.), *Communicator-in-Chief: How Barack Obama Used New Media Technology to Win the White House* (Lanham, MD: Lexington Books, 2010).
17. Aaron Smith, "The Internet as a Source of Political News and Information," *Pew Research Center*, April 15, 2009, <http://www.pewinternet.org/2009/04/15/the-internet-as-a-source-of-political-news-and-information/> (accessed June 13, 2018).
18. "The Facebooker who Friended Obama," *New York Times*, July 7, 2008.
19. "Barack Obama and the Facebook Election," *US News*, November 19, 2008, <https://www.usnews.com/opinion/articles/2008/11/19/barack-obama-and-the-facebook-election> (accessed June 13, 2018).
20. Claire Phipps, "Obama's Anti-racism Tweet after Charlottesville is Most Liked Ever on Twitter," *Guardian*, August 16, 2017.
21. Nicol Turner-Lee, "How the President's Twitter Account Affects Civil Society," *Brookings Institute*, <https://www.brookings.edu/

blog/techtank/2017/02/16/how-the-presidents-twitter-account-affects-civil-society/> (accessed June 13, 2018).
22. Brady Fukumoto, "Sid Meier's Civilization: Is it Educational?," *EdSurge*, August 14, 2015, <https://www.edsurge.com/news/2015-08-14-sid-meiers-civilization-is-it-educational> (accessed June 13, 2018); Kanishk Tharoor, "Playing with History: What Sid Meier's Video Game Empire Got Right and Wrong about Civilization," *Longreads*, October 26, 2016, <https://longreads.com/2016/10/26/what-sid-meiers-video-game-empire-got-right-and-wrong-about-civilization/> (accessed June 13, 2018).
23. Stephany Nunneley, "Two Black Ops Levels Getting Unlocked for the Weekend," *VG247*, <https://www.vg247.com/2011/02/18/two-black-ops-levels-getting-unlocked-for-the-weekend/> (accessed June 13, 2018).
24. Teabag_11 [user], GameFAQs, *Call of Duty: World at War*, 2009 (no precise date).
25. World Internet Usage and Population Statistics, March 31, 2017, <https://www.internetworldstats.com> (accessed June 13, 2018).
26. Jason Gainous and Kevin M. Webster, *Tweeting to Power: The Social Media Revolution in American Politics* (New York: Oxford University Press, 2013), 1.
27. Pew Research Center, "Social Media Update 2016," <http://www.pewinternet.org/2016/11/11/social-media-update-2016/> (accessed June 13, 2018). Statista, "Number of Monthly Active Facebook Users Worldwide," <https://www.statista.com/statistics/264810/number-of-monthly-active-facebook-users-worldwide/> (accessed June 13, 2018).
28. Statista, "Number of Monthly Active Twitter Users Worldwide," <https://www.statista.com/statistics/282087/number-of-monthly-active-twitter-users/> (accessed June 13, 2018).
29. Lesley Stahl, "Interview with President-elect Trump," 60 Minutes, *CBS*, November 13, 2016.
30. "All the President's Tweets," *Economist*, January 13–19, 2018, 35.
31. "Presidential Approval Ratings—Donald Trump," *Gallup*, <http://news.gallup.com> (accessed June 13, 2018).
32. Donald Trump, *Twitter*, February 15, 2016, 6.04 a.m.
33. Donald Trump, *Twitter*, October 1, 2017, 12.01 p.m.
34. Epic Rap Battles, "Donald Trump vs Hillary Clinton," *YouTube*, <https://www.youtube.com/watch?v=Kbryz0mxuMY> (accessed June 13, 2018).
35. "Presidential Approval Ratings—George W. Bush," *Gallup*, <http://news.gallup.com> (accessed June 13, 2018).

36. See, for example, John Edward Smith, *Bush* (New York: Simon & Schuster, 2016) and Jacob Weisberg, *George W. Bushisms* (New York: Touchstone, 2001).
37. Corky Siemaszko, "George Bush: Free Press Indispensable to Democracy," *NBC News*, February 27, 2017, <https://www.nbcnews.com/news/us-news/george-w-bush-free-press-indispensable-democracy-n726141> (accessed June 13, 2018).
38. Ibid.
39. Henry L. Roediger, III, and K. Andrew DeSoto, "Forgetting the Presidents," *Science* 346, no. 6213, November 28, 2014, 1108; Nate R. Silver, "Contemplating Obama's Place in History, Statistically," *New York Times*, January 23, 2013.
40. As might be expected, Americans often voted for the president they were most familiar with. Thus, the highest placed president amongst those aged 45–54 was Ronald Reagan. "Poll: Ronald Reagan Named Best President Since World War II," ABC News, <http://abcnewsradioonline.com/national-news/poll-ronald-reagan-named-best-president-since-world-war-ii.html> (accessed June 13, 2018).
41. Melvyn P. Leffler, "The Foreign Policies of the George W. Bush Administration: Memoirs, History, Legacy," *Diplomatic History* 37, no. 2 (April 2013): 191.

Epilogue: Confessions of a presidential biographer

H.W. Brands

One can write about American presidents historically without writing biographies. In fact, most presidential historians do not write biographies, preferring episodic accounts and policy-oriented analyses. But some do write biographies, for one or more of the following reasons.

First, biographies sell. This is no small thing. Many people develop an aversion to history, as history, in school. Perhaps their teachers are uninspiring; perhaps young people simply tend to look forward rather than back. But the result is a widespread belief that history is a dry collection of dates and facts. Biographies, by contrast, deal with living, breathing people—or people who were once living and breathing. Biography, of all the genres of historical nonfiction, is the one that most closely approximates the novel. It has a protagonist and often antagonists. Its characters speak, through letters, diaries, and other primary materials. The chore of the biographer is quite similar to that of the novelist: to place readers inside the head of another person. The result is that many people who would not think of picking up a history book are happy to read lives of important and interesting figures.

Second, presidents justify biographical treatment more than some other historical figures. A common critique of presidential biographies is that they tend to confirm the great man theory of history. And so they do. But if there are any great men in history, presidents are among the likeliest suspects. Presidents are more important than other people because their actions have large consequences. This is not a moral evaluation; it is simply a statement of fact. Historians, including biographers, seek to explain how the world has become the way it is. Insights into presidential minds and hearts provide greater leverage in this explanatory process than similar insights into people who wield less power.

Third, presidents generate profuse historical records. And these are generally preserved and made available to researchers. Governors, senators, business leaders, actors, athletes, and other celebrities also generate records, but the number of these records is typically smaller, their collection and preservation is more haphazard, and their accessibility to researchers is far from guaranteed. People who never achieve renown sometimes generate records, but these usually disappear before or after the death of the generator.

Until the twentieth century, presidential records normally wound up in the Library of Congress. This central location made studying presidents convenient. To be sure, the presidential records in the Library of Congress often did not include materials relating to the lives of presidents before and after their time in office. But they allowed a good start on a presidential biography.

Franklin Roosevelt was the first president to build his own presidential library. Since Roosevelt, every president has had a library of his own. And some presidents who served before Roosevelt have had libraries built in their names retrospectively. Presidential libraries take pains to gather all manner of materials a presidential biographer might desire. Pre-presidential papers are included, as are post-presidential papers. Papers of people who served with the president provide additional perspective. Oral history projects fill gaps in the paper record. Photographs, videos, and tape recordings supply visual and audial evidence of how the president filled his days. Presidential libraries make the work of the presidential biographer almost too easy.

And herein lies the problem. Or rather, herein lies a principal manifestation of the problem, of which the presidential libraries are a consequence as much as a cause. The problem is this: Americans devote far too much attention to their presidents. Presidential libraries and presidential biographers enable the excess.

It was not always so. The president was not originally the great figure of American politics. The Constitution relegates the executive branch to second place in the federal government, behind the legislature. Article One describes the legislature in detail; the framers intended and expected Congress to be the engine of the federal government. Article Two is almost an appendix to Article One, giving the president responsibility in foreign affairs but otherwise making the president little more than an executive agent of Congress.

For the first century of the operation of the Constitution, presidents stuck to the framers' script. With a few exceptions, presidents of the nineteenth century were unmemorable. Jefferson lucked into Louisiana, Jackson heralded democracy, Polk captured California, and Lincoln defeated secession and freed the slaves. Other presidents came and went, attracting modest attention and leaving minor wakes. Not coincidentally, biographers have had little to say about Monroe, Van Buren, Tyler, Fillmore, Pierce, Buchanan, and the rest. The giants of the age, the models of political consequence and the ones parents urged their sons to emulate, were members of Congress, starting with Webster, Clay, and Calhoun.

Things changed at the turn of the twentieth century. Starting with Theodore Roosevelt, presidents unfolded a cumulative coup against Congress, seizing the center ground of political visibility and initiative. Several developments encouraged the coup. The war against Spain signaled America's emergence as a world power and gave the United States an overseas empire. Foreign policy, previously an occasional chore for presidents, became a full-time job. Congress could still adjourn and its members go home; the president now was on constant call.

Evolving technologies amplified the president's voice. High-speed rotary presses reduced the price of newspapers, allowing presidents to reach wider audiences with their messages and actions. Theodore Roosevelt's knack for self-promotion made him the darling of reporters and the object of interest of their readers. Radio permitted presidents to eliminate the filter of reporters and editors and speak directly to voters. Franklin Roosevelt's Fireside Chats caused millions to think of him almost as a member of the family. Television put a face to the president's voice; John Kennedy made the president a star of the screen; Ronald Reagan, having been a screen star already, became president. The new technologies increasingly selected for skills of speaking ability and stage presence not demanded of nineteenth-century presidents. And they rewarded those skills with stature no member of Congress, one of a cast of hundreds, could approach.

Technologies of war secured the president's place at the center of American life. Harry Truman, a former senator and an avid student of history, had greater respect for the Constitution and the prerogatives of Congress than most other presidents of the modern era, but Truman recognized, upon the outbreak of fighting in Korea in 1950, that a president in the nuclear age had to be able to respond to crises swiftly and decisively. He ordered the United States to war without asking Congress for a war declaration, and the precedent stuck. The president became the protector in chief of the American people, the preserver of American lives and values.

During the Cold War the American president was the most powerful person on earth, acknowledged as such by Americans and others alike. American politics could be amusing, but it was not for amusement that people in many other countries followed American presidential campaigns as closely as they were followed in the United States. American elections were deadly serious business; who won the White House touched the fate of billions.

The growth of presidential power and consequence triggered a boom in the genre of presidential biography. Fat volumes on the Roosevelts, Wilson, Truman, Eisenhower, Kennedy, Johnson, Nixon, and Reagan rolled off the presses and onto the bestseller lists. The biographers turned to earlier presidents and gave similar star treatment to Washington, Jefferson, Jackson, and Lincoln. Even John Adams had his turn.

The biography boom was good for the biographers, some of whom became stars themselves. But it contributed to the exaggeration of the importance of the presidents. From about the time the president began to be called "leader of the free world," a subtle but fundamental misconception vexed American politics. The president was indeed the most powerful person on earth, but he was not *all*-powerful. Predominance was never the same as omnipotence.

Presidents knew this. Their biographers knew this. But neither group had incentive to stress it. Presidents and candidates for president were rewarded for projecting strength. The projection comforted Americans made anxious by the Cold War even as it enhanced Americans' views of themselves and their country. Presidents perceived as weak—Jimmy Carter and George H.W. Bush, to name two—didn't get re-elected. Candidates perceived as weak—George McGovern, Michael Dukakis—didn't get elected in the first place.

Biographers paid attention. Presidents seen as strong, or even simply as active, received greater coverage than presidents judged weak or passive. There were twenty biographies of Theodore Roosevelt for each one of Taft or Coolidge; books on Carter were similarly outnumbered by works on Nixon and Reagan.

The biographers contributed to the elevation of presidents in a manner peculiar to their genre. A biography by its nature places its subject at the center of the universe. No one is at the center of the universe, not even presidents. But biographies make them seem that way. When this warping of reality appears in a biography of a writer or an actor or an athlete, it has scant political consequence. But when the biographical subject is a president, the political consequence can be dramatic.

Most dramatic is the contribution to what can only be called the cult of the modern presidency. The cult is characterized, first, by the relentless attention paid to presidents in the media and by the endless coverage given to presidential campaigns, often starting years before the actual elections. Hardly a day goes by without prominent coverage of the sitting president or of one or more of the candidates striving to be next in the White House. Sometimes the coverage is justified by a particular action or statement; nearly always it reflects the consensus that the president is the prime mover of public American life and that 1600 Pennsylvania is the country's most important address.

The cult is characterized, as well, by the related belief that the president is the source of most good and ill in American life. Presidents get credit when the economy thrives and receive blame when it falters. Economists know that presidents have precious little control over the economy. But most voters aren't economists. George H.W. Bush did not cause the recession of 1991; if anything, his policies helped alleviate it. But Bill Clinton blamed him for the downturn and voters tossed him out of the White House. If a revolution in a foreign country overthrows an American ally, the president is criticized, even if the ally was corrupt and deserved his overthrow. Jimmy Carter was diplomatically prudent not to try to rescue the shah of Iran or Somoza of Nicaragua, but he was politically foolish, and he paid the consequences. Voters might or might not have made the right choices in boosting Clinton over Bush and Reagan over Carter, but they made them for the wrong reasons.

The most insidious consequence of the cult of the president is that voters chronically expect too much of new presidents. This expectation pushes candidates to make all manner of unrealistic promises in campaigns. A candidate who promises the moon loses to one who pledges to deliver the sun besides. A candidate who aims for objectivity is punished. In 1984 Walter Mondale, the Democratic challenger, told voters that the soaring federal deficits of Reagan's first term needed to be brought under control. Mondale wasn't averse to spending cuts, but tax increases, he said, must be part of the solution. There was no other way. The president knew this, Mondale said; he simply wasn't admitting it. Reagan scoffed, branding Mondale as another tax-and-spend liberal. Voters buried Mondale in a landslide.

And Reagan went on to raise taxes. The lesson future candidates took was that voters could be misled with impunity. Indeed, they *had* to be misled, lest the candidates suffer the fate of Mondale.

The promising continued, sometimes subliminally. Barack Obama campaigned in 2008 on the slogan "Yes We Can." Supporters projected their own dreams—of a post-racial America, of a liberal Eden of equality and tolerance—onto Obama. He rode the projections to victory and then disappointed many of those who elected him when he didn't deliver all they had envisioned.

The cult of the presidency has the effect of infantilizing voters. Voters refuse to be treated as adults who can handle the obvious truth that life requires compromises. Their refusal spawns a cycle of unrealistic promises, unfulfilled expectations, and inevitable disillusionment. It deters candidates and office-holders from acknowledging those compromises, for fear that voters will punish them and reward uncompromisers. Reagan used to say he'd rather get 80 percent of what he wanted than go over the cliff with his flags flying. But he didn't say this while he was campaigning, and he didn't say it loudly while he was president.

What is to be done? The cult of the presidency was a century in the making. It won't be unmade in a year or an election cycle. And it won't be unmade by presidential biographers, who continue to enable it, if only by their choice of genre. It might be undone by hard reality: by the shrinking of America's disposable national income, by the intractability of problems like climate change, by an unfavorable and undeniable tilt in world affairs.

If that happens, many of the biographers won't be there to report it. They will have found other subjects to center universes around.

Index

Abbas, Mahmoud, 68
Acheson, Dean, 141
Adams, John, 33, 41, 42, 61, 136, 280
advertising, 5
AECOM, 232, 234
Affordable Care Act (2010), 136, 182, 221
Afghanistan, 176, 178
A History of New York, 33
AIDS, 176
Air Force One, 159
Airoutdoor, 69
Alaska, 167
Alger, Horatio, 237
Alka-Seltzer, 59
Allen, Craig, 78
All the Way (film), 134, 146–52, 218
American Catholic League, 68
American Life, 26
American Revolution, 61; *see also* Revolutionary War
Anderson, Robert, 80
An Evening with Richard Nixon, 27
A New Literary History of America, 27
Anglo-American relations, 56; *see also* "special relationship"
Anheuser Busch, 61, 64; *see also* Anheuser, Eberhard; Busch, Adolphus
Anheuser, Eberhard, 69; *see also* Anheuser Busch

anti-Vietnam War protest, 2, 93, 95; *see also* Vietnam
A Pinnacle of Feeling, 47
Apocalypse Now (film), 138
Apollo moon landing, 63
Argentina, 166
Arthur, Chester Alan, 15
arts and humanities, 135
Assassin's Creed (game), 266
Atlantic, The, 106
A Woman Named Jackie, 137
Ayer, N. W. & Sons, 65

Baker III, James A., 245
Baldwin, Alec, 141
Baldwin, James, 46
Balkans, the, 171
Ballard and Ballard, 60
Bantham, Reyner, 19
Bataclan nightclub attack, 186n
"Battle Hymn of the Republic," 11
Baudrillard, Jean, 34
Baum, L. Frank, 26
Bell, Alexander Graham, 259
Bellow, Saul, 107
Benedict XVI (Pope), 68–9
Benin, 176
Benton, Thomas Hart, 17–18
Berners-Lee, Tim, 261
Berryman, Clifford, 59
bin Laden, Osama, 272
Bishop, Rob, 239, 241, 242

284

INDEX

Black Lives Matter, 185, 205n, 220
Blessing, Tim, 105
Born on the Fourth of July (film), 138
Bourguiba, Habib, 108–9, 123
Brazil, 166
Breuer, Marcel, 238
Brexit, 181
Brinkley, Alan, 106
British Petroleum, 56
Brown, Joe, 234
Brown v. Board of Education, 247
Brown, William Wells, 26
Buchanan, James, 279
Buchanan, Pat, 116, 119
budget, 85, 92; *see also* defence spending
Budweiser, 61, 69
Bullock, Helen Duprey, 60
Bunshaft, Gordon, 20
Burns, Ken, 16–17
Burundi, 172
Busch, Adolphus, 69; *see also* Anheuser Busch
Bush, Barbara (daughter of George W. Bush), 201n
Bush, Barbara (wife of George H. Bush), 11
Bush, George, H. W., 11, 19, 170
Bush, George W., 11–12, 19, 23, 33, 44, 120, 159, 160, 162, 163, 164, 165, 175–9, 180, 181, 182, 185, 198n, 200n, 199n 201n, 264, 269, 270, 271, 281, 282; *see also* Hurricane Katrina
 9/11, 14, 176
 Presidential Center, 11–13, 21, 22
Bush, Jeb, 265
Bush, Jenna, 201n
Butler, The (film), 133–4, 141, 142, 143

Cadillac, 67
Calhoun, John C., 279
Califano, Joseph, 134, 135, 137, 151, 152
Call of Duty (game), 258, 266
"Camelot," 107, 120
Camp David, 172, 195n
Canada, 169

Cantos, 33
Carey, Hugh, 210
Caro, Robert A., 20, 138
Carter Jimmy, 21, 44, 46, 120, 159, 168, 173, 183, 281, 281
 Carter Center, 21
 Carter Library and Museum, 19, 21
Carter, Rosalynn, 11
Castro, Fidel, 266
Chairman Mao, 22
Charles, Prince, 103
"Charlie Hebdo," 186
Charlotteville (clashes), 265
Chaucer, Geoffrey, 31
Chavez, Hugo, 68
Cheney, Dick, 94
Chicago Tribune, 16, 206, 208, 217
Childs, David, 234, 235
Chile, 166
China, People's Republic of, 115–7, 119, 123, 124, 173, 183
Chrysler Corporation, 55–6
Churchill, Winston, 103, 118
CIA, 14, 181
Citigroup, 63–4
Civilization (game), 258, 265, 266
civil rights, 7, 18, 45–6, 133–4, 135, 136, 137, 138, 143, 145, 216, 218
 Civil Rights Act (1957), 247
 Civil Rights Act (1964), 133, 138, 142, 144, 146, 148, 149, 151, 215, 219–20
Civil War, 15, 64, 173, 272
Claiborne, William, 35–6
Clark, Andrew, 56
Clay, Henry, 209, 279
Clifford, Clark, 140–1
climate change, 186n
Clinton, Chelsea, 201n
Clinton, Hillary, 11, 70, 174, 182, 183, 185, 264, 270
Clinton, William J., 11, 22, 159, 160, 162, 163, 165, 170–6, 179, 180, 181, 182, 194n, 195n, 196n, 218, 221, 261, 262, 263, 264, 265, 269, 281, 282

285

Clinton (cont.)
  Digital Library, 262
  Patients' Bill of Rights, 173
  Presidential Library, 12, 19, 263
Clotel, 26
CNN, 11
Coca-Cola, 58, 69, 72n
Cogliano, Francis, 209
Cohen, Eliot, 185
Cold War, 2, 14, 18, 58, 64, 66, 72, 78, 87, 88, 89, 92, 94, 95, 106, 109, 121, 142, 166, 213, 266, 280, 281
Cole, Bruce, 238
Columbine High School shootings, 173
Commemorative Works Act, 249n
Commission of Fine Arts (CFA), 232, 234, 235, 238, 240, 242, 244, 245
Conagra, 60
Confederate statues, 4
Congreve, William, 31
Conover, Willis, 117
conservation, 183
consumer protection, 135
Container Corporation of America, 65–7
containment, 76, 87
Conway, Kellyanne, 69
Cook, Fred J., 92
Coolidge, Calvin, 44, 260, 281
Cooper, John Milton, 120
Cosner, Kevin, 93
Cranston, Bryan, 146, 218
criminal justice, 135
Crocker, Betty, 60
C-SPAN survey, 121
Cuba, 158, 180, 181
Cuban missile crisis, 109, 110, 120, 139, 261
Czechoslovakia, 114

D'Addario, Daniel, 143
Daily Show, The, 63
Dallek, Robert, 135, 138, 141, 146, 151, 215
Darman, Jonathan, 217
Daughters of the American Revolution, 60

Davis, Aeron, 71n
Davis, Nathaniel, 113
Day-Lewis, Daniel, 153
D-Day, 238, 247
Death of a President, 33
Declaration of Independence, 17
Deepwater Horizon, 56
Deerhunter, The (film), 138
defence spending, 83–4
de Gaulle, Charles, 107, 108, 118
DeGeneres, Ellen, 271
Degman, Roman, 36–7
de Kooning, William, 65
Democratic Party, 81, 84, 174, 175, 211, 212, 216, 219
  National Convention, 182
Department of Defense Appropriations Act (2000), 230
DeSoto, K. Andrew, 272
Diana, Princess, 103
Diaz Ordaz, Gustavo, 112
Dirksen, Everett, 151
Disney, 58
Disneyland, 19
Dobrynin, Anatoly, 114
Dodge Challenger, 55, 58
domestic surveillance, 14
Donahue, Bill, 68
Dostoyevsky, Fyodor, 146
Dove (comestic products), 69
Dovere, Edward-Isaac, 220
Dromedary cake, 60, 61
drone strikes, 14
Dukakis, Michael, 281
DuVernay, Ava, 218
Dylan, Bob, 33, 50n

Economic Stimulus Act, 200n
education, 135
Egypt, 176
Eisenhower, Anne, 236
Eisenhower, David, 231, 235, 236
Eisenhower, Dwight D., 5, 18, 34, 81, 92, 133, 159, 160, 161, 162, 163, 165, 166, 167, 171, 175, 185, 191n, 192n, 201n, 227–40, 245, 246, 247, 260, 261, 280

Farewell Address, 6, 76–95, 165, 168; *see also* military-industrial complex
Foundation, 241
Library, 236
memorial, 5, 227–48
New Look strategy, 83, 85
Eisenhower, John S. D., 236, 239
Eisenhower Memorial Commission (EMC), 228–31, 235, 236, 237, 238, 239, 241, 243, 244, 245, 248
Eisenhower, Milton, 79, 85, 91
Eisenhower, Susan, 236, 237, 238, 239, 242
11.22.63, 214
Ellington, Duke, 117
Ellis, Sylvia, 144
Ellison, Ralph, 32
el-Tayeb, Ahmed, 68–9
Emerson, Ralph Waldo, 66
energy policy, 199n
Engelbrecht, H. C., 81
Enlightenment thought, 31
environmental protection, 135, 183–4
European Union, 181
Evans, Bill, 117
Excell Ogilivy, 73n
Eylanbekov, Sergey, 243

Facebook, 258, 264, 265, 267
Faith-Based Initiatives, White House Office, 179
Fannie Mae and Freddie Mac, 200n
Federal Communications Commission (FCC), 269
Federalist 70, 40
Feinstein, Dianne, 212
Fermi, Enrico, 7
Fillmore, Millard, 15, 279
financial crisis, 2008, 63
Finch, Atticus, 26, 32
First Blood (film), 138
Fisher, Eddie, 111
Fitzgerald, F. Scott, 30
Ford, Gerald, 19, 46
Forrest Gump (film), 137
Founding Fathers, 61, 209, 263
Fox, Frederic, 80, 86

Fox News, 212, 268
Foxworth, Bo, 150
France, 166
Franklin, Aretha, 118
Free Speech (movement), 93
Frost, Robert, 1, 7–8

G-7 meeting, 181
Gaia TV, 67
Gallup, 109, 120, 167, 268, 270
Gambon, Michael, 140
Garrison, Jim, 93
Gehry, Frank, 228, 229, 231, 232, 233, 234, 235, 236, 237, 238, 239, 240, 241, 242, 244, 245, 246
General Electric, 213
General Mills, 60
General Service Administration (GSA), 232, 241
Germany, 182d
Germany, Kent, 221
Gerry, Elbridge, 41
Ghana, 176
Ghosts of Mississippi (film), 137
Gingrich, Newt, 213
Glass, Loren, 107
Glassboro summit, 112–15, 123
Glory (film), 145
"Glory, Glory, Hallelujah," 11
Goldwater, Barry, 146, 148, 150
Good Friday Agreement, 172; *see also* Northern Ireland
Goodwin, Doris Kearns, 142, 148, 150
Gorbachev, Mikhail, 169
Gore, Al, 174, 175
Grant, Ulysses S., 15
Great Britain, 103, 110
Great Depression, 14, 44
Great Recession, 22
Great Society, 22, 135, 140, 144, 147, 150, 215, 217, 221
Greenberg, David, 123
Guantanamo Bay, 158
Guardian, The, 56
Gulf of Tonkin Incident, 150

Haliburton, 94
Halprin, Lawrence, 238

INDEX

Hamilton, 27
Hamilton, Alexander, 40, 79
Hanhimäki, Jussi, 123
Hanighen, F. C., 81
Harding, Warren, 207, 260
Harlow, Bryce, 81, 85, 90, 95
Harrelson, Woody, 149, 152, 218
Harris, Lou, 116
Harrison Wagon Company, 72n
Harrison, William Henry, 33, 62
Harris poll, 272
Hartstone, Joey, 152
Harvard University, 19
Hastings, Doc, 241
Hawaii, 167
Hawthorne, Nathaniel, 33
Hay, George, 51n
Hayden, Tom, 92
Hayes, Rutherford B., 14–15, 207, 259
Hayes, Webb, 15
HBO, 212, 218
healthcare, 135; *see also* Medicare; Medicaid
Hemings, Sally, 36
Hiawatha Bridge, 167–8
Hines, Duncan, 60
Hiroshima, 181
History Channel, the, 212
Holt, Rush, 246
Hoover, Herbert, 13, 23, 44, 211
Hoover, J. Edgar, 137
Hoover vs. The Kennedys (TV series), 137
HOPE NOW alliance, 200n
housing and urban affairs, 135
Howard University, 184
Hu, Jintao, 68
Hughes, Chris, 264
Humphrey, Hubert, 148, 150, 151
Hurricane Gustav, 178
Hurricane Ike, 178
Hurricane Katrina, 22, 44, 178, 270
Huxtable, Ada Louise, 19

Ideal Novelty, 59
immigration reform, 135
"imperial" presidency, 4, 14, 20

Inouye, Daniel, 239
Instagram, 265, 267
Interstate Highway System, 167
Iran, Shah of, 282
Iran-Contra affair, 22, 170
Iraq, 94, 176, 178, 216, 269
Irving, Washington, 33
Israel, 172, 181
Israel-Palestinian conflict, 175–6, 181, 195n
Issa, Darrell, 240, 242, 248

Jackie (film), 136
Jackie, Ethel, Joan (film), 137
Jackson, Andrew, 1–2, 43, 62, 70, 279, 280
Jackson Automobile Company, 72n
Japan, 166, 181
Jarecki, Eugene, 94
J. Edgar Hoover (film), 137
Jefferson, Thomas, 6, 26, 31–45, 51n, 54n, 61, 62, 66, 121, 208–10, 222, 280
Jefferson Memorial, 210, 234
Jencks, Penelope, 243
Jenkins, Walter, 146, 149
JFK (film), 93, 147, 214, 218
John Adams (film), 136
Johns, Andrew L., 135, 139
Johns Hopkins University, 79–80
Johnson, Lady Bird, 20, 146, 147
Johnson, Luci, 152
Johnson, Lyndon B., 5, 6, 7, 14, 33, 46, 84, 105, 110–17, 120, 121, 122, 123, 124, 126, 134–53, 156, 208, 215–23, 261, 280
  Building, 230, 234, 240, 244
  "Johnson Treatment," 151
  Library and Museum, 4, 19, 20–1, 22, 143, 152, 221
Johnson, Tom, 112
Jones, Steve, 68

Karsh, Yousuf, 257n
Katzenbach, Nick, 156n
Keeping Faith, 26
Kelly, John, 268

INDEX

Kennedy (TV mini-series), 137, 214, 218
Kennedy, Jacqueline, 19, 107, 108, 133
Kennedy, John F., 6, 44, 46, 62–3, 73n, 74n, 81, 84, 85, 87, 90, 93, 105, 106–11, 112, 116, 119–26, 133–4, 137, 139, 140, 147, 149, 153, 175, 201n, 208, 213–15, 222, 223, 261, 266, 267, 279, 280
   Amherst speech, 1–2, 7
   assassination, 1, 148, 214, 218
   Camelot myth, 107, 108, 120
   Kennedy Foundation, 9n, 214
   Kennedy Library and Museum, 19–20, 64
   Memorial at Runnymede, 2
Kennedy, Jr., John, 147
Kennedy, Robert, 137, 140
Kennedys, The (TV series), 137, 214
Kennicott, Philip, 234
Key, Francis Scott, 260
Khrushchev, Nikita, 109, 110, 166
Killian, James, 91
Kim, Jong-Il, 68
King (TV series), 136–7, 143
King, Henry, 136
King, Martin Luther, 136, 137, 143, 144, 145, 148
   King (mini-series), 143
   National Memorial, 253n
King, Stephen, 214
King Lear, 32
Kistiakowsky, George B., 91
Knights of Malta, 170
Knute Rockne, All American (film), 171
Korea, 14, 166, 280
Korean War Veterans Memorial, 253n
Kosygin, Alexei, 112, 123
Kotz, Nick, 137, 143, 144
Krauthammer, Charles, 158
Kuwait, 176

Lambert, William, 34, 42
Langella, Frank, 151
Laos, 181
Latin America, 166
LBJ (motion picture), 134, 149, 153, 218

LBJ Foundation, 216
LBJ's Neglected Legacy, 136, 215–6
LBJ: The Early Years (TV drama), 136, 138
Lears, Jackson, 57
Lee, Harper, 26
Lee, Myung-Bak, 68
Legend, John, 145
Lehman Brothers, 200n
Leigh, Catesby, 239
L'Enfant, Pierre Charles, 231
Leo, Melissa, 146
Levi-Strauss, 58
Lewinsky, Monica, 174
Lewis, John, 46
Liberia, 176
Library of Congress, 16, 278
LIFE magazine, 212
Lincoln (film), 139, 145, 149, 153
Lincoln, Abraham, 16, 46, 47, 62, 66, 70, 121, 124, 139, 148–9, 206–8, 217, 259, 265, 266, 270, 272, 279, 280
   Emancipation Proclamation, 149
   Gettysburg Address, 43
   Lincoln Centenary, 207, 223
   Lincoln Memorial, 15, 17, 206
Lincoln, Lincoln Motor Company, 72n
Lincoln, Mary Todd, 60
Lincoln, Robert Todd, 73n
Lincoln National Life Insurance Company, 72–3n
Linn, Maya, 229, 230, 234; *see also* Vietnam Veterans Memorial
Lippmann, Walter, 211
Little Rock crisis, 247–8
Livingston, Edward, 35–42, 45, 47, 51n, 54n
Livingston v. Jefferson, 27, 35, 36, 37, 44
Locke, John, 31
Louisiana Batture, 6, 35, 36, 37, 38, 41, 44, 45
Louvre, the, 20, 108
Lyndon Johnson (TV series), 136

MacArthur, Douglas, 79
McCann, James, 159

INDEX

McCann, Sean, 47
McCarthy, Eugene, 140
McCloy, John J., 84
McDonalds, 58, 72n
McGovern, George, 119, 281
Mackie, Anthony, 148
McKinley, William, 260
McNamara, Robert, 141, 150, 266
Madison, James, 36, 61
"Mad Men," 59
Magna Carta, 2
Malaria, 176
Malcolm X, 144
Malraux, André, 107, 108, 109
Manchester, William, 33
Mann, Abby, 143
Marbury v. Madison, 36
Marcus, Greil, 27, 34
Margolis, Michael, 264
Marmon Motor Car Company, 72n
Marshall, John, 51n
Medhurt, Martin J., 78
Medicaid, 152, 182
Medicare, 152, 173
Meier, Sid, 258, 265
Memoir of a Movement, 46
Merkel, Angela, 68
"Me Too" movement, 269
Mexico, 168, 169
Microsoft, 58
Middle East, 68, 113, 173, 181, 195n
Midway Island, 183
military-industrial complex, 6, 76–82, 85, 88, 90, 92, 93, 94, 95, 165, 167; see also Eisenhower's Farewell Address
Millennium Challenge Corporation, 176
Mills, C. Wright, 91, 92
Miroff, Bruce, 104–5
missile gap, 81, 84
Mississippi Burning (film), 137
Mitcham, Morris, 59
Mitchell, George, 172
Mona Lisa, 108
Mondale, Walter, 282
Monroe, James, 60, 61, 279
Montesquieu, Charles de, 31

Montgomery, Robert, 78
Moore, Henry, 65
Moos, Malcolm, 79, 85, 90, 91
Morgan, Iwan, 136
Morgan, J. P., 64
Morrow, E. Frederic, 257n
Mount Rushmore, 62, 210, 259
Mount Vernon, 15, 61, 209
Mr. Peanut, 59
Mumford, Lewis, 229
Murrow, Ed, 33
MySpace, 265

Nabisco, 60, 61, 64
Naftali, Timothy, 22
NASCAR, 213
National Aeronautics and Space Administration (NASA), 167
National Archives, 16, 20, 22, 23–4
National Archives and Records Administration, 3
National Association for the Advancement of Colored People (NAACP), 206
National Capital Memorial Commission, 249
National Capital Planning Commission (NCPC), 230–1, 235, 242, 243, 244, 245
National City Bank, 64
National Civic Art Society, 235, 238
National Gallery of Art, 19
National Intelligencer, 42
National Interstate and Defense Highways Act, 191n
national parks, 183, 241
National Review, 211
national security, 81, 82, 88
NBC, 271
Nelson, Dana, 46
Netanyahu, Benjamin, 68
New Deal, 26, 44, 216
New Left, 92
New York Metropolitan Museum of Art, 108
New York Times, 19, 21, 90, 92, 174, 183, 260, 268

INDEX

New York World's Fair, 260
Nicaragua, 282
Nigeria, 172
Nitze, Paul, 65
Nixon, Richard M., 14, 21, 33, 46, 85, 90, 105, 115–19, 120, 121, 122, 123, 124, 125, 126, 167, 168, 215, 222, 261, 266, 281; *see also* Watergate
  Moscow summit, 119
  Nixon Library, 22
  trip to China, 116–17, 119, 123
Nobel Peace Prize, 21
No Child Left Behind Act, 178
Norman, Peggy, 212
North American Free Trade Agreement (NAFTA), 172, 174, 178, 194n, 196n
North Atlantic Treaty Organization (NATO), 18, 169, 171
Northern Ireland, 172
North Korea, 269
Nuclear Non-Proliferation treaty, 113, 122
nuclear weapons, 83
Nunneley, Stephanie, 266

Obama, Barack, 3, 11, 14, 21, 22–3, 26, 33, 46, 68–9, 70, 133, 152, 158, 159, 160, 162, 163, 165, 179–85, 201n, 203n 204n, 205n, 212, 214, 216, 218–19, 259, 264, 265, 267, 269, 272, 282
  Dreams from My Father, 32
  Farewell Address, 185
  Obamacare, 182
  Obama Foundation, 3, 9n
  Presidential Center, 3, 12, 13, 22, 23
Obama, Michelle, 11, 219, 265
"Ode for the Fourth of July," 34
Old Crow (bourbon), 62
Old Hickory (whiskey), 62
Old Left, 93
  Omega, 62, 63, 74n
Oswald, Lee Harvey, 214
Oval Office, 17, 18, 20
Oyelowo, David, 143

Pach, Chester, 77
Paepcke, Elizabeth Nitze, 65–6
Paepcke, Walter, 65–6
Paine, Thomas, 40
Pakistan, 171
Palestine, 195n; *see also* Israel-Palestine conflict
Panagopolous, Costas, 105
Panama Canal, 64
Path to War (motion picture), 134, 136, 140, 141, 142, 146, 152, 218
PBS, 212
Pedersen, William F., 238
Pei, I. M., 19
Pelosi, Nancy, 217–18
Peres, Shimon, 181
personal diplomacy, 115
Peterson, Merrill D., 207
Philadelphia Whiskey, 61
Philippines, 166
Pierce, Franklin, 279
Pillsbury Doughboy, 59, 60
Plain Dealer, 117
Planter, 59
Platoon (film), 138
Plischke, Elmer, 125
Politico, 220
Politics as Usual, 264
Polk, James K., 62, 279
Polly, Jean A., 261
Port Huron statement, 92
Portrait of a President, 33
Portraits of Courage, 271
Pound, Ezra, 26, 33
Powers, Gary, 166
preparedness, 82
presidential diplomacy, 104, 106, 126n
presidential election (1960), 84
President's Daughter, The, 26
President's Day, 26
Prohibition, 61
public opinion, 4, 78
public opinion polls, 109–10, 122
Public Papers of the Presidents, 161

Quaid, Randy, 138

INDEX

race relations, 184–5, 220; *see also* civil rights
Randolph, Martha Jefferson, 60
Raymond, Jack, 90
Reagan, Nancy, 169, 213
Reagan, Ronald, 17, 21, 34, 103, 105, 133, 135, 159, 160, 162, 163, 164, 165, 168, 169–71, 180, 192n, 193n, 208, 210, 211, 215, 217, 221, 223, 228, 279, 281, 282–3
   centennial, 212–13, 219
   Reagan Foundation, 213
   Reagan Library, 19
   Reagan Revolution, 2
Reconstruction, 15
Reddel, Carl W., 238
Reddit, 270
Reiner, Rob, 134, 152
Republican Party, 84, 167, 185, 213, 217, 220, 228, 237, 242, 259
   Grand Old Party, 167, 177, 213
   National Convention, 167, 170, 177
Resnick, David, 264
Resolute Desk, 71, 147
Revolutionary era, 55
Revolutionary War, 18
RFK (film), 137
Richardson, Samuel, 31
Robbins, Jonathan, 42
Robert Kennedy and His Times (TV series), 137
Rockne, Knute, 171
Rockwell, Norman, 58
Roediger III, Henry. L., 272
Rogers, Hal, 244
Roman Empire, 13
Romero, Vidal, 120
Ronald Reagan (documentary), 213
Roosevelt, Eleanor, 16, 17
Roosevelt, Franklin D., 4, 14, 26, 34, 44, 103, 120, 121, 126, 175, 208, 210–13, 216, 223, 228, 238, 260, 261, 266, 279, 280; *see also* New Deal
   Roosevelt Centennial, 212
   Roosevelt Library, 15–17, 278
   Roosevelt memorial, 211, 238, 253n

Roosevelt, Theodore, 4, 26, 43, 59, 60, 62, 64, 66, 67, 72n, 175, 206, 209, 214, 265, 266, 267, 279, 280, 281
   Memorial, 253n
   statue at American Museum of Natural History, 4
   Theodore Roosevelt Association, 61
Rorschach test, 95
Rostow, Walt, 112, 113
Roth, Philip, 27
Roth, Tim, 144
Rothko, Mark, 107
Rousseau, Jean-Jacques, 17
Rove, Karl, 181
Rives, Tim, 102n
Rubin, Vera, 7
Rubio, Marco, 217
Rusk, Dean, 114
Russell, Dick, 151
Ruth, Greg, 67
Rwanda, 172, 176
Ryan, Paul, 217

St. George, Katherine, 167
Sam and Dave, 118
Samsung, 73n
Sarkozy, Nicolas, 68
Saturn V, 63
Saudi Arabia, 176, 181
Schlesinger, Arthur, 14
Schulz, Eric, 68
Selma (film), 134, 142, 143, 144, 145, 152, 218
72andSunny, 68
Shakespeare, William, 26, 31, 39
Sheen, Martin, 214
Shelley, Percy, 24
Shipley, Otto, 57
Shubow, Justin, 235, 239, 240, 241
Siciliano, Rocco, 231–2, 235
Sidney, Algernon, 31
Silver, Nate, 70
Skidmore, Owings & Merrill, 235
Smith, Jeff, 47
Smollett, Tobias, 31
Snapchat, 258

INDEX

social media, 258, 264, 265, 267, 271
social networking sites (SNS), 268
Sollors, Werner, 27, 34
Somalia, 172
Somoza, 282
Soviet Union, 18, 72n, 78, 103, 114, 115, 124, 169, 211, 261
"special relationship," 169, 181; see also Anglo-American relations
speeches, 79
Speedy, the Alka-Selzer Kid, 59
Spenser, Edmund, 38
Spielberg, Steven, 145, 148, 153
sputnik, 84, 87, 88
Stalin, Joseph, 103
Stern, Robert A. M., 11
Stewart, Jon, 63
Stone, Oliver, 93, 147, 214
Story, Joseph, 36
Students for a Democratic Society (SDS), 92, 93
Super Bowl, 213
Supremes, the, 118
Sutherland, Donald, 93, 140
Swatch, 62, 64
Swift, Jonathan, 31
Symington, Stuart, 84
Syria, 172

Taft, William Howard, 207, 281
Taiwan, 166
Tanzania, 172, 176
Tazewell, Littleton Walter, 51n
Tea Party, 56
Tehran (conference), 103
Telecommunications Act (1996), 262
Temple, Larry, 216–17
Tenpas, Kathryn, 159
Tet offensive, 222; see also Vietnam
The Help (film), 137, 143, 145
The Life of Franklin Pierce, 33
The Long Walk Home (film), 137, 145
The Plot Against America, 27
The Power Elite, 91
The Presidents We Imagine, 47
The Private Files of J. Edgar Hoover (film), 137

"The Swimmers," 30
Thirteen Days (motion picture), 137, 139
Thomas, Norman, 93
Tilney, Bradford S., 238
Titan missile, 90
Today Show, 271
To Kill a Mockingbird, 26
Top Trumps (game), 267
Toy Company, 59
Transcendental Can Corporation, 66
Travolta, John, 103
Tretick, Stanley, 147
Troubled Asset Relief Programme (TARP), 179, 200n
Truman (film), 136
Truman, Harry, 14, 17–19, 82, 87, 124, 136, 260, 280
Trump, Donald, 44, 45, 69, 70, 72n, 135, 152–3, 185, 258, 259, 267, 268, 269, 270, 271
"fake news," 268
Presidential Center, 12
Trump Foundation, 4
Tunisia, 107, 108
Twenty-second Amendment (1951), 159
Twitter, 265, 267, 268, 269, 271
Tyler, John, 209, 279
Tyler, Royall, 26, 28, 29, 30, 31, 32

UNHATE Foundation, 68
United Colors of Benetton, 68
United Arab Emirates, 176
United Kingdom, 181; see also Great Britain
United Nations, 158, 168, 186n
United States Information Agency, 78, 263
University of Massachusetts, 19
Updegrove, Mark K., 143
Uruguay, 166
US Constitution, 227, 278–9, 280
USS Abraham Lincoln, 176
US-Soviet relations, 114; see also Soviet Union

Van Buren, Martin, 279
Variety, 134

Vatican, the, 68–9
Vidal, Gore, 26
Vienna summit meeting, 109, 110, 123
Vietnam, 7, 22, 93, 94, 95, 112, 113, 114, 115, 120, 121, 122, 123, 134, 135, 137, 138, 139, 140, 141, 142, 146, 147, 150, 152, 172, 181, 194n, 216, 218, 219, 222; *see also* anti-Vietnam War protest
Vietnam Veterans Memorial, 229, 234, 253n
Voice of America, 117
von Bothmer, Bernard, 215
voting rights, 134, 216
   Voting Rights act, 7, 138, 142, 145, 147, 215, 218

Wallace, George, 144, 146, 156n
Warlick, Jim, 69–70
War of Independence, 56
War on Poverty, 217–18
War on Terror, 175
Warsaw Pact, 114
Washington, George, 15, 17, 26, 27, 28–31, 32, 33, 34, 36, 45, 47, 55, 57, 58, 60, 61, 62, 66, 77, 88, 120, 149, 208–9, 265, 266, 280
   centennial, 223
   Farewell Address, 30, 77–8, 86–7
Washington, Martha, 60, 61
Washingtonian magazine, 243
Washington Motor Company, 47
Washington Mutual, 72n
Washington Post, 158, 212, 217, 234, 263
Watergate, 21, 22, 119, 120, 124, 125, 223, 261
Webb, Craig, 245, 247

Webster, Daniel, 279
Weeks, Todd, 146
Weisberg, Jacob, 181
Wernick, Andrew, 57
Whitaker, Forest, 133
White, Mark, 121
White House, 19
Whitford, Bradley, 148
Why We Fight, 94
Wickham, John, 51n
Wild West, 58
Wilentz, Sean, 220
Wilkinson, Tom, 143
Will, George, 239
Williams, Ralph, 80, 81, 85, 88, 90, 95
Williams, Tennessee, 107
Wilson (film), 136
Wilson, Robert, 232, 233, 235
Wilson, Woodrow, 33, 124, 136, 206, 280
   Center, 235
Winchester, Lucy, 117
Wirt, William, 41, 51n
Wise, Ray, 151
Wolfe, Tom, 66
Wonderful Wizard of OZ, The, 20, 26
Woods, Randall B., 135
World Cup, 2010, 56
World Trade Center, 269; *see also* Bush, George W.
World War II, 14, 18, 58, 59, 65, 103, 210, 232, 238, 239, 247, 266
World Wide Web, 261, 263, 269
Wright, Mina, 246

York, Herbert, 91
Young, Hiram, 18
YouTube, 262, 270, 272

Zelizer, Julian, 135, 217

EU representative:
Easy Access System Europe
Mustamäe tee 50, 10621 Tallinn, Estonia
Gpsr.requests@easproject.com

www.ingramcontent.com/pod-product-compliance
Lightning Source LLC
Chambersburg PA
CBHW071805300426
44116CB00009B/1210